WALKING A FINE LINE

How to Be a Professional *Wisdom Keeper*

in the Healing Arts

Rosy Aronson, PhD

WALKING A FINE LINE

How to Be a Professional *Wisdom Keeper*

in the Healing Arts

Rosy Aronson, PhD

Berkeley, CA

For permission requests, write to the publisher, addressed "Attention: Permissions Coordinator," at the address below.

Seal Pup Press

PO Box 138

Berkeley, CA 94701

sealpuppress.com

Writing and design by Rosy Aronson

Cover design by Kim and Rosy Aronson

Muse Consulting and Editing by Pam DeLeo, LMT

Contributing Editor, Shandi Petersen, MSSc

Proofing by Evelyn Aronson

Ordering Information: This book is available on Amazon and **wisdomkeepers.net**

Walking a Fine Line/Rosy Aronson, PhD
ISBN 978-0-9970230-6-0

Also by Rosy Aronson

The *Wisdom Keepers Oracle Deck (Full color, and B & W limited edition)*

The *Wisdom Keepers Inner Guidebook (Paperback Edition)*

64 Faces of Awakening (Artwork)

The *64 Faces of Awakening Coloring Book*

64 Faces Projects (Global Outreach)

Designed to Blossom (Foundational Course and Workbook in Human Design)

Designed to Blossom (Resource Book)

A Tale of Serendipity (Part One of The Wisdom Keepers Adventure Tales Series)

Wisdom Keepers and Seekers: A Working Definition

For centuries, Native American and indigenous cultures have identified the elders and teachers in their communities as *Wisdom Keepers*. Wisdom Keepers have been revered and trusted not only for their sharp minds, but their compassionate hearts and strong spirits. Able to embody and impart sacred, holistic teachings, and to nurture a humble-yet-potent relationship with the Great Mystery, Wisdom Keepers have helped their communities through hard times for generations. Both spiritually and practically, they've served their communities by bringing everyone in the tribe closer together, as well as closer to the earth, and the cosmos.

Many people in today's world are *Wisdom Seekers*. We long for the healing and empowering guidance Wisdom Keepers have traditionally provided in the past, but we have lost touch with the ways of our ancestors. Very few of us still live in indigenous or traditional communities where elders are respected and responsible for passing down ancient, experientially-tested wisdom to the younger generations.

Because of this, many of us turn to modern-day professional Wisdom Keepers for support and inspiration. Professional Wisdom Keepers are today's therapists, healers, coaches, psychologists, bodyworkers, astrologers, psychics, spiritual counselors, yoga teachers, inspirational speakers, workshop leaders, meditation facilitators, metaphysical mediums, priestess circle holders, urban shamans, and more.

This book is dedicated to the
modern-day *Wisdom Keeper*s of the world,
and to the *Wisdom Seekers* they wish to serve.

"Love tells me I am everything. Wisdom tells me I am nothing. Between these two banks, flows the river of my life."

~ Nisargadatta

Author's Note

After observing diverse and evolving healing arts communities for decades, I've come to believe that an ongoing, nuanced and collective dialogue on professionalism is deeply needed. *Walking a Fine Line* was written to empower, inspire and support professional Wisdom Keepers and communities around the world. My hope is that together, through a shared and honest inquiry, we can raise the quality of our collective service and grow as a planetary family of creative, caring individuals.

An alternative healing arts movement emerged in the West well over a century ago, in response to a growing desire to acknowledge that we are more than our neuroses, psychological problems and material struggles. Many who became healing arts professionals felt called to honor the 'feminine,' the intuitive and the spiritual, to use modalities that bridged ancient wisdom with modern practices, and to embrace philosophies that transcended the intellect while acknowledging the manifesting power of Mind. They came to see their clients and students as Spirit in form, as empowered beings, fully capable of thriving—not as helpless patients, barely able to survive.

As a rich and multi-faceted community of practitioners, teachers, coaches and healers took shape, its members began to rely on holistic and integrative ways of working with people. No longer following purely illness-based models and symptomatic medical treatments, they embraced a rainbow of paradigm-shifting approaches to healing—like the expressive and dramatic arts, somatics and bodywork, meditation and mindfulness, shamanism and shadow work, divination tools and cosmically-inspired systems, and more.

Today, most professional Wisdom Keepers (standing gratefully on the shoulders of these brave pioneers) know the importance of making ethical decisions, holding conscious boundaries, and understanding the power dynamics that often arise within healing and teaching relationships. Intellectual appreciation, however, doesn't always translate into responsible and congruent action.

Although I wrote *Walking a Fine Line* back in the early nineties, I believe it holds special relevance in today's times. With the #MeToo and Times Up Movements gaining steam (reflecting the hard work of generations of courageous activists, whistleblowers and various human rights movements), we are being asked as a collective to better understand the emotional, psychological and socio-political forces that contribute to abuses of power and systemic inequality. Since many of us working as alternative professionals have no external authority to evaluate the quality of our services, and no checks and balance system to keep our egos (and shadows) in check, we are especially vulnerable to losing touch with our integrity, without even realizing it.

If you are a professional Wisdom Keeper, and if you live, work or serve in an alternative learning or healing arts community, my hope is that this book has some relevance for you. Though I explore therapeutic concepts and applications, you don't have to be a professional psychotherapist to benefit from what's inside. *Walking a Fine Line* speaks to the knowledge, wisdom, skill, art and balance we all need to be of true service to those who come to us, regardless of the technique or modality we use. Please join me in exploring what it truly requires to cultivate professional Wisdom Keeping integrity.

Table of Contents

CONCLUSION:

APPENDIX I:

APPENDIX II:

APPENDIX III:

A Prayer to the Quality Goddess

Quality Goddess, we ask for guidance.
May you bring us balance
as we strive to let spirit, inspiration and intuition soar freely through us,
so that at the perfect moment,
we can capture, channel and transform your energy
into high thought, deep insight, and right action.

Introduction

On September twelfth, 1967, I was born into a warm, lively, creative, socially and politically active, self-sacrificing and sufficiently neurotic Jewish-American family. It only made sense, coming from a family like mine, that I chose psychology as my major at the University of Michigan and engaged in many extra-curricular activities there which were service-minded, 'grass-rootsy' and focused on personal and political empowerment.

As I struggled for the rights of any potentially oppressed people (plants and animals) I could get my progressive hands on, I did my best to save the world, and myself. Eventually, I began to long for a more spiritual approach to social and personal change, and started to study transpersonal psychology. I searched for a spiritual teacher and started taking a different kind of responsibility for my life and my world.

At the University of Seville in Spain during my junior year, I met a free-spirited and artistic Dane who turned my relatively conservative academic life upside down. He helped me recall and reclaim my inner artist, the creative muse within that had always existed, but in subservience to the part of me believing I had to directly serve people to earn my right to exist. Instead of going down the expected care-taking PhD track, I decided to explore my artistic dreams with this tall blond fairytale and travel the world. As soon as I graduated, I stuffed my backpack with life's bare essentials and headed towards the land of the Vikings.

Although it was never our plan to stay in Denmark, we did, or at least I did—for eight years, the last seven without the blond. For one year, I focused on my artwork, painting and exhibiting my work. The life of an artist in a new country, however, began to feel lonely and meaningless. I missed people, the feeling of being of service and of belonging, so I began to study a form of Rebirthing, a gentle breathing technique combined with a philosophy used to heal birth traumas both physically and psychically, developed and taught by an American woman named Binnie A. Dansby. Inspired by her guidance, I was able to integrate a life-enhancing perspective to help myself and others, and found myself a community and a way to make a living as a professional breathworker.

Self-employed in 1991, I saw clients, taught and supervised in my private practice, and was a founder of *The Heart Chamber*, the Center for Water Rebirthing in Copenhagen. A short time later, I embarked on a 30-month training program at the Institute for Art Therapy in Kerteminde, Denmark, where I met my future husband. This training not only inspired me as an artist, but allowed me to bring a deeper understanding of the creative process into my work as a therapist, teacher and supervisor for professional Wisdom Keepers (as defined at the beginning of this book, before the Author's Note).

Eventually, my husband and I decided to move to the States. Kim's hunger for adventure joined my growing desire to be closer to my family and reconnect with my roots, so we sold our home, packed our bags, and prepared ourselves for a profound journey. The last thing I expected to feel—while surrounded by moving boxes—was inspiration to write a book.

I now understand that before I could take the next step along my journey, I needed to acknowledge where I had been and all I had learned during this formative period of my young adult life. Writing *Walking a Fine Line* offered me a sacred ritual, bridging past to future. It allowed me to express gratitude towards those who influenced me greatly, and to give back to the communities that had been my home.

Though I wrote these words so many years ago, and have learned so much since, I still feel their relevance, and hope you do too.

Revolution

The Human Potential and 'New Age' movements stemmed from a growing need among people to acknowledge that they were more than their neuroses, psychological problems and material struggles. This collective longing towards spirit provided the necessary fertile ground for the sexual, spiritual and psychological revolution which ultimately took place in Western civilization.

Like a big bang, hundreds and thousands of people gathered together, joined by a similar sense of spiritual emptiness and a deep desire to fill the void. Unsatisfied with the status quo's limited definition of who they were and their potential, they journeyed to learn the truth about themselves and others. These brave pioneers restored and brought to the forefront the 'feminine,' the intuitive and the spiritual, reacting to the overly masculine, one-sided and logical approach to healing acted out by the scientifically (or pathologically) oriented field of psychology at the time. They soon discovered the untapped treasures of their minds, hearts, bodies and spirits and delighted in their unlimited human potential.

Original thinkers and free-spirited forerunners courageously pointed the way towards new, more spiritually sound ways of working with people by accessing, reviving and modernizing ancient spiritual and mystical traditions. Freedom was the name, Anything Goes, the game. Hundreds of exciting new approaches were developed, and thousands of enthusiastic explorers jumped in.

Illness-based diagnoses and treatment plans no longer sufficed for most of these Wisdom Seekers. Their new goal was to reclaim their ultimate divine potential, the birthright of every human being. Repressing symptoms with medication was out and meditation, massage, and shamanism were in. People were no longer helpless patients, but empowered clients and students. The aim of therapy, coaching and healing was no longer mediocrity or to attain mainstream functionality, but to reach for the stars, living fully and joyously in the here and now as unique, creative human beings.

Consequently, many of the methods that we work with today came into being. Organizations were formed. Sophisticated certification programs, schools and centers were developed, so that newly discovered knowledge could be practiced by more and more people.

Like a giant tree, the 'New Age' grew branches and stems from which thousands of specialized dazzling leaves dangled. Each unique leaf ranged from the deep-psychological to the metaphysical in terms of focus. Eventually, a wondrously rich and diverse forest was born.

While I have thoroughly enjoyed this plush paradise, plucking my share of fruit from the magnificent Wisdom Keeping orchard, I've also found that biting into fruits of knowledge (as has been said for millennia) doesn't always bring the easiest or most comfortable consequences.

Many of us who are engaged in the healing arts (whether we are professional Wisdom Keepers, seasoned Wisdom Seekers or just starting out) find ourselves grappling with the responsibility which has accompanied the communal consciousness attained. We are blessed with the blissful wonders of our heightened awareness, yet cursed with the sometimes-heavy weight of personal and global responsibility.

If we want to co-create a new paradise here on Earth, we must unite our thoughts, feelings and actions for the sake of internal congruency and external harmony. Having gone with the flow, it's time to take stock, glean wisdom from our experiences and refine our methods. It's time to engage in a collective, continued dialogue focused on professionalism.

This is not to say that we who work in the healing arts are unprofessional, or that most of us are not already addressing many of the issues raised in this book. Most of us know the importance of ethical decision-making and practice the art of establishing healthy boundaries. Most of us are deeply familiar with the complex dynamics that can arise in any therapeutically beneficial relationship.

Some of the most professional people I know, in fact, are active, influential members of healing arts, alternative learning and spiritually-grounded communities.

There are also those whose work is less than professionally responsible. Since there is no single or higher external authority to evaluate the quality of our services, we professional Wisdom Keepers are often left to our own devices.

Instead of relying on a national certification board for guidance, we rely on The Universe Itself, or our Higher Self. Sometimes our inner sense of rightness, our conscience, is right on target. Sometimes it isn't, for we are only human. This leaves us with a collective dilemma. This book is my way of inviting all members of the alternative professional global community to a much-needed dialogue. Together, we can find working guidelines and practices for professionalism which apply to us all, and can raise the quality of our work to a level of which we can all be proud.

Walking A Fine Line

Look at someone balancing on a tight rope; notice that they never stand still. They're constantly shifting their weight from one side to the other to remain balanced and centered. Their concentration must be impeccably focused, as their life depends on their ability to be in the here and now. They must also be keenly aware of their current position in relation to where they have been and where they are going. They must have a sense of direction, but must never allow their mind to get too far ahead of their body or too far behind. They move towards their destination, legs flexibly yet firmly planted on the rope, taking one step at a time.

We, as professional Wisdom Keepers, must also operate like the tightrope artist. We must know where we come from and where we are headed; yet must firmly, flexibly plant ourselves in the here and now, taking one step at a time. Though our lives and livelihoods may not always depend on this ability, our sense of inner peace, our self-respect and the quality of our service most definitely do depend on our ability to stay focused, moving and balanced.

Knowing a technique well and sharing it is only half of our task. Discovering how to share it, with whom, when, how much, why and where make up the other portion, and the answers to these questions are not always simple.

A myriad of polarities must be acknowledged and integrated if we are to give our students, clients and ourselves what we all deserve. We must be able to use the left and right sides of our brains, just like the tightrope walker who leans to the left and right at the appropriate time. We must be intuitive, yet think analytically. We must honor our sense of certain universal Truths, yet acknowledge the specific universe of each individual we meet. We must hold the highest visions for ourselves and for those we work with, yet be realistic and emotionally honest. We must work towards spreading and focusing on the light; yet we must befriend, understand, and uncover the treasures hidden in the dark. In other words, we must aim towards enlightenment, yet accept and love our humanness.

As we attempt to unite our spirits with our minds, bodies and hearts, as we move towards wholeness ourselves and assist others in the same process, we begin to fathom the vastness of our task. Should we become overwhelmed, we can do one of two things. We can give up, ignoring what is being asked of us—either by continuing our work the way we always have without question, or by quitting. Or, we can rise to the challenge. We can gently remind ourselves that no matter what happens to us and no matter what we discover about ourselves, we are still worthy and lovable people. We can confirm that embarking on such an ambitious journey towards balance is about the willingness to grow, learn, explore and have some fun.

Our Journey Together

Walking a Fine Line is more than a book; it is a journey. This journey was intended for people who have been drawn to Wisdom Keeping (and Seeking) terrains and have encountered *Light* and *Shadow* there. It is for those of us who feel ready to stretch our minds and hearts, increase our capacity for questioning, and engage ourselves in an honest process of self-discovery and professional maturation. It is for anyone wanting to join and contribute to an ongoing dialogue about embodied integrity, a conversation which has relevance in just about every arena of human interaction.

As mentioned earlier, my background is in expressive arts therapy. I have tremendous faith in the power of storytelling and the creative process, and in their ability to reveal things to us which would otherwise be inaccessible. Because of this, throughout *Walking a Fine Line*, I've sprinkled in illuminating stories (with details changed to protect the identities of those involved), personal experiences, and in the Appendices, creative explorations from my life including from my own expressive arts journey. My intention is to inspire you along your path, and to give you permission to uncover your own story through honest sharing and self-expressive experimentation.

Our journey together will begin with **Part One**, where I share my story as a means of opening up to the larger question of 'quality control' in the context of professional Wisdom Keeping. We'll explore the benefits of supervision and mentorship for those of us who find ourselves offering a unique service that doesn't easily fit into mainstream professional environments.

In **Part Two**, I will be introducing a five-phased model of the psyche developed by one of my cherished Danish mentors, Vibeke Skov—taking us from *Emptiness, Idealization, Confrontation,*

Forgiveness, and ultimately to *Freedom*. I've found this developmental prism, inspired by Carl G. Jung, to be particularly helpful in my work with clients and students. It illuminates the inherent strengths and challenges of each developmental stage that Wisdom Seekers and Keepers commonly experience.

In **Part Three**, we'll apply an understanding of the individuation process and a wholeness-oriented approach to the psyche (also inspired by Jungian theory). We'll consider ways in which the *ego* gets a bum rap in Wisdom Keeping circles and how the *shadow* deserves our special attention.

In **Part Four**, we'll bring to light how important it is, especially in spiritually-oriented environments, to learn to discern between Truth with a capital 'T' and the honesty of the inner child, as well as to move beyond principles.

In **Part Five**, we'll delve into the important subjects of non-attachment and creative insecurity. We'll look at the fine line between learning to trust, and staying awake.

In **Part Six**, we'll inquire into the utterly human experiences of grief and suffering. We'll explore how spiritual teachings aimed at empowering us can either serve to open our hearts through compassion, or close our hearts through 'explaining suffering away.'

In **Part Seven**, we'll examine the exceedingly important role Timing and Transitions (and slowing down!) can play in our work as professional Wisdom Keepers, as well as in our Wisdom Seeking self-development paths.

In **Part Eight**, we'll sift through the 'good' and the 'bad'—and the fine line between—when it comes to the relevant Wisdom Keeping themes of *Guilt, Blame, Resistance* and *Positive Thinking*.

In **Part Nine**, we'll take a deep dive into the subjects of personal and professional boundaries, as well as cross-cultural and social boundaries. We'll explore some of the challenges that arise when we make transitions—from one modality to another, as well as from one role to another (such as from professional Wisdom Keeper to friend).

In **Part Ten**, we'll identify the many gifts and challenges that arise when learning and working inside of Wisdom Keeping communities. For example, we look at the art of role-juggling, the hazards of hierarchy, the problem of overpopulation, the challenge of speaking out, and the professional Wisdom Keeper/Leader's special role in letting go.

Finally, in **Part Eleven**, we'll move through some of the most common traps that emerge in spiritually-oriented healing relationships, trainings and communities, such as: *The Self-absorption Trap*; *The Peaceful-Loving-Kindness Trap*; *The Martyr Trap*; *The Money Trap*; *The Love, Attention and Approval Trap*; *The Charisma Trap*; *The Forgiveness Trap;* and lastly, *The Perfection Trap*.

While a journey such as this requires motivation, right timing and full-heartedness, how you approach the reading of this book is up to you. You can read it on your own, as part of a group, or with a friend, colleague or mentor. You can read it from cover to cover, following the path that has been laid out for you, or you can allow your intuition to guide you to the parts that feel especially relevant or resonant with your current work or life situation. You can keep a written journal as you move along. You can engage in some of the expressive arts processes that I share from my own life experience in the Appendices, should you feel inspired.

Whatever your approach, I encourage you to pay special attention to the parts of the journey that bring about resistance, or feel particularly easy to skip over. It is often the very places we tend to avoid that hide the most precious gems.

PART ONE
QUALITY CONTROL

Quality Control is an Oxymoron

Controlling quality is a paradoxical idea by nature. Quality lives in the fluid, subjective world of the individual, its very nature, uncontrollable and unmeasurable. What might be of high quality to one person might be of low quality to another. What might be high quality one moment might be low the next.

Quality cannot be measured; it can be intuited, experienced and hinted at. In our attempts to define quality, we are like small children trying to catch a butterfly with our nets. We watch the butterfly carefully, looking for patterns of flight, trying to predict its every move. To our dismay, its moves are as unpredictable as the wind itself, just as its true beauty cannot be caught or harnessed, or determined by its color or the spot pattern on its wings. If the essence of quality had a name, it would be love—or inspiration, enthusiasm, presence, the spark of creativity.

Just as the ultimate spark of quality belongs to the world of spirit, control belongs to the world of form. Control compares one thing to another based on concrete measurable details. Where quality flows, control structures. Where quality flies freely, control makes solid. The task of becoming objective about something subjective, the task of controlling quality is a highly challenging one, in some ways, impossible. In the healing professions, it is especially difficult.

Human interactions are complicated and multi-faceted. The essential tools for providing quality service can differ from moment to moment, service to service, and server to served. Yet, human interactions do take place; therapeutic ingredients, healing tools and inter-personal guideposts do exist, impacting the quality of the services professional Wisdom Keepers provide. Good will and sincerity can only get us so far. I believe that a willingness to consciously explore guidelines contributing to our work can, at the very least, improve the quality of what we do.

My Own Story

When I started out, I pursued a more mainstream academic career in the States. Although a good student, I experienced the American approach to learning as somewhat poisonous to my free spirit. The pressures to perform, compete and constantly compare myself with others distracted me from my innate desire to learn for the sake of learning. I found the requirements harsh and rigid, and not conducive to creativity.

Surely, my pressured experience of academia was greatly influenced by my family—a fun-loving and creative group of people who also happened to be ambitious over-achievers. We all found it difficult to resist the cultural temptation to equate our self-worth with *how we did* in the eyes of the teacher, the grader, the institution—the mainstream culture. While both of my parents are highly intuitive and have each pursued their creativity in their own ways, neither valued their non-conforming spirits as much as they could have.

My older sister experienced a similar struggle and pressure to achieve in the mainstream academic world. Also like me, she suffered from what has been called the 'impostor complex.' Doing well academically rarely made either of us feel secure about our abilities or our worth.

Perhaps because we are sisters, we ended up exploring and living out opposite sides of the same coin as young adults. While she plunged her way through the academic world, trying to keep her spiritual and creative core intact, I prioritized my spiritual and creative core and put my academic career on hold. I was equally determined not to change the system from the inside, but to make my own rules and find another way of living, learning and working than the one I knew. While my sister was willing to gain from a certain amount of pain and effort, I dedicated my life towards proving that success could be struggle- and pain-free. I convinced myself that any goal worth reaching had to include an enjoyable process, and left the States to find myself.

In my new European home, I sought out alternative learning environments which taught me effective ways to serve others without putting me through academic torture. I practiced my skills, enjoying relief from unbearable forms of supervision. Teachers did observe me working and provided me with useful feedback, but I was not constantly evaluated, scrutinized or put in situations where I had to defend my position. Any assignment I was given, I was invited to do for my own sake.

Pleasurable learning was not only possible, but effective. I even completed writing assignments and past-dreaded tasks with much less resistance than ever before. The process of learning felt as rewarding as the actual goal I was working towards. My innate talents and learned skills were recognized, acknowledged and appreciated without my having to continually prove myself through excelling in standardized tests and getting skyrocketing grades. I did not have to back up every move I made or justify everything I said with scientific research or materials written by Freud or Skinner. I was not ranked in relation to those with whom I studied.

I attracted the clients and students that I needed when I was finished studying, finding numerous and exciting ways to serve people and challenge myself. My experiences in alternative learning environments taught me that life did not have to be a struggle; I could do what I loved and make a decent living; and I could provide quality service without having to be anyone other than myself, and without having to go through years of bureaucratic anguish.

For several years, I thrived in Copenhagen's alternative community, surrounding myself with creative, free-spirited and well-traveled friends, most of whom thrived in the budding and blooming alternative Danish world just like I did.

I also began to notice the professional pitfalls alternative teachers, guides, coaches and practitioners tended to fall into, and the consequences which seemed to result from the general lack of quality control. As I refined my own skills and increasingly incorporated traditional psychotherapy practices into my work, I began to see how much a basic understanding of traditional depth psychology was missing in many spiritually-oriented trainings and communities. Ironically, I came to miss the psychodynamic professionalism, the very same academic, ethical and theoretical standards I had fled!

Over time, I began to appreciate my past, my academic background and solid family structure, realizing that if my parents and sister had something in common, it was their high level of professionalism. Perhaps I still thought that they had paid too high a price for that professionalism, but I also came to value the hard work, dedication and willingness to move through discomfort for a deeper satisfaction, which went into earning their degrees and positions. Clearly, freedom and ease could exact their own price—accountability.

Different Ways of Learning

Back in the eighties, a favorite professor at the University of Michigan in Ann Arbor, Richard Mann, gave me some valuable feedback. He said, "Rosy, what I wish most for you is a frame. You've got all this energy, so much to say and feel, but you seem to be missing a container, something to help you channel it all in a structured way." His statement was right on target, defining one of the major lessons I have had to learn over the years: discipline and structure.

I have always tended to be an intuitive learner, a brain- and body-stormer. I learned and performed best when following an inner creative impulse. Happily jumping on my surfboard, I'd ride a wave of inspiration and usually experience a high level of learning and productivity. When the wave subsided, I felt helpless. Being productive turned into a struggle. I remember envying my friends who never seemed to have the trouble with discipline that I had. They could accomplish things regardless of their moods and momentary impulses, effortlessly taking care of the general maintenance of their bodies and studies, never having to crash-diet or pull panicky all-nighters.

Over the years, I've had to work towards two distinct goals: to accept myself as I am by learning to make the most of my somewhat unpredictable creative nature; and to gently guide myself towards greater balance by befriending the arts of discipline and maintenance work. Though I still prefer to be carried by a strong creative impulse, I've gained an appreciation for the less glamorous but essential parts of the creative process. I now trust myself and my basic commitment to the work that I do. No matter how much resistance surfaces, I eventually get back on track.

The process of healing my wounded willpower has allowed me to maximize results from spontaneous spurts of inspiration, and to take them one step further towards deeper learning, integration and completion.

People seem to benefit from a healthy combination of inspiration and willpower, along with a good dose of receptivity. Without inspiration and free space to explore, people striving to learn new skills, complete creative projects or fine-tune their work often find that originality, vision, and fun vanish into thin air. Without willpower, discipline and perseverance, however, the same people learn that inspiration is rarely enough to get the desired job done. Though all people learn best when they can balance these two aspects of the learning process, not all people need the two in the same order.

Some are like me: intuitive learners who need a structure. They approach learning in the same way I have written this book. They first experiment and express intuitively without censorship, and then they examine the results in search of structure. They look for red threads, sort the appropriate from the inappropriate, determine what is useful to others from what is only useful to themselves. Eventually, an outline and form are born, and their creative mission is complete.

While a lack of boundaries can make intuitive learners feel safe when they embark on a project or process, it can leave more methodical learners feeling insecure. Methodical learners appreciate guidelines, recipes and general rules to start their endeavors. A more controlled setting specifically designed for method mastery is often exactly what they need to feel safe and progress towards a more experimental state.

Both ways of learning are valid, and both kinds of learners have something valuable to teach. Eventually, all can benefit from the lesson of the tight-rope walker. We can strive towards achieving a state of balance, where quality and control, *feminine* and *masculine*, inspiration and willpower, experimentation and technique, imagination and theory, intuition and knowledge, freedom and structure are all given equal attention. Ideally, as we learn to move between opposites, as we make subtle adjustments, we discover the unique quality of what we do, and we keep that quality in check with the skills, tools and disciplines that we learn.

While we all aim towards achieving a state of balance, a simple yet profound question arises: *What do we do in the meantime?* In the alternative professional world, I've seen what can happen when people freely follow their impulses without supervision, evaluation or quality control. They stick with what feels good and ignore what feels bad, avoiding many of the less comfortable but crucial parts of the learning process.

On any number of occasions, things have gone haywire. Egos have gotten out of control, and many clients and students have wound up leaving their professional Wisdom Keepers with problems much larger than their original ones.

At the same time, I have also seen (and experienced) the negative consequences which can arise from too much control. In more mainstream settings, people who are constantly watched, evaluated and monitored by others in authority can easily lose touch with their own inner authorities. They can become crippled with self-doubt and the constant fear of making mistakes. Having to constantly define themselves and their work in relation to others, they learn to hide behind rigid models and theories. They become cut off from their gut and their joy, and the road which would otherwise lead them towards their authentic genius is blocked. Each form of imbalance takes its toll.

I come up with more questions than answers when I think about what is needed in the alternative professional world in terms of quality control. I find it a tricky business to suddenly make demands for more rigid requirements for the education, testing and supervision of others, since I have benefited so much from the professional freedom I've been given.

Being forced through a purely methodical track would have stomped out my creative seeds before they had a chance to sprout. Freedom to explore was the only way for me to be responsible to myself, to my work, and ultimately to my clients and students. Yet, the boundary-less nature of many alternative healing communities seems to be calling out for form and structure, for the same frame I've needed in my own life.

People listening honestly to their own hearts and intuitions know when they are ready to work professionally and under which circumstances. As a rule, I think most professional Wisdom Keepers fall under this category. I also believe that generally speaking, the people who think they are ready but are not, do not attract the clients and students they need to support themselves.

We still cannot ignore the exceptions to the rule. Too many people are out of touch with their intuitions, dishonest with themselves, and too charismatic to turn people off who would be better off without them.

The natural and spiritual balances that we often count on in our alternative healing professions do not always do the job. Without judgment or blame, I see a need for discernment. Sometimes an ability to distinguish between adequate training and care, and inadequate training and care is essential. Everyone makes mistakes. I have made plenty, and all of us can get in over our heads. A certain number of mistakes should be accommodated, even encouraged, because we learn so much from them.

There is also a fine line between making just enough mistakes to grow, and making enough to do major damage. When it comes down to it, we must be held accountable for our actions and their consequences. Our ability to respond appropriately to the consequences catalyzed by what we do (or don't do) determines the level of our professionalism. This book is dedicated to exploring what it means to be professionally 'response-able.'

The Psychic and the Psychotic

Nancy was an alternative practitioner who combined kinesiology with clairvoyance. Like many people using alternative healing modalities, she was used to working with people who were relatively stable psychologically. Perhaps they suffered from bouts of low self-esteem, depression, grief or anxiety, but rarely if ever from what could be called clinical psychoses.

One day, a man walked into her office. Having had bad experiences with the mainstream psychiatric world, he came to her because he longed to receive help from an alternative practitioner, someone who had an understanding of the spirit world, and who would not automatically judge him or put him into a pathological box.

Despite the fact that he mentioned having been institutionalized and diagnosed with schizophrenia at one point, Nancy did not feel the need to investigate further into his background. Instead, she took what he said at face value and began to do her thing, treating this man as she treated all of her clients.

During the session, the man began to tell her about the voices that he heard, introducing her to the invisible beings surrounding the two of them. Nancy, quite comfortable with the spirit world, confirmed that the beings he saw were real, that he wasn't seeing things, and that his earlier psychiatrists were likely the crazy ones.

Perhaps the beings he saw were real. Maybe he truly was surrounded by guides and spirits. Or, it is possible the beings he saw represented undigested parts of his personality which were most safely experienced as distinct external individuals. Or perhaps he was delusional.

It's hard to know the truth about this particular man, given the limited amount of information we have. It was probably just as impossible for *Nancy* to know the truth about him—considering she had only known him for a matter of minutes before assuming all was well.

It is concerning when traditional psychiatrists only see pathologies, not potentials, or when people undergoing spiritual emergencies or crises are automatically and unnecessarily diagnosed and drugged, without any acknowledgement of Spirit. Traditional psychiatry certainly has its limitations just like everything else.

This book, however, wasn't written to address what can go wrong in the psychiatric community, but rather the potential pitfalls that arise in Wisdom Keeping communities.

When a professional Wisdom Keeper (like Nancy) with no training or knowledge of the phenomenon of psychosis and all it encompasses feels they can work with anyone, without taking time to explore the client's psychological history or consider their own professional limitations, it can be dangerous and inappropriate.

As professional Wisdom Keepers, it is important that we have conviction in our work and belief in our competence. It's equally important that we know our limitations. When it comes to the human psyche, things can be more complicated than some of us spiritual students would like to believe. Unfounded conviction can become unhealthy naiveté if we are not careful.

As professional Wisdom Keepers, let's be honest with ourselves when we enter into unknown territories. If we truly rest in our inner authority, we will welcome the expertise from those who are exploring the human psyche from another perspective. We won't be afraid to say, "I need to know more about your history before I can serve you," or "I think this is beyond my scope."

Supervision & Mentorship

Supervisors can help those of us who teach, coach, guide or counsel others to raise the general quality of our work. Good supervisors or mentors, provide us with a place where our work is seen, acknowledged and supported, where our batteries recharge, and where all of our questions are welcome. They also support us in discovering our own answers, giving us guidance, insights and technical tips which we might not have discovered or known on our own. They help us look at our own personal challenges and blind spots in the specific light of how these limitations may be affecting our work and how we can avoid this from happening.

At their best, supervisors' observations and feedback increase our compassion for ourselves, our willingness to grow and change, and our ability to provide our students and clients with the best possible service. They also help us feel less isolated.

For several years before I became an art therapist, I had been working as a breathworker with plenty of professional and peer supervision as I advanced. When I began work as an art therapist, I could not use my Rebirthing teacher or colleagues for supervision. The only supervisor I felt comfortable with was Vibeke Skov, the founder of the Institute. I used her as much as I could, but because of the physical distance between us, not as much as I would have liked. Looking for potential supervisors in my area was difficult since expressive arts therapy was such a new field in Denmark.

As Vibeke and I explored reasons for my unusually lengthy client notes, we saw I had been desperately missing supervision. In that moment, I realized how lonely being a therapist, guide or teacher can be without appropriate and regular supervision or mentorship. Though we are with people all day long, we are still alone in our experience of what happens in our confidential sessions.

Finding the appropriate professional guide can be challenging— especially when we work with two or more modalities. In my case, I chose less frequent yet appropriate supervision instead of frequent supervision which was either poor or misaligned. I needed someone who could mirror, contain and inspire me in a way that honored my eclectic, multi-modal style.

Finding the perfect mentor or professional guide is like finding a partner, or a really good therapist. The fit must feel right in the core of our beings. Trust, safety, devotion and surrender all play a part in solidifying the somewhat magical match between an alternative professional and their very own Wisdom Keeper.

A profound match, however, does not mean the two beings must be exactly alike. On the contrary, a certain amount of difference can be healthy and constructive. Often, a fresh new perspective applied to an old problem can be the key to a creative solution.

That said, it is best when our professional guides have a solid grasp of the nature of our work. Supervision is challenging enough. Having a mentor with no clue about what we do or why we do it can turn into a field day for defenses. Only you know what feels right for you. You may find that a little bit of perfectly-matched supervision is better than none, or that frequent supervision is more important than custom-designed supervision. If your practice is eclectic, you may choose to have more than one guide. Or, if you're blessed, you may find one that meets all of your needs.

Whatever your situation, if you are a professional Wisdom Keeper without a mentor or guide, I invite you to give finding one a try. You deserve to be supported in your work. If for some reason, this isn't possible, consider receiving some form of personal counseling or support.

When helping others through deep developmental journeys, we need to remember self-care. Having a good counselor can also be a model. Nothing is as effective as experiencing helping relationships and healing tools firsthand.

Now that we've acknowledged the importance of receiving support as Wisdom Keepers, let's turn our attention to the journey of self-development. I'd like to share with you a theoretical model which I have found to be quite helpful over the years. This five-phased archetypal—heroic—path has equal relevance to professional Wisdom Keepers and the Wisdom Seekers we serve.

PART TWO:
THE HEROIC PATH
A Model

As mentioned, Vibeke Skov is the founder of the Institute of Art Therapy in Denmark, and she developed a theoretical model I have found especially useful. It describes the heroic path taken by all human beings—whether we know it or not, and whether we find ourselves at the beginning stages of the process or near its final destination. The model has five phases and acts as a metaphor for the creative process as well as the therapeutic. The first phase begins with emptiness, and the last completes the circle with freedom. This archetypal and cyclical pattern reveals an ideal journey towards wholeness.

Whether you are an alternative professional, a student of life, or both,
you are a hero in the process of self-realization.
Your life is your work of art.
It deserves to be seen, appreciated and experienced as such.

The Five Phases

This five-phase process must be appreciated for its essential components, each with the potential for a healthy and shadow-laden expression.

Emptiness: Phase One

The Emptiness Phase refers to the first experience on every hero's journey: the beginning of life, the first spark of the creation process, the moment when all is chaos.

In the same way that emptiness is said to have birthed the universe as we know it into existence, people entering the Emptiness Phase find themselves on the edge. They stand on the very fine line dividing exhale from inhale, the old from the new. All is empty, wiped clean, fresh and unknown. The earlier state of total Oneness, of symbiosis with the *Great Mother*, with life as they know it, ends. One chapter in their lives closes and a new one begins. The heroes become new born babies again. The symbolic newborns are left open, unconscious, on their own in an unformed world, without direction or ideas—just unlimited amounts of untapped potential.

Idealization: Phase Two

Typically, the Idealization Phase follows quickly after the Emptiness Phase. The Idealization Phase refers to a filling of the void, the time when the chaos is channeled into a form, a direction, an ideal or purpose.

Someone finds themselves growing tired of life's routines and longing for greater meaning. A friend loans them an inspiring self-help book which provides tools for change and turns their life around. A lonely person falls hopelessly in love with someone, believing their new partner is perfect and capable of fulfilling their every desire. In both cases, light is brought into darkness. Order is brought from chaos. Idealization is set in motion.

Many people enthusiastically pursuing an alternative path reap the benefits from the Idealization Phase. Uplifting courses, inspiring books and life-transforming philosophies fill people with hope and a sense of purpose. They become one with the beloved. Spring fills the air with the scent of new life.

The idealizations experienced in this phase can be as negative as they can be positive because those in the beginning stages of their journeys are often so busy bringing order out of chaos that they have little time, background or desire to think in nuances. Instead, they exaggerate during this phase.

People in the Idealization Phase may not understand or focus on the complex mystery of life. Instead, they tend to see simplistically and one-dimensionally. Like the young child who idolizes one parent and despises the other, the world's objects and beings take on 'good' and 'bad' auras. During the Idealization Phase, heroes temporarily lose themselves in order to find themselves.

Confrontation: Phase Three

The Confrontation Phase is not the most comfortable or pleasurable of the phases to move through, since disillusionment is at its core. Confrontation knocks at the heroes' door the moment they realize that their perfect lovers never wash the dishes, their favorite self-help book can't answer all of their questions, and their chosen spiritual system won't solve all of their problems.

This phase persistently and mercilessly confronts romantic thinkers with the fact that no one and no thing is perfect, nothing is simple, and no one is to blame. This phase is associated with the fall from Eden. If people were blind, blissful, or self-righteous in any way before, they become awake, somber and humble now. If they had placed anyone or anything up on a pedestal of perfection, their admired objects will come crashing down. Whether they like it or not, the truth will come out. Daddy does not always know best, and Mommy is not the witch that she has seemed to be.

Forgiveness: Phase Four

The Forgiveness Phase refers to the time when heroes learn to accept and embrace whatever they were presented with during the previous phase. During this time, they use their sharpened vision to explore and practice their compassion. They learn to understand, contain and allow—even when the objects of their attention are mysterious, multicolored and complex.

They may suddenly feel love for those who have failed to live up to their idealized expectations. Their increased understanding opens their hearts, allowing old weights to fall away and ancient feuds to be resolved. Their own and others' good intentions, which have been lying beneath the surface, are revealed. Parents and other people are restored to their rightful human place. Heroes can finally forgive without having to distort the truth, deny their feelings or sacrifice their honesty. They begin to give back to those who once hurt them, either directly, symbolically, or by setting them free energetically.

Most importantly, during the Forgiveness Phase, heroes repair the areas of self-trust damaged during the Confrontation Phase. Seeing themselves with the same compassion and clarity they have gained in relation to others, the heroes-in-training come home. They experience a deeply loving acceptance for themselves and their humanity, no longer feeling the need to accuse, blame or judge themselves for imperfections. During this phase they become adults, taking responsibility for the reality in which they find themselves.

Freedom: Phase Five

Freedom happens when heroes invite all of their old projections home. People integrating their missing, hidden or rejected parts enter the Freedom Phase, making it possible to look clearly at the world and the people around them. Freed of the past's blind idealism, and of the guilt and disappointment which followed, they are energetically liberated by their increased understanding, compassion and ability to let go of old struggles and grudges.

Finally, heroes accept their strengths and limitations. They embrace paradox. They acknowledge the value of lessons learned, and have the energy necessary to share their wisdom with others when called for.

During the Freedom Phase, heroes become the lovers, the teachers, the healers and the Wisdom Keepers they have been seeking. Their own inner family structure is intact, their vision cleared. Ultimately, they know when it is time to be and only be.

Here heroes become powerful, influential participants in their creative life paths. Their timing is impeccable; for it is sourced in the moment, not in dogmas or principles. They know when to surrender to a new emptiness, when to fill themselves up with new inspiration, when to confront and be confronted, and when to forgive and let go. As they commit themselves to this journey home towards their very center, their right spiritual expressions and social roles come into place, enabling them to support others on a similar path towards authenticity and freedom.

When heroes arrive at Freedom's destination, they are reborn into Emptiness, beginning a new cycle. With each new cycle, their consciousness is sharpened; their path more flowing and their new emptiness more transcendental in nature.

Applying the Path to Our Work

Theoretical models help us structure phenomena which would otherwise remain chaotic and incomprehensible. At the same time, if we expect real life and real people to reflect the exact patterns written in our textbooks, we will be disappointed or confounded.

Life, growth and the human psyche are as multi-faceted as the multiverse itself. With endless layers of existence and experience intertwining, interacting and operating simultaneously in our lives and psyches, our journey towards wholeness is everything but linear.

We may go through the five mentioned phases once in five minutes, once a day, once a year, or once in a lifetime—or all, depending on the nature of the process and of our person. We may use the stages to make a sandwich, a baby, a vocation, or a work of art, like life itself. Some of us might hop back and forth between the developmental stages, skipping over a phase or two, only to return to it years later. Others might occupy two stages simultaneously. Others might remain at one stage during an entire lifetime, or more!

Take this model with the appropriate grain of salt that all models deserve, seeing the five steps as a metaphor for life, which just like birth, is a highly unpredictable and paradoxical phenomenon.

Before applying the specific phases of this creative process to your current work as a professional Wisdom Keeper, please note that any given phase has both positive aspects and potential pitfalls. No one phase is better or worse than any other. Each is a necessary and integral part of the whole; each serves a valuable purpose.

From a personal perspective, you can use the theory not only to gain understanding into the creative process in general, but to find your present position on your path. Allowing yourself to witness your own personal growth and creative development within this larger context, you can learn to view your life with more clarity. Although you will still be living your life, you can rise above it when you get in a rut or could use a different point of view. From your cloudless perspective, you can see where you have been, where you are, and what options are available. You will also have a better sense of what you and your developing Higher Self truly need, even when your little self feels a bit resistant to a healthy change. When you can do this, you are much more equipped to give yourself the appropriate mirroring, encouragement and gentle kick in the bottom that your Self sees fit.

From a professional perspective, you can use the five-phased model as a general guideline and point of reference for your work. If you are an alternative practitioner, guide, coach or teacher, you will undoubtedly find that the people who come to you will be unique, making your job of meeting their differing needs more challenging and rewarding.

Some people in 'the soup of life' need to learn the same old lessons many times over before taking the next step. Such people will need your patience above all else. Other people already have a deep sense of what they need and their position on the path. They have access to the big picture just as you do, and know their ultimate goal is achieving a sense of freedom, connection and creative autonomy in their lives. For these people, your willingness and ability to engage in inspiring conversations and experiences, and to help them do some fine-tuning and subtle adjusting, may be all they need from you.

Other people may come to you while they are completely in the dark. They will need you to hold the vision of their ultimate freedom even when they have lost or forgotten it. They will need you to temporarily guide them, and listen to them, until they can discover their own inner source of wisdom and power.

You will also meet people who have already experienced degrees of mastery in several of the five phases, but somewhere along the line, managed to skip over an entire phase of the process. These people need help to fill in their developmental gaps. They will need you to kindly escort them back to the neglected areas so they can experience more wholeness in their present-day successes.

Others who come to you will understand everything in their heads, but not in their hearts or bodies. They will need you to slow down the process so their emotional selves can catch up with their racing minds.

Many people who seek your help will be in transition between phases. Transitioning is often accompanied by a feeling of loneliness, fear, emptiness, loss, or a deep longing for some kind of change—whether it be greater intimacy, creativity or inner authority. Keeping the infinite possibilities in mind, here is a straightforward summary of how this model can work in practice.

A Word About the Types

Certain client/student personality types or 'states of being' correspond to each of the five phases, just as certain professional methods, styles or orientations correspond to the five phases. Some professional Wisdom Keepers work well with all types of clients and students, for they have the skills, knowledge and creative flexibility to meet the needs of people moving through many stages of development. Such professionals can assist a person or a group of students on the journey from preconscious emptiness to psychological freedom, to a new, more transcendental experience of emptiness or oneness.

Most professional Wisdom Keepers, however, tend to specialize. They are equipped to bring clients and students from one particular phase to the next, but not any farther. Whether you are a professional specializing in any one phase, or an expert juggler of all of the phases, learning how to recognize the particular stage in which your clients and students find themselves can be helpful.

If you do have the skills, experience, know-how, and desire to shift your style of service to accommodate your clients' and students' changing needs, this model will be useful in helping you to know what function to play, and when, in relation to those you serve. If you are a phase specialist, having a working knowledge of this model can help you know when it is time for you to refer your clients and students to another place where their changing needs will be met more effectively.

Being a heroic professional Wisdom Keeper does not require that we be everything for everybody all of the time. In fact, it requires the opposite. It asks us to let go of that ego-driven expectation that we should be able to do it all and become non-attached.

Exploring Client and
'Therapeutic Approach' Types

Utilizing Strengths and Minimizing Weaknesses

Clients and students are often served well by professional Wisdom Keepers whose styles are inspired by the stage which succeeds their own. For example, a client feeling empty will likely benefit from an idealistic (body conscious) therapy or coaching style, whereas an idealistic client will benefit from a confrontational (imaginative) therapy or coaching style.

The Emptiness Phase Client

When clients in the Emptiness Phase reach out for help, they do not often know what kind of help they need. They just know that something is wrong, and they want it fixed as quickly as possible. If they are in touch with feelings, the feelings will most likely take the form of chaos, fear, anxiety or underlying depression.

It can take time for helping professionals to get a sense of such clients' needs. If professional Wisdom Keepers feel safe with emptiness themselves, they will be able to contain the not-knowingness that often arises in the beginning of any therapeutic, growth or healing process. Instead of panicking or trying to fill in the emptiness immediately by analyzing the situation too early, promoting a system too strongly, or attempting to make the client feel better, these guides can slowly follow their natural curiosity, listening and questioning until a more solid, intuitive sense of what is needed evolves.

All helping professionals deal with emptiness at some point, for it holds hands with all beginnings. Chaos is a natural state of being which requires a certain amount of time and space before it can take form.

If professional Wisdom Keepers feel too uncomfortable with the empty phase of their work with people, they may turn into 'empty healers' themselves—rushing to fill in the void instead of hanging out in the unknown with their clients. Although this can temporarily make clients feel better—in the sense that the clients are suddenly given a function (or a meaning in life), to save or help their healer understand them—it is rarely the best solution in the long run. This dynamic is particularly destructive when helping professionals unconsciously use their client's emptiness in order to escape from their own. They end up merging with their client's situation to such an extent that they cannot gain the distance necessary to be of true service.

Though *emptiness clients* can join forces with 'empty helpers,' most do not. Most empty-phase clients tend to attract or seek out professional Wisdom Keepers who work idealistically. Because such clients often lack a positive self-image, they find themselves longing for positive attention, for positive parents—for people who can help them see their problems in a new light, and who can help them feel safe, loved and worthy. They need guides who are there for them, who can remind them that they have the right to live and that their lives are worth living.

Although there is an infinite variety of idealistic professionals, they tend to share certain common traits. They truly believe in their method or teaching transmission, whatever it is. They embody the knowledge and faith that their method can and will work. Effective idealistic coaches, practitioners and guides are motivational, enthusiastic and optimistic. When they model an ideal for those they serve, and when they believe in their clients when the clients cannot believe in themselves, they ultimately enable their clients and students to internalize the positive function that they, the professional Wisdom Keepers, have lived out for them up until this point.

Many professional Wisdom Keepers tend to fall under this particular category of idealism. What these professionals (and their communities) have in common is an ability to give hope, to uplift and to provide their clients, students and community members with a sense of direction and an opportunity to build self-esteem. Such supporters also provide clients with the concrete tools necessary to positively influence their futures.

When idealistic professionals do their jobs well, they work miracles. When they become overly-identified with the ideals they promote, they can risk creating a compensatory shadow which can subtly sabotage their work. Without realizing it, they misuse their power and their exalted positions to serve their own egos, doing so in a variety of unconscious ways.

Since idealism is often born from an experience of being abandoned, of being left 'empty,' people who work in a purely idealistic manner tend to have some resistance to using a depth-psychology or existential approach to their work, where early experiences of abandonment and rejection, or the deep, underlying fears faced by all human beings are explored at length. Certain that everything can be healed by love, high thinking and spirit alone, they see everything else as unnecessary.

Many purely idealistic professionals solve the 'problem' of emptiness in their own lives by filling up their own psychic holes with idealistic pictures of themselves and others. When they assume helping positions and cling to ideals or systems too tightly, they can end up giving inappropriately, or failing to give what is needed. The problem with adopting systems on which people base their entire lives, work and identities is that when those systems fall apart, so can they.

In Part Eleven, I will take a more detailed look at the traps idealistic professionals can fall into if they are not careful. For now, just know that the *ideal* idealistic professionals can present the ideal to those who need it as long as they need it, and no longer. They can distance themselves (and believe in themselves) enough to know when their clients and students are ready to move on to something more nuanced, because they have come to trust themselves sufficiently.

When idealistic professionals fail to acknowledge and encourage their clients' growing independence, they risk perpetuating an unhealthy and no-longer-necessary dependency—simply because they are themselves dependent on their clients, whose continued presence help them avoid their own unconscious emptiness. They risk giving all of their enthusiastic teachings, not because their clients need them, but because they need to be giving them, because *they need to be* the ideal.

The Idealization Phase Client

Typical *idealistic clients* come to their practitioners, guides and teachers feeling frustrated or stuck. They may carry narcissistic wounding, or a deep sense of powerlessness, hopelessness and repressed anger. Their anger often hides behind their idealism.

If over-idealism has been a life-long pattern for these people, they may have had cold or distant parents. Idealistic clients can have a deep and fundamental expectation that they will not be seen or understood. An example of an idealistic client would be a person who has been leaping from one workshop to the next for years. They have written countless affirmations and mastered countless systems, and yet, they still feel like they're getting nowhere. They come to their fifteenth Wisdom Keeper and say, "Well, I've tried everything and nothing works. You're my last hope, even though I doubt you can help me."

In this person's case, their idealism has turned into a dream, isolating them more than helping them make true contact. People in this situation can maintain a reasonably positive self-image when they are alone with themselves, or in their own fantasy world, but when they go out and meet others, they can experience losing themselves and their confidence. Sometimes they can be a little hard to relate to. They can seem distant, lost, and/or immersed in their inner world.

What idealistic clients need are professional Wisdom Keepers who can confront them, people who are not afraid to look behind their positively or negatively idealized pictures of themselves and others, in order to uncover hidden emotions and release unhealthy patterns.

Since idealistic clients and students are by definition idealistic, they often have false or distorted pictures of themselves. Either they think they are much greater than they are in reality, or much worse, or both. They may resist being confronted with the nuanced truth. The fact that they may resist a helper's invitation to gain a more realistic picture of themselves and their world does not mean that they do not need the confrontation.

For many of these isolated people, learning to see themselves and their surroundings clearly and honestly is exactly what they need to end the loneliness. Confrontation assists them in regaining a sense of connection with themselves and with others. Eventually, they learn to stay connected with themselves and others simultaneously. They learn to give themselves the experience for which they have deeply longed.

Effective *confrontational professionals* resist accepting the false self-pictures of their clients and students. They see right through the idealism and into the sadness, loneliness and anger beneath. They avoid the temptation to live out their clients' and students' expectations of distance and coldness. They continue to care, stay open, and show their desire to understand. Most of all, effective confrontational professionals feel and are safe enough to contain the emotional energy resulting from confrontation. Gestalt, psychodrama, primal therapy and family constellation work are all great examples of confrontational modalities or counseling styles which can be effective and helpful to idealistic clients.

Often, confrontational approaches to the healing arts use imagination. They encourage people to confront or express their deepest thoughts and feelings on the symbolic plane, so that real results can manifest on the physical plane. (Imagination is not the same as fantasy, since fantasy often brings people farther away from reality and has more of an idealistic function than a confrontational one.) Such professional Wisdom Keepers help people get in touch with and work through psychologically problematic areas so that they can symbolically release, destroy or sacrifice the old inner family structures and intrapsychic counterparts which no longer serve them. Effective confrontational therapists are not afraid to frustrate, for they know frustration can lead to growth.

At their best, confrontational professionals understand that one person's truth is not necessarily another's, and that learning to survive and heal our deepest wounds is more important than being right. If confrontational professionals tend to fall into a trap, it is usually an intellectual one, where their inability to fully embrace their own emotional life can turn them into self-righteous intellectuals.

The Confrontation Phase Client

Typical *confrontational clients* walk in through the doors of their professional Wisdom Keeper's clinic already working hard on solving their problems. They are analytical, self-aware, and ready to roll up their sleeves and dig.

An example of such a client would be a mentally active and highly intellectual person who is dissatisfied with their relationships and work life. Demonstrating little feeling or emotion, they remain busy analyzing themselves, without asking for their therapist's, healer's or Wisdom Keeper's help. They've got zillions of opinions about what is wrong with their current life situation, and their mental cup is brimming over with ideas about what to do to make it better.

For these people, *forgiving professionals* can be exceedingly helpful. They need guides who can contain, care for and nurture them, without feeling obligated to cheer their clients or correct them in any way. They need positive *parenting*, professionals who can hold the space for them so that they can go deep and release, so that they can begin to feel without having to carry around so much responsibility and burden. They need to be reassured that they are not alone, that they are acceptable as they are, and that there is help to be found.

If such clients are contained and energetically held long enough, if they are listened to, validated and reflected without judgment, they eventually learn to treat themselves more gently, following in their practitioners' footsteps. While psychoanalytic, Rogerian, Jungian and existential-humanist therapists commonly provide this kind of listening, mirroring function, so do many other kinds of professional

Wisdom Keepers. One does not necessarily need years of a specific kind of training to be fully present, empathic or a good listener. What matters is that these clients are deeply seen and heard.

Something to watch out for in this type of therapeutic or helping relationship is the possibility of energetic stagnation. If the flow of communication only goes one way, the professional Wisdom Keeper can risk losing interest or enthusiasm, bringing about a lack of dynamic energy between them and their client. If forgiving professionals, however, can remain free, present and alive, and if they can find creative ways to engage in the dialogue, as real people, this potential problem can be avoided.

The Forgiveness Phase Client

Typical *forgiving clients* are people who have never really learned how to confront. An example of such a client would be an alternative student or longtime Wisdom Seeker, highly skilled in their ability to understand and take care of others, and infinitely willing to listen and put their own needs aside. They probably have a difficult time setting limits and often allow themselves to be stepped on or misused in their relationships with others. They are especially protective of those who have hurt them. They are experts at finding brilliant reasons and spiritual rationalizations to explain all events, and to disregard their feelings and needs. They are filled with guilt and have a tendency towards martyrdom. They might even try to parent their helpers. Beneath the guilt and goodness can lie a great deal of pain and anger.

Often, the best kind of therapeutic or healing approach for forgiving clients is a regressive one which assists such people in learning how to confront, so that they can go through the five phases in the proper order—but with a deeper and more authentic experience of forgiving themselves. Forgiving clients typically do best with free and flexible therapists, guides, teachers and coaches. They come alive in the presence of professional Wisdom Keepers who feel safe and comfortable moving in and out of the different phases according to what they can see is needed.

Ideally, free Wisdom Keepers are creatively oriented. They feel safe exploring the magical and unpredictable space which exists, and constantly changes, between themselves and their clients and students. *Free professionals* are unbound by their clients' and students' expectations of them. They are not afraid to surprise themselves or those with whom they work.

Many forgiving clients are attracted to and seek out *idealistic professionals* who can reconfirm and keep in place that which is most familiar to them. Unfortunately, for these people, the familiar is not generally what is best for them. If they continue to surround themselves with idealistic helpers who tell them "Keep forgiving!" they risk never experiencing the authentic forgiveness for which they long. Their already sizeable sense of guilt will only be magnified by the pressure to be good, and to be even more understanding and containing than they already are.

Many idealistic professional Wisdom Keepers make the mistake of holding forgiving clients and students in place by discouraging them to deal with their anger. Too caught up in their own idealism, such helpers cannot see what is necessary for these self-sacrificing and guilt-ridden people to heal their wounds. They forget how important it can be for clients to learn to confront and dis-identify with their inner and outer parents as an example. Inadvertently, they prevent their clients from developing an inner authority, making the creation of a more positive and appropriate inner family structure impossible.

When forgiving clients are helped by professionals who are as resistant to confrontation as they are themselves, they can easily wind up spending the rest of their lives avoiding the essential steps which can bring them the healing and wholeness they desire.

The Free (Multi-Phased) Client

A place, time, client and professional exists for every kind of therapy, modality and healing approach. What matters most is that people are encouraged to be *Free Clients*—to move through the various phases in ways which are most aligned with their unique and authentic growth process. It is important that they stay in healing environments as long as they are supportive, and no longer. When clients and students stay longer than needed in any environment, no matter how wonderful the environment, they do themselves a disservice.

Some people do need lots of building up, so much that they can spend whole lives going from one idealistic course to another without doing anything unhealthy. Most people though, at one time or another, become ready to move on. When their helpers recognize and support this natural, healthy need for growth, even if the recognition means losing the client or student, this is very good. When helpers are so attached to being helpers that they ignore their clients'/students' growth signals, this can be highly detrimental.

Again, although it is often desirable for a client to move from one phase to another, this does not mean that every counselor, teacher or practitioner needs to shift from one style to another. Many professional Wisdom Keepers have found their home or calling in one of the several styles, and they do beautiful, transformative work. They are able to go deeper and deeper into one method for years and keep getting inspired. Others feel the need to shift in style and approach in order to follow the thread of their inspiration. We're all different.

Note: *This model is to help you gain an awareness of the function you are providing as a professional Wisdom Keeper, and to help you keep an eye on the big picture, the bigger context in which you and those you support stand. This greater awareness can help you meet your clients'/students' needs. When the time comes that your clients and students are ready for something new, you are much more likely to know it. When you know what they need, you can either meet the needs yourself, or realize that it is time to refer those you help to someone better qualified to meet their needs.*

In Appendix III, you'll find 'A Guideline for Parenting Professionals,' where you'll have the opportunity to see how this five-phased theory can be used as a means of exploring your own strengths and challenges as a 'professional parent,' and how these strengths and challenges may relate to your own experiences growing up.

An understanding of Carl G. Jung's model of the human psyche can help us navigate our own self-development journeys, as well as support those we serve along a healthy individuation process. As we get to know some of the psyche's main archetypal players—the ego, persona (mask), shadow, Anima/Animus and the Self, we can better understand the difference between a healthy and unhealthy ego, the shadow's role in the healing arts, and how a creative process can facilitate a greater sense of wholeness.

PART THREE:
THE PSYCHE
WORKING TOWARDS WHOLENESS

The Ego Gets a Bum Rap

In many spiritual circles, the ego is seen as the ultimate enemy, the Darth Vader of human potential. The ego is defined as the illusion-buying part of us that worships and breeds separation, a greedy inner devil forcing us to cling to the material world and false self-pictures, distracting us from spirit. No wonder Wisdom Seekers are constantly encouraged to keep our egos in check, to sacrifice our personal needs for the whole and to dissolve into the One.

While the collective and individual egos of human beings have certainly done much to live up to their lousy reputations, the ego has gotten an unnecessarily bad rap in many spiritual communities. Unfortunately, in their sincere efforts to provide Wisdom Seekers with a much-needed alternative to Western society's materialistic ego trip, some Wisdom Keepers have brought forth a counter-culture superego, one which judges and rejects the ego and its value totally, replacing one set of oppressive rules and values with another. As it often does, the truth lies somewhere in between the two extremes.

Psychologically speaking, the ego has a very important function. Here's a straightforward description of the human psyche, inspired by Carl G. Jung.

The Ego (the small 'self')

The ego, linking the conscious with the unconscious, is often referred to as the center of consciousness, the all-around communicator, the small 'self.' (This is in contrast to a more whole, or Higher Self discussed later.) The ego represents everything we identify with, everything that makes us feel safe about who we are. When faced with too much confusion, we can always return to the ego, remembering our identities (as we understand them) and beliefs.

The ideal ego is balanced—strong but flexible. If an ego is too strong, it can become easily isolated. Like a person who lives on a deserted island without a boat to allow them to explore the surrounding islands and inhabitants, people with rigidly strong egos remain alone and out of touch with life and relationship. Their fixed state may keep them safe from negative influences, but it also keeps them stiff, unyielding and untouchable. People with egos that are too strong for their own good always know exactly what they think and why, and are always ready to defend themselves and their unswayable positions. They are unable and uninterested in being influenced by those around them.

People with egos which are too weak, on the other hand, risk living the bulk of their lives on symbolic boats, their inner and outer life courses determined by the wind. Having little if any inner conviction, they are easily swayed by others with stronger egos. They think and do what others think and do; they continuously venture out into new and unexplored territories, but rarely return to their own islands, their own centers. People whose egos are too weak can only connect with their world at the expense of themselves, at the expense of their Selves. They are self-less, lost and far away from home.

One of the primary goals of depth-oriented counseling is to help people balance the ego. Many therapists focus on assisting their clients in grounding themselves in their own identities, so they can safely return to their centers, when necessary.

Equally important to these therapists is helping clients (with overly strong egos) learn how to feel secure while exploring the outer world. As these clients learn to temporarily 'leave behind' rigid self-pictures, they open up to new experiences, which ultimately enhance their attitudes, expand their identities, and widen their worldview. Without this kind of flexibility, such clients can have trouble making use of their unconscious, engaging in intimate relationships, and having meaningful experiences wherever they happen to be. Healthy and motivated egos are behind the decision to embark on a self-development journey in the first place. They make the necessary phone calls, sign up for the workshops, and set in motion all creative processes.

The Persona (mask)

Like 'ego,' the word 'mask' also gets a bad rap in some alternative environments. Masks are often looked at as unnecessary, as the false faces hiding our authentic self. While it is often true that the masks we wear can falsely represent us and be used for hiding purposes, masks can and do have a healthy function—like the ego.

Jung called the mask that all people wear the persona. Psychologically speaking, our personas are our social identities—similar to our ascendants, if you're into astrology. The persona's ingredients include the way we look and dress, the work we do, the roles we play, the way our homes operate, as well as our general lifestyles.

Whether we like it or not, having a persona is a human necessity, especially if we want to function in society, which most of us do. Through our masks, we express our creative qualities and connect with the outside world, learning to communicate with those around us. Without the persona, we are isolated. Problems arise when the masks we wear do not belong to us, but to our parents or other influencers.

Many people make the common mistake of identifying with our personas completely. We think that we *are* our social identities. We live and make choices as if we are our jobs, our bodies, our outer shells. When we then lose our jobs, for example, or when our bodies begin to age, we can feel as though we are losing ourselves. This is unfortunate, for masks are meant to be our servants, not our masters, changing over time and reflecting our authentic, evolving inner selves.

The Shadow

Later in this section I will be addressing the shadow in greater detail, for I believe it is one of the most important parts of the psyche for professional Wisdom Keepers to come to terms with. For now, I'll describe the shadow in relationship to the ego to demonstrate its fit into the psychic scheme of things.

The shadow's role in the human psyche is the opposite to the ego's. Where the ego holds something to be positive, the shadow holds it to be negative and vice versa. The shadow represents the rejected and/or forbidden parts of the personality; the qualities, traits or tendencies in us which were, and still are, seen as unacceptable, and are thus repressed.

Therapists and self-development teachers must deal with the shadow if they want to support themselves and others in developing a balanced ego. By cultivating the art of shadow exploration, qualities that were once forbidden and distorted have the potential to become valuable assets. Whether people choose to work with their shadows or not, shadows inevitably express themselves in people's lives.

One of the best ways for people to get to know what lies in the shadows of their psyche is to work consciously with projections. If clients and students are encouraged to pay attention to who and what fascinates—and irritates—them, they are already halfway there. People thought repellent as well as people found attractive are often persons capable of mirroring back to clients lost parts of themselves. These split off parts need integration.

Issues of self-esteem and self-confidence often surface when working with the relationship between the shadow and the ego. A wonderful way to establish a balanced relationship between the ego and shadow is by exploring the ego's attitude towards the shadow. If professional Wisdom Keepers, for example, work with expressive arts therapy techniques or imaginative modalities, they can encourage their clients to create or find symbolic representations of their shadows, and then pay attention to the attitudes clients have towards their creations.

If clients' attitudes seem too rigid or too judgmental, therapists can try to help their clients soften up, expand their flexibility and make space for a more nuanced self-image. If the attitudes seem too soft, on the other hand, therapists can assist their clients in coming forth with concrete opinions about their work, thus stabilizing and building their confidence, helping them move toward center. Because it can be so difficult to know whether people's actions or creations reflect their ego-identities or their unconscious shadows, it is essential to explore people's opinions and thoughts about what they do and why.

The Anima and Animus

The Anima or Animus—also referred to as the Inner Partner—guides the ego. The Anima is the Jungian term traditionally used to describe a man's 'inner woman,' or the feminine elements within him. The Animus is the term Jung used for a woman's 'inner man,' or the archetypally masculine elements within her.

Note: *Personally, I am of the belief that all beings, regardless of gender, have an Anima and Animus within them, although depending on our unique nature and specific conditioning, one of these intrapsychic beings might be more loaded, or hidden, thus worthy of exploring. Women are typically socialized to suppress qualities that are often associated with the Animus, so they often find balance through an exploration of the Animus. Men are typically socialized to suppress qualities associated with the Anima, so they often find balance through an exploration of the Anima. Of course, this is not always the case. We all have unique conditioning experiences, and not all of us fit into a binary model of gender. What matters is that we each move towards balance and wholeness.*

The entire concept of gender, and gendered qualities like 'feminine' and 'masculine,' are culturally relative and often associated with a dualistic model which is becoming increasingly outdated. Just as an example, modern Western culture tends to emphasize more passive expressions of the 'feminine,' as opposed to more dynamic, powerful and fierce expressions, which are just as relevant to the archetype. Unfortunately, it's beyond the scope of this book to delve into the ways Jungian discourse has evolved over the years, largely thanks to the birth of modern, feminist theory. I ask that you please keep this in mind as I continue to share about the inner partner, knowing that I wouldn't be sharing this information if I didn't feel its usefulness, even though we've still got a long way to go!

This psychic archetype of the Anima gives men a sense of compassion, caring and inspiration, connecting them to their feelings, inner lives and intuitions. A healthy Anima can help men realize themselves and their goals in a way which not only brings results, but emotional satisfaction and genuine happiness. If a man's inner partner is repressed or rejected, she often shows up in dreams as an evil witch or consuming monster, or she expresses herself in his waking life through a violent, irrational or explosive temper, or partner.

On the other hand, the Animus helps women set empowering goals for themselves, hold onto their visions, and realize themselves in the outside world. A healthy Animus listens devotedly to the feminine voice of intuition, dutifully acting on what he hears with impeccable timing in relation to the external environment. Ultimately, the Animus assists women in trusting their own authority and healthfully using their willpower. If he is repressed, however, this potentially life-affirming psychic being is transformed into a destructive inner voice of judgment and criticism, or an equally destructive outer partner, sabotaging women as they work towards self-empowerment and actualization.

Just as the attainment of a balanced and integrated ego is needed to enhance people's self-esteem and self-confidence, the cultivation of a healthy relationship between the ego and the Anima/Animus (whichever is needed to bring about balance) is equally important in people's self-development.

When professional Wisdom Keepers help their clients and students create healthy relationships between their egos and inner partners, they help them nurture their growing spirit of independence, and obtain a sense of individuality as they journey down their paths towards wholeness. Such professionals also help their students/clients hear and follow their own inner authorities, as opposed to outer ones. The easiest way to assess a client's ego/inner partner relationship is by exploring their ability, or lack thereof, to manifest themselves and their inner wishes in the outside world in a fulfilling way.

The Self

Finally, let's look at the indescribable Self—that part of the psyche in which many Wisdom Seekers and Keepers enjoy basking (and, though not the same, can be associated with the Higher Self). Simply put, the Self, according to Jung, refers to the center of the psyche, the personality as a whole, including both conscious and unconscious aspects. It is that spiritual, divine part of us often depicted by beautiful pictures of pearls, rubies, gurus and avatars. During the moments when we sense and know that we have more possibilities than we ever realized, we are in connection with the Self. This linkage, this widening of horizons, is often the motivating factor in choosing the journey of creative and spiritual self-development.

No matter how we access the Self, the Self is here to provide us with valuable guidance, with divine inspiration, with a sense of connection and soulfulness. The Self often appears in our lives just when we find ourselves experiencing emotional chaos; it comes to bring balance to the psyche.

The Dangers of Identification

When people rag on the ego, what I believe they are truly and justifiably ragging on is an unhealthy *identification* with the ego. When we are identified, or possessed by something, this means that 'something' is still lying in our unconscious psyche. If we identify with an object, no matter how wonderful it may be, we are a slave to it, powerless to use it consciously and wisely.

Let's say I hold an orange in my hand, and that by some twist of fate, I feel I *am* that orange, and that the orange is me. One could say I have become identified with the orange, possessed by it. In thinking the orange and I are one, I cannot use this orange. In fact, I will have no idea that it is an *it* at all.

If, on the other hand, a person comes close and whispers into my ear, "You know what? That orange is not you, not who you are. You *have* an orange, but you are not the orange," my situation will be instantly and completely changed. Suddenly, an entire world opens. The orange which was once identical with myself becomes a separate entity with which I can develop a relationship. I can explore the orange, bring it to my nose and smell it. I can peel and eat it. I can hang it from a string and decorate a tree with it. I can squeeze it into juice. I can juggle it, play catch with it, paint a picture of it, converse with it. I can receive the wisdom of it and use its color to dye my clothes. I can compare it with apples, pears and elephants, and I can use it to learn even more about the world around me. Once I understand our separateness, my orange and I are free to explore the unlimited possibilities presented by our new relationship.

So it is with everything. If I think I am my thoughts, I cannot choose them. If I think I am my feelings, I cannot explore, express or transform them. If I think I am my body, I cannot care for it properly, nor can I maximize its potential as an instrument for my inner self. On a path towards self-development, the ability to separate, take distance and dis-identify is what makes dialogue possible; for true healing and change often take place in the magical space between two entities.

Even if the ultimate truth is that I am the All and the All is me, if I do not at least momentarily buy into the illusion of our separateness long enough to receive and make use of the All's gift, or hear the All's voice, I may end up with nothing. If you can believe in two-ness while still understanding that on a higher plane, the two are just different aspects of the same One, you will be in fine shape. It takes two beings to give and to receive. If you can do this as an alternative professional, you will also be able to do your clients and students a lot of good.

Ego Identification

People can run into problems when they totally dismiss the value of the ego, since anything they are *unconsciously* identified with takes on a shadow expression. When people reject the ego, they push it into the dark alleys of their unconscious minds, forcing it to express itself in twisted and destructive ways. This same psychological phenomenon works across the board. If I am identified with any one part of my personality or psyche, I cannot make proper use of all the other, equally important parts. If I identify with my persona, I cannot use my shadow. If I am identified with the Self, I cannot use my ego to manifest the Self, nor can I use the Self as a guide, for dialoguing with it will be an impossibility.

A healthy ego dis-identifies with its parts, but befriends them as listener, witness and decision-maker.

A last example: if I were too identified with the alternative movement, I would never be able to write this book. I would be it, and it me, and I couldn't look at it critically or objectively. Accepting and working with the ego is a prerequisite to transcending it. As Ram Dass says, "You've got to become a somebody in order to become a nobody." It takes a highly-developed ego to get rid of itself!

The Shadow's Role in the Healing Arts

Most people have one childhood experience in common. They learn that if they act or feel one way, they get the love, safety and attention they need; and if they act or feel another way, they are disapproved of, rejected or unsafe. Because children depend on their parents or primary caregivers for love, approval, and for their physical survival, they quickly learn to reject parts of themselves in order to stay physically alive and emotionally safe in their families (as well as in their social, cultural and political environments). Most children take some of their very human and natural impulses, feelings and desires and cast them into the darkness of their unconscious. There, banned from the light, all of their forbidden feelings and wants live as shadows.

Shadows can be either 'positive' or 'negative' qualities. Common shadows in our Western society include angry, playful, intuitive, creative, selfish, sexual, sensual, sensitive, shy, 'primitive' and childlike qualities, among many others. What all shadows share is the fact that they are forbidden to us, and forbidden by us. Some of our shadows, in fact, have been so banished, so hidden, that we have absolutely no idea that they exist as parts of us.

Jung taught that our psychological and spiritual well-being is greatly connected to our ability to both integrate and use our shadows in constructive ways. He believed that forbidden feelings, desires and thoughts kept hidden continue to express themselves, but in destructive, indirect, and inappropriate ways. His intensive and deep work with symbols, dreams, and archetypes revolutionized our way of perceiving the human psyche and its infinite potential. Jung believed that our true Self longs for wholeness, that what we contain within us must somehow be expressed and eventually integrated—no matter how much we may try to fight against it.

Many professional Wisdom Keepers working in the field of depth psychology and self-development today recognize this truth. They understand that when people are able to see and accept their shadows as valid parts of themselves, the shadows often miraculously turn into some of their greatest qualities, the very qualities which bring their personalities and lives back into balance.

To clarify, when I speak of shadows here, I am not talking about archetypal or collective beings like the devil, for example. Such beings are not to be integrated into the psyche of individuals. On the contrary, such shadows need to be cast back into the collective realm where they belong, or shrunk into a more appropriate size.

Like Jung, I believe that beholding our deepest, darkest, and riskiest thoughts, desires, dreams and feelings without judgment sets us free. As many people say, "Once something dark is brought into the light, it is no longer dark." When in the light, we more clearly see how these aspects of ourselves can be used to promote our general well-being.

Because shadows are what they are, shadows, they can be slippery and sneaky; they can elude even the most perceptive of us. Often, we do not know that shadows exist until we meet them in other people, representing qualities and potentials we possess which have not yet reached the level of total consciousness. The people to whom we react the most strongly are often the ones who allow themselves to act out the very impulses and desires we have ourselves, but dare not live out.

When we work on integrating our shadows, we allow others to inspire us. We observe those we admire or find irritating and ask ourselves what we can learn from them. We choose to see them as our mirrors—not just so that we can take 'responsibility' for what happens in our lives, not just to 'heal' whatever unaccepted parts of us have been exposed, but to *bring home the lost parts* of ourselves. We ask ourselves how we might allow ourselves to become more 'like' the others. Of course, becoming more like them does not mean transforming into them! The aim of shadow integration is balance and wholeness, not switching over to the other extreme.

In Appendix II, I demonstrate how a Jungian model of the psyche can work in practice by sharing about my own expressive arts journey.

Unlikely Shadows

For many people, some of the most positive, pleasurable aspects of being alive in a body have been rejected and turned into shadows. As children, we can experience our joy, enthusiasm, self-love, creativity and passion as somehow threatening, either to our primary caregivers, siblings, or our familial, cultural, religious and socio-political environments. Naturally, if those we depend on are threatened by our uniquely beautiful spirits, our own survival becomes endangered.

In alternative or spiritually-oriented communities, many of us with shadows around self-love have the wonderful opportunity to bring our joyous selves out of the closet. Perhaps for the first time in our lives, we experience legalized self-honoring. It is not only allowed; it is encouraged, fostered and praised. This is one of the most liberating and beautiful gifts provided by alternative Wisdom Keeping cultures.

Some alternative communities and healing professionals, however, end up going overboard. They become new family systems with new rules. While they elevate and praise our self-love and high thinking, they can also directly or indirectly shun our anger, confrontations, and less 'happy' or 'adult' states of being, creating new shadows.

Replacing one shadow with another doesn't solve any problems for anyone. The ability to meet the needs of students and clients who long for wholeness will largely depend on our willingness to make space for our 'dark' or more 'childlike' sides. I'll go into greater detail regarding shadows that arise in spiritual communities in Part Eleven.

Most Wisdom Keepers and Seekers have inner children (or less 'polished' and spiritually-refined qualities) that have been forced into the shadows. (They don't call us Wounded Healers for nothing!) If we want to meet the needs of these inner children, we must first learn to listen to them; we must meet them where they are. Sometimes it can be hard to tell the difference between 'Truth' (with a capital 'T') and the honesty of the inner child. Let's explore that difference together.

PART FOUR:
TRUTH, HONESTY
& THE INNER CHILD

The Limitations of Truth

When we work so intensively with the 'Truth' as we do in alternative communities, we can risk losing touch with our honesty. Honesty can be called the language of the inner child. It is not always pretty, but it is direct. It does not always take the entire context into consideration, but it does say what is on its mind and in its heart. While not always rational, controlled or polished, its primitive essence can lead us to a deeper emotional truth.

If we are too well-trained at speaking in affirmations, too good at thinking and expressing our highest thoughts, we risk unknowingly coating honest feelings with sugar and stifling our inner children with 'better-knowingness.' Our intentions may be good. We may want to affirm the uplifting thoughts that we think. The problem is that energetically and emotionally, we often end up communicating something much less lofty than our eloquent words.

The wise Jiddu Krishnamurti once said that "fear and love cannot co-exist." Similarly, *The Course in Miracles*, a channeled work used by many wise beings, teaches that "nothing real can be threatened, and nothing unreal exists." There is beauty and profound truth in these statements. In the end, all that exists is Love. Everything else—all that belongs to the world of perception, all that is dualistic in nature, all that is founded on the misguided belief that scarcity, loss, separation and death are real—is a manifestation of Fear, and thus, an illusion.

As deeply as I resonate with these ultimate truths, sometimes when we try to apply them to our everyday lives and human relationships, we run into problems. Whenever people only allow themselves to see and respond to life's challenges from a spiritual perspective—when anything other than an experience of love is considered to be unreal, thus not worth tending to—they lose touch with the human perspective which also exists. This ultimately results in their isolation, for they cannot come 'down to earth' in order to have honest conversations, from one human being to another. They end up experiencing the opposite of what they seek: disconnected from their own inner children, they are un-relatable and even more alone.

Most people suffer from ambivalence. Although some of us may be farther along on the continuum of personal and spiritual evolution than others, we each have our own little tricky areas and blind spots to deal with. While it can be wisely argued that love and fear cannot co-exist from the highest-frequency spiritual perspective, when it comes to the psychological plane, love and fear almost always co-exist.

I have found that people can move more quickly towards the ultimate Truth of connection and love once they have first made space for their honesty. When people are allowed to express their candid feelings in a place of acceptance and non-judgment, they eventually find the loving and valid essence of what they are really trying to express, the heart which opens the door to discovering solutions which are good for the whole.

Alternative professionals trying to bring their clients and students 'into the Truth' may hurt them more than help them by constantly correcting their 'limited' expressions of honesty. Learners may wind up feeling so guilty about their feelings that they learn to speak the Truth in words, while putting a lid on the underlying emotional charge. If their feelings are denied in this way, no real healing can take place. However, encouraging emotional catharsis and only emotional catharsis is rarely enough to bring about true healing. When clients and students are continually encouraged to express their raw feelings without any regard for the effect their words have on themselves and those around them, this can hurt them as much as repression can.

There must be a time and a place for letting out poisonous thoughts, for inarticulate and unsophisticated inner children to speak their minds and hearts without censorship. If no release is ever allowed, if low thoughts are banned from the tongue, the honest energy remains inside the emotional system, taking up the space and sitting on the throne which was ultimately meant for love.

Another mistake some professional Wisdom Keepers make is to be so utterly devoted to the Truth that they become dishonest with themselves when it comes to their own human feelings.

Imagine, for example, that you are an inexperienced student wishing to communicate some honest feelings to your alternative teacher. Let us say that something the teacher did troubled or hurt you, and you want to clear the air by expressing yourself and opening up for a dialogue. Your teacher is so highly trained in controlling their choice of words that their verbal expressions are spiritually immaculate. When they respond to your communication, their words, as always, are positive and loving. Beneath their words, however, you feel something else. Perhaps you hear anger in the tone of their voice, or you see defensiveness in their glare. But their words are perfect. You sense that your teacher is being dishonest. What do you do?

Do you respond to their high thought with another equally high thought? Or do you respond to their tone, the underlying emotion that you sense is there, with even more honesty? If you decide to share what you sense, what do you do if they deny feeling anything other than love and compassion for you? What do you do if they claim that whatever you think you are sensing is a mere projection? How do you know if your intuition is correct, or if you are just projecting something onto your teacher? How do you know if they are being honest?

Ambivalent communication is confusing. Whenever one person says one thing but means something else, it can be difficult for anyone to know how to respond. This kind of confusion is only increased when the messenger is in an authoritative position. When the messenger is in a *spiritually* authoritative position, trusting one's intuitive feelings and staying centered in one's honest truth can be even more challenging.

There is an unspoken and understood deal existing between all teachers and their students—between all helpers and 'helpees.' This deal is based on the simple understanding that the teacher (the leader, parent, practitioner or therapist) is here to support the student (the follower, the child, the client). Because of this unspoken agreement, most students assume that their teachers are there to help them and want what is best for them. Students also assume that their teachers have the surplus of energy, wisdom and insight required to respond to them as experienced, service-minded adults.

Spiritual teachers are human beings with good and bad days, adult and childish responses, lucid and blind moments. No guarantees exist that teachers and helpers can or will always respond in the most respectful, clear and conscious way when engaging in human interactions. Even if teachers like to think of themselves as equal to their students, they and their words still have a certain power over their students—whether they want that power or not. When teachers send out mixed messages by combining their Truthful words with their unassimilated emotions and powerful positions, their students are not always emotionally strong or mentally clear enough to respond to what they sense is being said in a self-supportive way.

People involved in the alternative culture can learn to cultivate safety with simple, unadorned honesty. Teachers can catch themselves when they hide behind their spiritual know-how. They can respond to students' honesty with greater compassion, humanity and honesty themselves. In cases when teachers are too unaware to do so, students can then support each other in learning to trust their intuitions. Together, they can make space for their honesty and gain enough emotional confidence to eventually respond to their teachers as centered adults, not children, and to make a positive difference for each other.

Truth is grounded in the moment.
Truth connects genuine feeling with the spoken word.
Truth is both 'true' to the self, and respectful of the whole.
Truth tends to be tactful.
Truth makes room for paradox.
Truth usually results in an open heart.

Ginger Sticks her Foot in her Mouth

Steven was studying to become a healing massage therapist. In the three-year training he attended, more experienced members were encouraged to practice their skills on the newcomers, just as the newcomers were encouraged to learn from more seasoned students by making use of their services. Steven decided to receive and pay for a series of sessions provided by Ginger, one of the more experienced massage therapists-in-training in the community.

Since a healing massage therapy session involved conversational counseling as well as bodywork, Steven and Ginger had many deep and intense talks. For quite a long time, they were able to gracefully shift between the personal work they did together in Ginger's private practice, and the group work they did together as members of the same training. It was not until later that problems began to develop.

During one of their most intense sessions, Steven revealed to Ginger his deepest fear. Ever since he could remember, he was afraid that others would find him boring. A great deal of sorrow and shame surfaced as he shared painful experiences from his past. Ginger did a beautiful job of affirming Steven, letting his mind and his body know that he was an interesting man. As she looked into his eyes, spoke loving words and laid healing hands on his shaking and saddened body, Steven began to feel loved and appreciated in such a way he had never before felt. He literally experienced being and feeling interesting in Ginger's presence; he went home feeling different that day. He felt happy, excited and exciting.

The next weekend, both Steven and Ginger participated in a massage training module. Everything went smoothly, until Steven overheard a conversation between Ginger and the other more experienced course participants, also her good friends. At first, he just thought they were all laughing and having fun. It wasn't until he heard what she was saying that his heart was crushed.

Ginger was telling a funny story about a time she practically fell asleep during a session with a client. She said her client was so boring she had to muster up all the strength and acting abilities to stay awake and look interested. There was no way of knowing whether Ginger was referring to him or another client. It didn't matter. Just knowing she could have such thoughts was profoundly upsetting to Steven.

Ginger was likely just kidding around. Most professional Wisdom Keepers who spend a great deal of time supporting people in an intense way need opportunities to blow off some steam and laugh at themselves, together with people who know they really don't mean what they say. Of course, if Ginger had any idea that Steven could hear what she was saying, she wouldn't have said it.

The problem was that he *did* overhear what she said, and whether she liked it or not, whether it was intentional or not, she crossed a line that would be difficult or impossible to repair. Steven had put his trust in Ginger, and that trust was damaged.

During their next session, Steven told her about what he'd heard and how it made him feel. He was giving her a second chance, a wonderful opportunity to right a wrong. All she needed to do was listen and empathize with him with sincerity, to take some responsibility for her own less than professional behavior, and to ask him what he needed from her to feel safe with her in the future.

Instead of rising to the occasion, she put on her 'spiritual hat' and asked him to see how and why he'd attracted this situation to himself. If he 'changed his mind' and stopped thinking of himself as boring, she would either not have said what she said, he would not have heard what she said, or he would have been able to resist taking what she said personally.

Since Steven still looked up to Ginger and had internalized similar Law of Attraction philosophies, it took him a very long time to see through her cowardice and limitations. In fact, he spent a long time being angry at himself for not being able to trust her and for not thinking more highly of himself.

Even when we believe there is one Higher Truth, finding our way to it can involve different, sometimes contradictory methods. Often in our work with clients and students, we discover that Truth is more fluid than we think, and that what is true in one moment might not be true the next.

The Truth Test

Bjorn was a client who alternated between thinking he was totally damaged because of his tragic past and thinking he was powerful, strong and well on his way towards healing.

Bjorn felt frustrated because he did not know what kind of support he needed. Earlier in his life, he had seen a psychiatrist who gave him the diagnoses he thought he wanted. To his dismay, however, the diagnoses left him feeling misunderstood and unseen, for deep down, he knew that he was much more than the labels he was given.

In an effort to break free of pathologically-oriented self-definitions, he spent years seeking out alternative coaches, healers and teachers who were all happy to provide him with uplifting perspectives on his life and potential. While he took inspiration from these positive reframes, they didn't always resonate or help him cope during difficult times. Though he intellectually understood that defining himself as 'sick' was not conducive to his healing, he still found himself occasionally longing for a sick diagnosis.

What Bjorn really wanted was for an external authority figure to tell him what the ultimate truth was about his mental health. Was he sick or healthy? Was his life hopeless or hopeful?

Lucky for Bjorn, he found a professional Wisdom Keeper who was less interested in providing him with the definitive Truth, and more interested in helping him discover his own, more nuanced understanding. With open minds, they explored why he was so attached to his 'negative' diagnoses. They found that being seen as sick increased his level of compassion for himself. Receiving a diagnosis was like receiving an indisputable, scientific and concrete acknowledgement of his illness, a confirmation that the pain he felt was *real*, not imaginary or exaggerated in any way. It helped him see the validity of his suffering and gave him permission to be patient and accepting of himself.

Together, they realized that his longings for a negative diagnosis came during certain times and not others. They came during life phases when he was experiencing a rise in ambition; when he was pressuring himself to succeed spiritually, psychologically and/or vocationally. During such times, entertaining a 'doomed' diagnosis had a slowing down effect, a grounding function. It provided Bjorn with a safety net, a supportive frame. In a way, it was a way for his 'Self' to call him back towards wholeness, to prevent him from developing an over-inflated ego, or 'small self.'

Acknowledging this gave Bjorn a deep sense of relief. Suddenly, something he'd been judging as a negative obsession became associated with something constructive. There was a self-loving, compassionate Bjorn who had been trying to get his attention all of those years.

Similarly, Bjorn realized the time-sensitive nature of his occasional longings for positive, uplifting and 'high-frequency' messages. Whenever he was stuck in a self-negating rut, opportunities to focus on his successes and strengths felt encouraging and utterly Truthful. Such positive reinforcements gave Bjorn courage. They reconnected him with his potential and visions for the future.

Together, Bjorn and his Wisdom Keeper found that the best support possible for him was *whatever helped Bjorn open his heart to himself*. Depending on his changing needs and emotional state, his heart could be opened by seemingly opposite support tactics. For Bjorn, Truth's fluid reality shifts depended on his needs.

Bjorn no longer demands that what is true about him right now must be true tomorrow. The more he understands this, the easier it is for him to support himself. Whenever he begins to feel a familiar longing or confusion, he uses the *Truth Test*. If a supportive strategy opens his heart to himself, he knows that the strategy contains sufficient truth. Instead of looking to his fluctuating mind for the stamp of approval, or to outer authorities, he looks to his heart. He knows and understands that the heart never lies.

Remembering the Inner Child

Even the wisest people on earth have inner children who need and deserve attention and love. In our current culture, many people put so much energy into gaining spiritual insights that they end up with much more knowledge than they are prepared to deal with on an emotional level. No matter how they may be feeling, they can instantly see the big picture, provide a karmic explanation for their situations, and pull out a long list of spiritually sound reasons why they should forgive, praise and be thankful. At any given moment, they know exactly what they should be thinking, and how they should be relating to their feelings and other people. These people set the highest standards for themselves in virtually every area of their lives. They demand that they be loving, compassionate, aware, non-attached, positive, optimistic, present, open, successful, generous, healthy and helpful.

In other words, those who have been steeped in wisdom seeking cultures often require themselves to be very *adult*. While their goals are noble and worth striving for, I have found that a fine line exists between aiming healthfully high and being downright masochistic. Too much knowledge about 'right living' can create even more problems than a good dose of ignorance. I am not advocating for ignorance as the desired pathway to bliss. I am saying that consciousness—our ultimate bliss ticket—can be a real pain in the you-know-what, especially when we have not yet learned the essential arts of patience, compassion, and parenting the inner child.

Another problem I've noticed is that many of us make the mistake of using our spiritually sound and compassionate philosophies against ourselves. We dislike ourselves for not loving ourselves enough, or for not being as in charge of our feelings and emotions as we wish we were. We judge ourselves for not being able to forgive or understand others enough. We criticize ourselves for criticizing ourselves, blame ourselves for feeling victimized, and punish ourselves for acting childish when we 'know better.'

When we treat ourselves in this way, we are no better off than we were before we started. We're still hitting ourselves over the head with baseball bats. Our bats may be made of crystals and smell like lilac, but we cannot escape the unavoidable fact that amethyst bats hurt just as much (if not more) than wooden bats. Crystals, although spectacular, healing and beautiful, can also be hard and sharp—as seeing with crystal clarity can be.

I have witnessed many people on an alternative path mistakenly spending too little time with their inner children. I have also watched countless numbers of alternative practitioners overlooking the needy inner children hidden inside of their impressive and spiritually literate clients and students. If professional Wisdom Keepers' clients do not consider their own inner children's feelings, fears and doubts, if they are too busy thinking high thoughts, professionals can easily be seduced by their clients' lofty goals, neglecting the parts of their clients not yet safe or ready to take such ambitious spiritual leaps.

The self-development process is not just about building up and creating positivity. It is also about letting go and destroying. When we ask ourselves or our clients to peel off layers of false identities, we must realize that sensitive, feeling people are being asked to say goodbye to old inner, and sometimes outer friends. Of course, we do what we do because we know that it is ultimately for the benefit of all. We trust that such a revelatory, releasing journey leads us collectively to the core of our true Selves. When we encourage the release of old patterns and ways of perceiving reality, we make room in our inner and outer lives for new patterns, thoughts, possibilities and creations, ones which rest on solidly authentic foundations. All of these long-term rewards, however, cannot diminish the pain of making the divine journey towards the Self.

The more deeply people work with themselves, the more deeply they feel, and the more sensitive the child within them becomes— whether the child is listened to or not. In order to encourage a child to come out of hiding, one must be willing to give that child the love, attention and compassion it needs to flourish. If a child does not feel safe, it does not express itself fully. If an inner child does feel safe, however, it can connect people to old wounds, and even more importantly, it can become a source of healing.

I have seen that people who have reached a certain level of Self-consciousness have inner children suffering from loneliness. They often feel the pain and isolation which comes with sharing lives with people who they love deeply, but who can't share their multi-layered understanding and heightened experience of life and relationships. When such people are seen and mirrored by others who understand them at a deep level, their inner children bloom, uniting them with their creativity, inspiration and individuality.

I invite all professional Wisdom Keepers and students to join me in remembering the inner child in each of us. Whether we are clients, students, teachers or guides, let's remember our abilities to become truly centered and strong individuals. Let's reflect our abilities to care for the children within us. As time passes, our needs for 'false' or inappropriate protections may fall away, but the children are here to stay.

You are a worthy being, exactly the way you are.
You deserve to be loved, supported and accepted right now,
without having to change a thing.

In Appendix I, I share about a deeply personal expressive arts process, where I had the chance to encounter (and heal my relationship to) my own inner child.

Moving Beyond Principles

Back in the mid-eighties, I took a class in transpersonal psychology at the University of Michigan. Using a fascinating culture depicted in Ursula Le Guin's *Always Coming Home* as a model, eighteen students formed a group. The wealth of the group and its members was determined by how much was shared. Just as Ursula Le Guin so beautifully demonstrated in her novel, the more we shared, the wealthier we became as individuals and as a class culture. For a long time, we shared poems, songs, works of art, thoughts and experiences, and we enjoyed the harmonious, supportive and nourishing group environment. We were all greatly inspired, and for the most part, whenever we shared from our inner wells of creativity, we felt spiritually received and understood by those around us.

There had been no conflicts in our group until the topic of abortion came up. Actually, I raised the issue. I had written a poem about an experience I had defending an abortion clinic, and I shared it with the group. The poem reflected my mixed feelings about participating in such an action.

Although I felt strongly about supporting a woman's right to choose at the time, I was also deeply disturbed by the warring atmosphere the event generated. The *pro-choicers* and the *pro-lifers* were all at each other's throats. Wearing bands and symbols which made it clear whose side they were on, the two armies, each sure of their cause, strategized and planned to defeat each other. I had an especially difficult time making peace with the fact that my own 'army' seemed just as self-righteous and dogmatic as the opposing army.

My intention in sharing the poem was not to discuss abortion, but to use my experience as a metaphor, a way of shedding light on the dynamics of war and the prices we all pay when we stick so solidly to our Truth or to principles that we become blinded to our "enemy's" humanity. To my surprise, a very charged dialogue about abortion developed in the group. Strongly opposing opinions and feelings were expressed, and the general atmosphere turned from one of ease and mutual affirmation to one of tension and confrontation.

Just when I was feeling most confused—and in a way misunderstood—by the group's intense reaction to my sharing, our transpersonal psychology professor, a very wise man named Richard Mann, shared a true story which has stuck with me to this very day. I've probably left out or changed the details because it has been a long time since I heard it, but the story's essence is:

One day, a very wise guru named Muktananda was sitting in his office providing spiritual counseling for couples seeking guidance. His translator, who was present during the sessions, witnessed all that took place between Muktananda and his devotees. In the morning, one particular couple who was contemplating getting an abortion went into Muktananda's office to ask him for advice. When they came out of the room, the translator went over to Richard Mann and whispered, "I had no idea Muktananda was so opposed to abortion. I've never seen him so furious with anyone before."

Later that day, another couple contemplating making the very same choice went to Muktananda for help. When they left, the translator came out of the guru's office looking even more surprised. She went over to Richard Mann again, and this time she said, "I had no idea Muktananda could be so supportive of a couple's decision to get an abortion!"

This simple story helped me move beyond the stiffness of principle and into the fluid truth residing in each unique moment and situation. Although principles and philosophies can provide all of us with valuable guidelines for living, they can also become prisons if we adhere to them with rigidity.

"I'd rather be true to myself than be consistent."
~ *Ram Dass*

Now that we've explored the fine line between Truth and honesty, embraced the inner child, and released ourselves from the grip of rigidly-held principles, let's take a look at the equally delicate theme of Non-Attachment. We serve our clients and students best when we can keep our *human heart* soft and compassionate, and our *service eye* objective and awake!

PART FIVE:
NON-ATTACHMENT

A Fable

Once upon a time, a person walking through a desert dragged their tired, thirsty body toward a well with all their might. When they approached the well, they looked into it and saw a fly struggling in the water. Irritated, they grabbed they fly, squashed it against the rocks and threw its dead body onto the ground. They took a drink and quenched their thirst.

Twice upon a time, a person walking through a desert dragged their tired, thirsty body toward a well with all their might. When they approached the well, they looked into it and saw a fly struggling in the water. The person nudged the fly a few inches over to the left, and then they took a drink. Their thirst was quenched.

Thrice upon a time, a person walking through a desert dragged their tired, thirsty body toward a well with all their might. When they approached the well, they looked into it and saw a fly struggling in the water. This person smiled at the fly, took a sugar cube out of their pocket, and gently placed it underneath the nearly drowned fly's body. "You must be hungry, little one," said the person to the fly in a tender voice. After they could see that the fly was happily eating and safe from harm, they took a drink themselves, and their thirst was quenched.

The first person's response to the fly reflects a combination of what a Buddhist might call *attachment* and *aversion*. Caught up in their own thirst and suffering, they cling to the water and reject the fly. They are too consumed by their own sorry state to accurately see the fly as a being with needs and a life which has value. Instead, they perceive the fly as an unwelcome competitor, an object in the way of their desire.

The second person's response to the fly could be called a *detached* response. This person feels no irritation towards the fly, nor does this person feel compassion. They are detached. They feel nothing for the fly whatsoever. The fly's business is the fly's business, and the person's only responsibility is to serve themselves.

The third person's response to the fly could be called a *non-attached* response. This person is just as thirsty as the other two people, but is able to rise above the predicament to see the fly for what it is, a fellow creature with needs and inherent worth. This person's heart, already open, feels a natural desire to help the fly. Without even thinking, the person gives the fly the food and physical safety it needs. There is no sacrifice, no irritation, and helping is no big deal. The person lets the moment tell them what to do, and the moment makes sure that everyone is taken care of. Though the person is not attached to the fly, on another plane, they and the fly are One.

A Delicate Balance

All professional Wisdom Keepers want to serve their clients and students to the best of their abilities. Non-attachment is one of the most important practices for them to cultivate. Non-attachment in the healing arts requires both an open, joining heart, as well as an objective, witnessing eye. This essential practice allows teachers, coaches and counselors to give what is truly needed, even when something else is expected.

If you are a professional Wisdom Keeper, chances are that most of your clients and students come to you with their own sets of expectations. The majority of those expectations will be positive—at least consciously. They'll expect you to be wise, understanding, loving, compassionate and helpful. Some of those expectations, however, will be less than ideal, and will be operating on an unconscious level. The more traumatic your clients' and students' histories, the more 'negative' their expectations will be.

The Bottom Line:

The people who come to you expect you—both consciously and unconsciously—
to treat them in the way they are accustomed to being treated.
The stronger their expectation and the deeper it lies in their unconscious,
the more powerful and magnetic the expectation will be.

The expectations of our clients and students can be powerful forces. Without sufficient distance and objectivity, we can easily fall into the trap of giving exactly what's expected, and the opposite of what's needed, despite our deep desire to do otherwise.

The dynamic in which one person unconsciously lives out the unconscious expectations of another is a natural one. In fact, this process takes place between people all of the time, whether noticed or not.

Since most of us yearn for wholeness, we often attract others whose personalities complete our own, or make up for our perceived deficiencies. Opposites do attract, and we make unconscious contracts with each other to secure the establishment of (at least a feeling of) wholeness.

One person may live out the bold qualities for their partner, while their partner lives out the sensitive qualities for them. One sibling might play the role of 'responsible one,' while the other plays the 'rebel.' As long as these complementary pairs remain together, they experience a seeming wholeness. If the rebel leaves home, becomes a doctor and settles down in the suburbs, the responsible one is suddenly faced with two options. Either they discover, own and integrate their own inner rebel, or they find themselves a new rebellious friend or lover to continue where the sibling left off.

In truth, there are responsible, rebellious, bold and sensitive parts in all of us. If we only feel safe owning certain qualities, we inevitably get others to embody our more forbidden qualities for us—as long as we keep our end of the bargain, and do the same for them.

When people come to us for professional support, they don't only bring expectations that reflect behaviors or qualities of their family members. They bring repressed parts of their own personalities. Whether these 'parts' are objectively wonderful or horrific, they will likely have been experienced as either forbidden by our clients and students, or as ineffective survival strategies.

Our clients and students may subtly expect us to live out some of their shadow material for them. A basic understanding of how 'projection' works can help us avoid blindly hopping on the expectation train.

In the world of depth psychology, people talk a lot about *transference* and *counter-transference*. Simply, transference occurs when clients 'project' or attribute motives, qualities and attitudes to their therapist which do not necessarily belong to the therapist, but to someone else. When this happens, clients often see and respond to the therapist as they would to their parent, sibling, and/or another central figure from their life, usually childhood.

If a client, for example, has parents who have always strongly disapproved of their sexuality, they might easily assume that their therapist will also disapprove of their sexuality. If they feel tempted to share about sexual longings or fantasies with the therapist, they'll likely expect a negative reaction. If their expectation is too strong, they may decide not to talk about sexuality at all, and end up living out the same repressed pattern in the therapy room that they've done with their parents.

When clients see positive qualities in their therapists (and the therapists genuinely embody these qualities), a 'negative' transference (or expectation) like the one described can become quite useful. When the client feels safe enough, they can share their fear that if they talk about sexuality in the therapy room, they might be shamed or criticized.

Healing begins the moment the client dares to share their fear, and realizes that they are not being responded to as expected. Something new is happening. They begin to understand how old conclusions, drawn from past experiences, have been (unnecessarily) interfering with their present moments. They may not need to protect themselves as they used to, at least not in every situation. Slowly, over time, as they practice communicating openly in the presence of their accepting therapist, they make friends with their sexuality.

Projective identification refers to what takes place when the therapist comes to identify with and/or live out the client's projections—taking on the motivations, qualities or attitudes, which are unconsciously expected by the client.

Wise therapists take a good look at their own motivations when they find themselves giving their client what the client expects. Are they fulfilling a client's expectations because they're unconsciously living out the client's shadow material—their unassimilated or unloved personality parts? If therapists are working with sexually repressed clients, do they find themselves being inappropriately (and unusually) flirtatious, obsessing about sexual topics, or demonstrating disapproval, rigidity, embarrassment or evasiveness whenever the issue of sexuality pops up?

Or are they acting in similar ways for different reasons? As opposed to acting out their client's shadow material, are they acting out a part of their own unresolved sexual wounds? Are they experiencing *counter-transference*, projecting aspects of people from their own past onto their client and the current situation? Who knows? Maybe one of their own parents was sexually repressed, and they resented or identified with them for that, or maybe their parent was a sexual dynamo, and they idealized or judged them for that.

Whatever the therapist's background, if it's unconscious and undigested, it will likely blur their vision, causing them to act inappropriately or miss the boat. Their unconscious behavior will end up either solidifying or justifying their client's negative transference onto them.

If you are a professional Wisdom Keeper, it doesn't matter which technique you use, or whether you're even aware of the dynamics of which I speak. Transference and counter-transference occur automatically in most, if not all relationships between professional helpers and their clients. You certainly don't have to be a therapist to experience these challenging, and potentially transformative, dynamics.

Keep in mind that these dynamics can actually be golden grist for the healing mill, as long as we remain awake and honest with ourselves.

The point of therapy is not to avoid
the transference and counter-transference dynamic,
but to learn to use it consciously, wisely and as a tool for growth.

It often takes a strong, positive transference between therapists and their clients to bring old wounds to the surface for healing. Without genuine caring and affinity, there may not be enough of a rapport or secure attachment to make healing possible.

If you are a professional Wisdom Keeper who tends to go deep, I invite you to pay special attention to your emotional responses, mental activity and visceral reactions when with clients and students. Notice how being with them makes you feel. Do you find yourself feeling irritated, bored or impatient? Do you feel a strong pull to provide constant reassurance? Do you find yourself feeling inadequate, envious, or comparing yourself negatively to your client? Do you feel attracted beyond the usual positive rapport? Do you struggle setting healthy boundaries?

By watching your own reactions, you can become much better at recognizing when you are doing your own dance, and when you and your client are doing a tango together. When it is your own dance, you can work on learning a new one, in another context, and on your own time. When it is a duo, you can learn to use the arising dynamic as a territory you and your client or student can explore together.

Sometimes it's hard to tell what's going on. This is where supervisors and skilled mentors come in. Please don't be afraid to ask for help, ideally from someone who knows you well (blind spots included), can be objective and compassionate, and who understands the nature of the *co-transference* phenomenon. It's important you feel safe with this person. Sharing our counter-transference experiences with others can feel very vulnerable.

Take an example from my life. I tend to feel uncomfortable when it's time to end sessions with clients, especially when they're in the middle of a deep share. This makes sense, given the fact that setting limits and saying 'goodbye' weren't particularly encouraged in my family growing up. In fact, goodbyes were dreaded, boundaries were experienced as hurtful, and ending contact led to guilt and feelings of rejection.

Now, I pay more attention when I'm having a hard time ending a session, or am working overtime. I catch myself projecting feelings of rejection onto my clients. Recognizing this tendency allows me to reality-check with clients, as well as to end sessions more cleanly. It also helps me to know when it's time to make the theme of endings and limit-setting a prioritized focus in counseling.

Sometimes, professional Wisdom Keepers find ourselves feeling or acting in unfamiliar ways with our clients and students. I tend to be quite interested and alert during my sessions with clients. If a client walks through my doors, starts to talk, and I suddenly feel unusually sleepy, I pay special attention.

To make the best use out of this particular reaction, I cast a wide net for possible causes. If I instantly conclude, "I'm just tired," or that my response is a sign of my own resistance, without also exploring the possible relevance my sleepiness might have to my client, I risk missing out on some important information. My sleepiness might be just the clue I need to gain insight into one of the main reasons my client came to me in the first place. Perhaps for their whole lives, they've thought that they're boring. Or, perhaps they're afraid of powerful feelings lying just below the surface. My sleepiness may be my way of embodying their resistance to dealing with those feelings. Or it may be my *own* resistance to dealing with them. Or both!

If I can approach my own reactions with an open mind, and in the right time gracefully explore some of my hunches with my client, we have the chance to unwrap the mystery together.

I might ask my client any number of questions, if it feels appropriate, like "How are you feeling about this conversation? Are you finding it interesting?" I could also ask, "What is it that you really want me to know right now?" or bring our attention to the client's body. "Just for a moment, would you check in with your body? Notice your breath. Your belly. How is your body doing right now?"

I could share about my own experience, "You know, I am sitting here with a strange feeling of tiredness, and I'm wondering why. Do you feel sleepy yourself, or can you resonate with the feeling of tiredness?" Under very special and safe circumstances, and if this is a pattern I experience with this client in particular, I might even ask, "Have you ever had the thought or fear that you are boring?"

Of course, there are no guarantees that we'll pin the tail on the epiphany donkey. This is all intuitive guess work. My client may not relate to any of my questions or hunches. If they don't, I know that either I am off the mark, and picking up on something which belongs to me and not my client—or that my client isn't yet ready to deal with whatever I'm sensing, so I need to contain my intuitions for a bit.

When we as professional Wisdom Keepers share our exploratory questions from a space of innocence, non-judgment and genuine curiosity, we often find that our candidness has a resonating and releasing effect. Sharing our experiences of our clients can allow us to become a mirror through which they can see themselves more clearly. Through us, lost parts can be found, half-felt feelings can be more fully experienced, and unconscious thoughts can be made conscious.

Let's go back to my sleepy experience. Let's assume I asked my client, "How are you feeling about this conversation? Are you finding it interesting?" My client could easily respond saying, "Well, you know what? I'm not interested in this subject at all. I actually wanted to talk to you about something else today, but you seemed so interested in this story, I thought I owed it to you to finish it."

Ah ha! Now we're onto something. "Ah, I see. So, you were telling me this story for *my* sake, more than your own. I wonder whether this is something you've done before. Do you often feel responsible for entertaining or satisfying others, at the expense of your own needs?"

If my client recognizes this as a pattern, a rich dialogue can follow. If I'm not willing to take my sleepy response seriously enough to do a little sleuth work, we might miss out on a relevant and profound exploration.

If I feel too guilty about my sleepiness and boredom, if I judge it as 'unspiritual' or unkind, I won't be able to gain enough distance from the situation to learn from it. If I manage to move through the guilt and judgment and ask the first question, but get distracted by my client's response to my question, I also risk missing the boat.

In a case like this, I might be easily distracted by my own defensiveness, or desire to be accurately perceived. When my client confesses that they've been sharing for my sake, not their own, I might feel insulted or misunderstood. If I'm not able to contain these feelings, I might be tempted to say, "By all means, don't do anything for my sake. I don't need you to take care of me. I'm here for you." While it's important my client know that I'm not there to get my needs met, and that they don't need to entertain me, my rush to 'set the record straight' can prematurely cut off our exploratory path.

Most professional Wisdom Keepers feel best when we're actively engaged in our work. Genuine interest, loving kindness and unconditional love are qualities that we expect from ourselves. Many of us haven't been trained to consciously work with co-transference dynamics, and we can easily feel guilty and judge ourselves when it seems we're losing interest in our clients, feeling judgmental towards them, or experiencing anything other than pure compassion.

If we feel irritated, bored, impatient, or angry with our clients, we can mistakenly think we're not good enough, or that there is something wrong with us. We can assume that the best and only way to deal with the situation is to change our attitudes towards our clients and ourselves, and decide to think high-frequency thoughts. If no matter whom we're serving, and no matter how high we're thinking, we continue to be hard on ourselves, it might be worth seeking out extra support.

> *A healthy self-esteem can only improve the quality of a person's service,*
> *no matter what that service is.*

If, however, we continually stop at our own navels, (work only on our self-esteem issues, and never consider the possibility that our inner experience might—also—be reflecting something in our client's experience), we can miss out on valuable insights for healing.

The Dreamer Who Jumped the Co-Transference Gun

Joshua sought the help of a professional Wisdom Keeper. Never having tried anything like this before, he felt a bit vulnerable—understandably so. Speaking with the practitioner on the phone, the two found a time to meet the following week. On the day of the appointment, Joshua arrived at the practitioner's office on time and ready to go.

The practitioner sat him down with a very grave expression on his face. He'd had a nightmare about Joshua the night before which he believed revealed all he needed to know about Joshua and his serious problems. Needless to say, Joshua was frightened and ashamed—because he believed in the practitioner's authority. It took Joshua a long time to get over the doom-filled welcome of that first (and last) session.

I believe that our dreams are loaded with useful information. Discovering what our dreams are trying to tell us and how we should use that information is an art form. Some dreams can have clairvoyant aspects. They point to real people, real lives and real world events. Some dreams link us to collective truths and archetypes, connecting us to our divine Selves and universal themes affecting those around us. Other dreams can act as channels through which physical and non-physical beings can speak to us.

Most of our dreams, however, show us what is going on in *our own* lives, or compensate for what is *not* going on. They reveal to us our deepest fears and longings, or our past, present and future conflicts; as well as possible solutions. Many of the characters in our dreams reflect aspects of ourselves, and not necessarily the people we dream of.

Whether dreams are clairvoyant, cosmic, lucid, archetypal, self-reflective or life-compensatory, they all communicate to us through symbols. Symbols, by their very nature, stand for something other than what they are. Symbols are not meant to be taken literally. If our dreams wanted us to instantly understand them, and if we were always ready to hear, digest and make use of their intricate messages, they would probably have chosen another mode of communication than the symbolic! It can take a long time to fully understand a dream—especially highly impactful ones, like this practitioner's nightmare.

As professional Wisdom Keepers, our own dreams can be fascinating and revealing co-transference tools—especially when we respect their inherent mystery and approach them with curiosity and a degree of humility. Remaining open to the possibility that our dreams are telling us something important about ourselves, about our clients, and/or about the hidden dynamics within our professional relationships, can be very helpful. That said, being open and curious should not be confused with being overly-assured.

No matter how much or how little you use your dreams in your work with clients and students, please practice healthy restraint. Sharing intense and unprocessed dream material with clients and students can be both frightening and unfair. Much of the time, any quick conclusion drawn will likely be inaccurate, distorted or unhelpful. If you are sitting with a feeling or a powerful dream that you sense has relevance to your client, keep sitting with it for a while, until you can use it constructively. If you really want to share it, then share it in a way which allows the client the freedom to not relate, to disagree or to send it back to you.

Creative Insecurity
Combining Humility with A Healthy Degree of Skepticism

Effective therapists, coaches, teachers and practitioners don't fear insecurity. They're not afraid to ask themselves, "What the heck am I doing?" or "What's going on here?"

If you're a professional Wisdom Keeper, each person you meet and each group you teach will be unique, and they will also require something unique from you. If you insist on delivering the same old trusty routine, no matter who you're with, you can risk getting rusty and crusty! (Either that, or you'll bore yourself to smithereens.)

Many years ago, I attended a workshop taught by an American man. The workshop focused on the common popular theme of moving out of victim consciousness and into creator consciousness. This man had taught this same course for years, in many countries. He introduced thousands of people to the fundamental philosophies lying at the core of the human potential movement. I still feel grateful for the catalyzing role he played in my life, and for the good he's done around the world.

Unfortunately, I'm not so sure how much good he was doing for himself. I couldn't help but notice how bored he looked throughout the entire workshop, which he probably could have delivered blindfolded, while singing Madame Butterfly. I wondered how long he was going to last. For his own sake, I hope he's changed a thing or two in his act.

Personally, I'd prefer a professional Wisdom Keeper who isn't afraid to make mistakes and who's willing to try something new, over one who's 'got it all together,' but looks like they're holding down a nine-to-five job in an insurance office.

True healing usually takes place during the magical and unpredictable moments of the here and now.

Learning to Trust, While Staying Awake!

Trusting people, their innate wisdom and healthy core is one of the most important gifts we can give to those we serve. At the same time, it's important to recognize that not all who come to us have consistent access to their most authentic, empowered Selves.

In fact, many of us still strongly identify with what could be called 'false' or conditioned selves. These selves reflect the children we once were—the children who struggled to survive in less than ideal environments, who were defined and molded by the adults around them, (who were similarly influenced by the adults from *their* past).

Sometimes as professional Wisdom Keepers, we must be willing to second-guess our clients and students, to look beyond their limited or distorted definitions of who they are in order to reunite them with their true nature. We might need to combine a healthy degree of skepticism with our open hearts and deep respect for our clients' sovereignty.

Imagine you are a spiritual coach or guide, and a client comes to you for help. This client is absolutely convinced that they need you to provide answers to all of their questions. They need you to make suggestions and provide explanations for every experience. They even go as far as saying, "I *need* you to tell me what to do. I really do."

If you take what they say at face value and believe them unconditionally, you may end up giving them the opposite of what they actually need. When a client insists on answers from you, it's likely they've got a pattern of asking others for advice, and not trusting their own authority. Though they may think they need your direct advice, what they may really need is your trust, patience and willingness to guide them back to their own wisdom. They need to learn it's safe to feel uncomfortable and, ultimately, to find their own answers.

Giving what is needed, as opposed to what is expected or wanted, is not always easy, especially if you're a harmony lover. Clients can feel hurt, cheated, angry, judged, frustrated, shamed and rejected when you don't give them what they're hoping for.

Take the client who just wants you to tell them what to do. Even if you know you'd serve them best by not doing so, they may still insist on answers, or provide powerful arguments for why doing so would be good for them. They may show real signs of distress if you don't come through. If you're not careful, you might give in, subtly sabotaging their healing process, and keeping them stuck in an old pattern of disempowerment.

Say you have a gay client who's been strongly conditioned to see their sexual orientation as a problem. They may be very convincing when they share how many ways their sexual orientation has made their life painful and complicated, and why they need you to 'fix' them. What they truly need, however, is for you to reflect the truth that they are healthy and whole exactly the way that they are, despite the realness of their suffering. They need you to help them change their *attitude* about the orientation, not the orientation itself.

This is a perfect example of how a person can internalize destructive and painful conditioning messages. If, in your efforts to validate your client, you buy into their inherited worldview, you risk doing them a great disservice. If you can instead tolerate a little interpersonal discomfort, if you can live with a client temporarily resisting and feeling frustrated with you, you can then empower them to release painful conditioning, and become a Wisdom Keeper in their own right.

Sometimes the most loving and difficult thing we have to do as professional Wisdom Keepers is to let certain clients hit rock bottom.

I once had a client who struggled with alcoholism. He was a very sensitive, wise and intelligent man, and in many ways, quite receptive to counseling. Unfortunately, despite his powerful wish to heal his wounds, he had an even more powerful fear of feeling his pain and facing his life. At first I felt optimistic. We had several sessions where he opened up, gained great insight and took responsibility for his situation. With the agreed-upon help of an intensive support group for alcoholics, I felt I could serve him as a supplemental counselor. For a while, it looked like this was possible.

In the end, he was not able to keep his end of the deal. When we explored why he stopped going to the group, he claimed he could control his drinking—which he obviously couldn't, since he had come to our session 'under the influence' despite our agreement. Though I truly wanted to help him, I also knew that as long as he refused to acknowledge his addiction, and as long as he still lied to protect himself, the addiction was stronger than his ability to deal with it, and thus, stronger than the healing potential of our relationship.

Telling this man that I would not be his counselor until I could see he'd taken responsibility for his alcoholism was one of the most difficult things I've had to do. I felt the pain of his loss and abandonment, and yet I needed to step out of a codependent pattern in relation to him. My willingness to let him hit rock bottom was the most loving thing I could do for him.

Staying Awake While Remaining Humble

As important as it is for professional Wisdom Keepers to trust ourselves, it's equally important that we remember how little we actually know about the people who come to us. If you are a professional Wisdom Keeper, follow your curiosity, but if your curiosity leads you and your clients nowhere, or into a great mystery, drop your agenda. Spend time simply being with whatever is happening, even if what's happening is pure confusion.

Our relationships with our clients and students are partnerships. No one ever said we have to know everything. Letting go of being the eternal expert allows our clients and students to go where they need to go. I actually like to remind myself before my clients or students walk in through the door that I know very little about them. I say this to myself even when I have known them for years. This helps all of us to explore with an open and non-attached mind.

Our clients and students are our teachers. Never underestimate their brilliance. Remember to honor the vastness of their very beings.

The Unprepared Hypnotist

Carol struggled with her weight and body image since adolescence. She decided to seek out a well-known hypnotist to help her take off what she believed were excess pounds. The hypnotist was very good at what he did. His voice was calming, his words encouraging and his experience vast. Everything went splendidly for Carol during their first few sessions together. As long as all she needed was his technique, there was no problem at all.

After just a few visits, she was delighted to watch the numbers on her scale slowly descend towards her desired goal. Her hypnotist was also happy to have such a satisfied client; she was living proof that his technique worked.

Every once in a while, Carol would look in the mirror and wonder why her weight loss wasn't more apparent. Instead of resorting to old patterns of self-criticism, she'd think to herself, "These things take time. As long as I'm weighing less, it's working and I'm happy."

One day she discovered that the battery in her electronic scale had been running out. The numbers were going down, but not because of her weight loss. She panicked. Feeling sad, disappointed and frustrated, she called the hypnotist. Unfortunately, since conflicts between himself and his clients rarely, if ever, arose, and he had no real knowledge of co-transference dynamics, he was unprepared to deal with her panic. Instead of empathizing with her or exploring the deeper emotional material that was emerging for her, he felt immediately defensive and accused of doing a bad job. He got cold and formal.

Carol was an intuitive and sensitive woman who could instantly hear in his voice that he took offense. She spent the remainder of the call apologizing for her behavior.

This story illustrates the fact that being good at a technique isn't always enough. As professional Wisdom Keepers, we also need to learn how to receive uncomfortable or unexpected feedback, without dropping into a state of self-defense. Wonderful breakthroughs can occur during those unpredictable moments in our work, when clients take risks and expose new (sometimes raw or unpolished) parts of themselves.

In Wisdom Keeping circles, we often define responsibility as 'the ability to respond.' When we can respond to whatever happens in our work with a clear head, open heart, and an appropriate degree of non-attachment, we are embodying the spirit of responsibility.

If there ever is a time to practice compassionate non-attachment, it's when we are confronted with grief and suffering. Whether the suffering is our own, a loved one's, or a client's, we have a choice about how we meet, understand and respond to emotional, physical and spiritual pain. Let's take a look at the many gifts our Wisdom Keeping allows us to provide those who are hurting, as well as the pitfalls we can succumb to if we're not careful.

PART SIX:
GRIEF & SUFFERING

Success is getting what you want.
Happiness is wanting what you get.

The Humbling Truth about Conscious Creation

Many Wisdom Seekers are encouraged to stop being powerless victims, and to become conscious creators. Presented with a buffet of powerful manifestation tools, we're told to go for what we want, to aim for the highest. When our wishes are aligned with the good of the whole, wonderful dreams come true.

Manifestation-oriented philosophies become problematic when they act as cover-ups for misguided materialism and over-inflated egos. When greed and grandiosity take over, we lose our ability to discern between what's good for us as individuals, and what's good for the whole. We obsess over what we can get from the universe, instead of what we can give. I'm not saying that Wisdom Seekers and Keepers should be poor, sacrificing martyrs. I am saying that there are different kinds of wealth, one kind rooted in generosity, and another in greed or fear.

Service-oriented people are more likely to invest their resources into products and initiatives that benefit our planet and its inhabitants. Those who are more driven by the fear of losing than the love of giving are likely to invest their wealth in ways that deplete the environment and add to imbalances already at play. Their wealth often hides an inner emptiness and loneliness.

When we hold on to rigid pictures of our chosen desires, we unknowingly miss out on countless opportunities to receive the actual *experience* that we're longing for. Unable to receive pleasure from the symbolic world, and unwilling to receive what we want from unexpected places, or through unimagined forms, we experience dissatisfaction.

We can make an even greater mistake when we fail to manifest exactly what we want. We can judge ourselves to be failures. Either we're hopeless visualizers, inadequate affirmers or unworthy beings.

When Wisdom Seekers and Keepers are unreasonably hard on ourselves, we're more likely to apply the same misguided logic to those around us, passing blanket judgments. If we see someone who is physically ill, we think, "That person's health must be reflecting low-frequency thoughts." If someone is poor, we think, "They lack prosperity consciousness." If someone feels lonely or is sad that they have no romantic partner, we think, "They'll never attract a partner until they integrate the qualities they're looking for." No seeming 'fault,' no undesirable reality, escapes our high-standard stare and harsh sentence.

For thousands of years, shamans and mystics worldwide have understood the spiritual value of darkness and the act of descending into the unknown depths to uncover lost pieces of the soul. Many of us brought up in Judeo-Christian traditions (not the mystical ones) have learned to idealize light and demonize darkness. As a result, we've come to deify the heavens and diminish our humanness. We relish ease and reject conflict, crave the known and avoid the unknown, cling to control and shrink from change—the essence of life.

The truth about our abilities as 'conscious creators' holds a paradox. We have much more influence over our lives than we realize, yet none of us are all-powerful. When we forget this humbling truth, and when we devalue the profound lessons awaiting us in the dark, we lose track of the fact that getting what we want doesn't necessarily bring us the joy, power and fulfillment we expect.

Genuine fulfillment often comes during the most commonplace, unexpected moments. While brushing our teeth one morning, tears of gratitude well up, for no particular reason. A bird chirps outside our window, and our hearts expand. A stranger smiles at us in an elevator, and we remember that we are not alone. Even at a funeral, in the midst of our deepest grief, we can be struck by the feelings of aliveness, connectedness and peace. When loss and bliss, pain and humor, our utter humanness and our eternal divinity, all blend together in these inexplicable yet grace-filled moments, all we can do is surrender to the mystery of life.

Over time, we learn that love, peace and joy are unconditional states of being, independent of circumstance. The key to our increased fulfillment lies not only in our ability to visualize positive outcomes or set lofty intentions, but in our willingness to stay open, flexible and ready to be inspired by life.

As we begin to appreciate the possibilities hidden in every situation, from the most mundane to the most tragic, we eventually learn the art of *wanting what we get*. We experience a kind of serenity that is no longer dependent on the physical or provable world, a serenity—and freedom—that cannot be taken away from us.

As I strive to unite my personal will with the will of the Great Creator,
I acknowledge my humble yet important place in this collective dance.

Listening and honoring my intuitive voice,
I strive to influence that which I can and accept that which I can't.
When or if I receive something other than I have asked for,
I remember that true fulfillment lies in my ability and willingness
to find gifts in the least likely places.

Suffering

When it comes to the art of grounding high thinkers and conscious creators, few human experiences are as effective as suffering. With its sometimes merciless and seemingly random tactics, suffering pulls us down from our sky-soaring flights and rips open our hearts to the pain of the here and now. Even the most impressive Wisdom Keepers cannot escape the grips of suffering. Our loved ones die, marriages fall apart, and our children grow up, leaving us with empty nests. We look around us and witness one tragedy after the other, one meaningless act of cruelty after the other, and our hearts cannot help but break.

Whether the cruelty we see affects us directly or not, whether it is purposeful or accidental, whether 'people-made' or by 'natural causes,' it takes its toll. No matter how hard we work to raise our frequency, or respond with grace, we are often left with a deep sadness and a hole in our hearts.

Despite our sincere efforts to positively influence our lives, our efforts sometimes fail. Even the most conscious and creative of us don't always get what we want. We may be quite gifted at drawing meaning out of personal and human tragedies. We may strive to understand and grow from all that we are given. And yet, our talents and intentions still might not remove all pain. They can't make certain tragedies any easier to grasp or accept.

Sometimes things happen in our lives that we don't understand. Such things not only seem unfair but *are* unfair, at least on one very real plane of existence. Professional Wisdom Keepers might try to remind us, during painful times, that *we always get what we need*, that *all suffering is an illusion*, or that *everything that happens to us is a teaching in disguise*. Despite their well-intentioned attempts to put things into a higher perspective for us, we are not helped one bit. We still feel like we're falling apart; our wounds are still raw and wide. Instead of bringing us comfort, these spiritual slogans leave us feeling guilty for having the nerve to suffer at all. We feel embarrassed for being so 'unspiritual' and attached to victimhood.

I have seen two main approaches to suffering in Wisdom Keeping communities. One reflects the belief that people need not suffer, that suffering is an illusion, an unconstructive and correctable habit, with little to no value for human beings. Members of this Wisdom Keeping club tend to think suffering can be relieved and released with an enlightening conversation, a change of mind, or adjustment of perspective.

Members from the other club believe we need to befriend our suffering, to allow it to burn through our hearts. They believe embracing, as opposed to ridding ourselves of suffering expands our capacity for compassion and self-understanding. They believe suffering is grace. It is what makes us human, connected and real.

Whichever orientation you embrace, if you are a professional Wisdom Keeper, you can be sure that you are going to deal with suffering, one way or the other, since suffering remains an integral part of our human experience.

Many mystical teachers like Ram Dass speak about suffering. They say that the cause of all suffering is the act of wanting what one does not have. A person is starving when they want to eat. Someone is dying when they want to live. Someone's lover leaves when they wish the lover would stay. A person is jailed when they want to be free. Such wish-conflicting cases provide the perfectly fertile ground for suffering.

One fascinating thing about suffering is its relative nature. Since desires differ so greatly from person to person, culture to culture, and moment to moment, suffering will be experienced differently by different people, in different places, at different times.

My breathwork teacher, Binnie Dansby, liked to talk about the relativity of the birth experience, depending on the culture and environment in which it occurred. In Judeo-Christian cultures, for example, where our own bibles demand that birth be a painful experience, and where we call birthing women's physiological process 'labor pains,' it's no wonder so many of us experience birth as excruciatingly painful and very hard work.

There are still cultures in our world that aren't impacted by Western conditioning. Binnie shared about one culture that didn't even have a word for pain. The women in this culture give birth. Surely, they experience the same physical sensations of birthing women anywhere, and yet, there is no word for pain. Since language reflects a culture's experience of reality, we can only wonder how the absence of this word reflects and affects women's actual experience of birth in that part of the world. Perhaps they feel it all, cry and scream, but—because they're not taught to judge their experience as 'wrong,' as hard work, or as a sign of divine punishment—do not suffer. Fascinating to think about.

Whether or not these women suffer during birth, it seems clear that the cause of one person's suffering does not necessarily constitute another's. Similarly, what makes some people suffer during one moment does not necessarily make them suffer the next.

When discussing the mysterious nature of suffering, Ram Dass has shared how people's differing desires and agendas can have an enormous impact on whether and how much they suffer. Take someone who deeply wants to maintain their youthful appearance, but is aging. Powerless to reverse the body's inevitable aging process, this person—like so many of us impacted by a 'youth-obsessed' culture—may suffer a great deal.

Another person's body might be gathering just as many aches and wrinkles, and losing just as much strength and elasticity, but not be suffering at all. Approaching the aging process with curiosity as opposed to shame, they are able to acknowledge the value of their increased wisdom, vast experience and well-earned place in their *elder-honoring* community.

Similarly, someone who is not eating because of a cleansing fast or a politically-inspired form of activism may feel hungry and physically weak, but they won't suffer like someone starving in a refugee camp or because of a drought. Someone choosing to experiment with sleep deprivation to learn about natural hallucination techniques will not suffer like someone who's living with chronic insomnia or being tortured. When we choose our circumstance, our discomfort takes on deeper meaning, and we suffer less.

Stanislav Grof researched babies' experiences while moving through four distinct phases of the birth process. I'll briefly describe the second and third phases to shed light on the subject of suffering. During the second phase, contractions begin, but the cervix remains undilated. In other words, the baby is being pushed and pulled, but there is no opening, no direction, no light at the end of the tunnel. The baby struggles, but to no avail. They are helpless, hopeless and powerless. When complications occur during this phase, for the baby or the mother, it can have grave consequences later in life. This part of the birth process—and if one uses birth as a metaphor, the life and creative process as well—is equated with torture and suffering.

It is not until the third phase that the pain of contractions takes on meaning. The cervix is dilated; the door is opened; the way has been paved. The baby still feels intense pushing and pulling, still must be squeezed through a small passageway, but there is movement, growth, optimism, and a reason for the suffering. The struggle becomes an empowering one as the baby struggles towards life.

A Bit of Mathematics:
Pain minus Meaning = Suffering
Pain plus Meaning = Growth

When We Don't Choose Our Suffering

Unfortunately, in life, we rarely consciously choose our painful conditions. Most of us need more than intellectual explanations and spiritual platitudes to heal and grow from difficult experiences. With the right support, our suffering can open our hearts, burn through our defenses, release us from isolation, increase our compassion and enhance our ability to serve others. Suffering has the potential to turn Wisdom Seekers into Wisdom Keepers. The quality and kind of support we receive can make, or break, our ability to turn life's tragedies into heart-opening triumphs.

Resisting the Temptation to Explain It Away

A Tale

There once was a great spiritual master who taught his students about the illusions of the ego and the ego's world. One day, his own child died. For the first time in his students' lives, they saw their teacher sobbing with grief. Several students approached him, confused by their master's emotional reaction. "Why do you cry?" they asked. "We thought you said that death was an illusion, and that suffering belonged to the world of the ego. We don't understand."

The priest answered, "It is true, my students. Death is an illusion, just as our world is built on illusions. But losing my child is the most painful illusion of all."

Years ago, I heard Ram Dass tell a story about a woman who lived in a big city in the United States. Every day, on her way home from work, she passed by a homeless man who lived on her street corner. One day, she decided to commit herself to doing something concrete to support this person. She set aside a budget just for him, and every day, she gave him a certain amount of money. This made her feel a little better, but somehow, not totally.

When she shared this story with Ram Dass, he asked her if she ever took the time to sit down with the man and have a talk, human being to human being. No, she had never done that. He then asked her why she never did that, if she was afraid of something. After contemplating the answer, she said, "I was afraid that if I sat down and acknowledged him as a human being, I might end up inviting him to live with me."

I was touched to hear this woman's testimony. She revealed that what often lies behind a closed heart is a heart which is painfully open. We are not as cruel and rejecting as we sometimes seem. We do care. We care so much, in fact, that caring hurts.

Thanks to our technological advancements, we have more access to tragedy today than ever before. It's no wonder so many of us feel overwhelmed. In Wisdom Keeping communities, we're often encouraged to solve the problem of over-exposure to negativity by surrounding ourselves with positivity. Understandably so, many of us choose to stop watching the news and spend time with people doing the same. We understand that taking charge of what we put in our minds is as important as choosing what we put in our bodies.

Focusing on what inspires us can release us from 'hopelessness paralysis' and empower us to carry out our life's work. When we nourish ourselves with uplifting images and environments, we more easily avoid the common trap of merging with heaviness and fear. As we increase our resiliency and spiritual surplus, we bring hope to others and find creative solutions to seemingly impossible situations, even in the face of tragedy. We are able to be of service wherever it's needed.

We walk a fine line as we learn to distribute our attention in a conscious manner. While taking a break from negativity can be just what we need to open our hearts, it can also provide a convenient excuse to shut them down.

Since we are in the business of healing hearts as professional Wisdom Keepers, we can mistakenly think we're incapable of closing our hearts. This is not true. Like everyone else, we risk stepping over homeless people on our way to work, without making contact. We can avoid, deny or devalue the pain of those we serve because we're afraid of being engulfed, destroyed or smitten by it. We can do so in the name of spirituality.

In a way, our heart-closing methods can be more damaging and confusing than more blatant ones, for they can be exceedingly subtle.

In fact, we can make our hearts look wide open when they're bolted shut. We explain our clients' and students' pain away with sophisticated karmic theories. We tell them all they need to do is change their minds. We remind them that they've created their situations, so have nothing to complain about. We convince them that their suffering is just an illusion. While there may be elements of truth to all that we say, if our timing and underlying motivations are off, our guidance becomes either useless, dismissive, hurtful, shaming or guilt-provoking.

I'll never forget the day I bumped into someone who was a well-known journalist at a spiritual magazine and 'New Age' radio host. Somehow the subject of starvation in Third World countries came up between us. What left the deepest impression on me was not only what this person said, but how they said it. They shrugged their shoulders, laughed and flippantly stated, "Well, that's their karma. Their souls must need to starve." I was stunned by the callousness in this statement and took it as a potent invitation to find those places in me that shut down when faced with suffering.

Most Wisdom Keepers become healers, coaches and guides because of a deep desire to relieve the pain of others. We want to share the very philosophies and practices that helped us deal with our own suffering, and to spare our clients and students from having to go through what we went through. We can live up to our Wisdom Keeping potential when we can cultivate these three skills:

- an ability to slow down
- a willingness to feel safe with a wide range of feelings (including our own!)
- a keen sense of timing

When we slow down, we temporarily release our spiritual ambitions and allow our clients and students to move through the stages of grief at their own pace. We show our respect for their inner rhythms and natural abilities to heal. If and when we feel deeply moved or triggered by their experiences, we can choose to make room for our inner experience, acknowledging that our clients and students are often our most powerful mirrors, and teachers. Together, we practice stretching our hearts, while remaining objective.

A keen sense of timing is key for all professional Wisdom Keepers. Just as there is a right time to share a possible meaning or uplifting perspective, there is a right time to be silent, to allow the tears of meaninglessness to flow.

When at our best, we catch ourselves when feeling a premature urge to 'explain away' someone's pain. We ask ourselves *why* we're in such a hurry to understand or interpret their suffering. Are we afraid of feeling our own sorrow? Are we afraid of hanging out in the unknown? If we are, we work towards raising our comfort level with discomfort. We take deep breaths as we open to the mystery, allowing whatever is arising to arise, without rushing to explain or offer a quick fix.

Waiting for the right moment to deliver our wisdom doesn't require that we let go of our high visions for those we serve. On the contrary, it allows us to get even better at spotting those just-right moments, when we can beam light through openings and cracks as they appear. In the meantime, we relate to suffering without merging with it. We support where we can, doing our humble best to provide what is needed, when needed.

Humility is key. Becoming a competent professional Wisdom Keeper is a life-long journey. Some of our experiences will be more successful than others. Sometimes our timing will be impeccable and wisdom-delivery just right. Other times, we'll act too quickly, get too involved, or not get involved enough. When things don't go so well, let's be gentle and compassionate with ourselves for we are only human. Opening our hearts in the face of suffering (on a daily basis) is not easy. As my old professor, Richard Mann used to say, "No blame. No shame." We just get back up on our Wisdom Keeping horse and keep on trying.

My own compassion makes it possible for others
to transform their suffering into compassion.
I give myself and others the time and space needed to feel our feelings.
I don't have to have all the answers.

Giving and Receiving are One and the Same

Here in our earthly existence, we may need to temporarily buy into the illusion of separateness in order to keep the give-and-take ball rolling. But there really is no difference between giving and receiving.

I remember Ram Dass, one of my favorite Wisdom Keepers as you can see, using the simple metaphor of hunger to drive this point home. He asked the question, "What do most people do when their stomachs tell them that they're hungry?" For those of us blessed with shelter and food, the answer is easy. We walk over to our refrigerators or kitchen cabinets, grab something that looks appetizing, and we eat it. If we're feeling extra ambitious, we cook it.

Although the process of satiating the body's hunger is relatively simple, it actually involves a great deal of cooperation between our body parts and biological systems. The stomach must send the hunger signal to the brain; the brain must receive the hunger signal; the brain must then send the appropriate signals to the rest of the body to take the appropriate actions. The legs must walk the body over to the refrigerator; the arms must reach out towards the refrigerator handle; the hands must open the door, grab the food, prepare it, and then bring the food to the mouth. The mouth must chew the food, the throat must swallow it, and the esophagus and other organs must carry the food to the stomach, where the hunger is eventually satisfied. The intestines must absorb the nutrients into the body and push out the waste.

Acknowledging this complex string of events, Ram Dass asks us to imagine what each of our body parts would say if they could talk.

Would our stomach be so grateful to the legs, arms and hands for bringing it food that it would feel eternally indebted? Would the hands and legs quarrel over whose role in feeding the stomach was more valuable? Would the esophagus send the stomach a bill for its hard work? Would the brain resent the stomach for being hungry so often, forcing it to work so hard on the stomach's behalf?

The answer to all of these questions would most likely be 'no.' This is because every bodily 'part' involved in the process of satisfying the stomach's hunger would understand one important fact: if the body isn't nourished, they're all in trouble. They're all intricately connected and interdependent, part of the same body.

Ram Dass then draws the analogy between our bodies and our planet, also a singular living organism. Just as our hearts, elbows and toes are invaluable parts of the same body, all plants, minerals, mountains, sentient and non-sentient beings are essential parts of Earth's planetary body. If any 'part' of our Earth is suffering or in need, then it is everybody's business. With this in mind, how thankful should hungry planetary citizens be for food provided by those who easily have the means to give them what they need? How superior should those in a position to give feel in relation to those they serve? When we truly acknowledge our Oneness, such questions seem silly.

Although Buddha was born into a wealthy family, he understood from a very early age that as long as someone was suffering, he was suffering too. He understood and came to teach the paradoxical truth that we are each simultaneously part of a whole, and the whole itself.

As we strive to master the art of giving and receiving as professional Wisdom Keepers, let's remember that when we give to someone else, we are in fact giving to ourselves. When we remain aware of this truth, we understand that there is no reason why someone in a receiving position should ever have to lose their dignity in order to meet the ego's needs of a 'giver.'

Although gratitude is a wonderful practice and powerful prayer, we are all working for the same Employer and will get the big bonus in the end. It has always been, and will always be, in *all* of our best interests, that we *all* get what we need.

Lastly, something that Ram Dass and others emphasize is the importance of giving in a way that genuinely empowers people, that honors their sovereignty. Assessing someone's real need can take more time than quick fixes allow. It requires developing a keen ability to listen, to get to know the people we aim to serve, and to be honest with ourselves about our motivations and hidden agendas.

I once heard a story about a prestigious American charitable organization which brought tons of grain to a third world region. When the 'helpers' returned to the region months later to see how the new crops were growing, no grains were left, and none had been planted. Confused, the volunteers asked the people who received the grain what had happened. They said that the grains were cooked and eaten. No one had ever taken the time to tell them that the grains were to be planted, or how to plant them. This is a good picture of what can happen when we are in too much of a hurry to give, and too out of touch with those who we aim to serve.

When Personal Hang-ups Get in the Way

Carrie saw a homeopath to bring her body, thus self, back into balance. She had a history of under-eating. Unlike an anorexic who uses their conscious willpower to attain the 'ideal' state of thinness and assume control over their eating habits, thus their life, Carrie experienced her thinness, general lack of appetite and physical resistance to eating as undesirable. She had always wished to be heavier and to eat more. Not being able to do so, and being surrounded by people who not only didn't understand her frustration but felt envious of her, had been a source of pain for her for many years.

While generally a healthy person, the homeopath herself had struggled with weight issues for years. When Carrie shared that she'd been going through an exceptionally difficult time, and that she had almost no appetite at all, the homeopath jokingly responded, "If only I had your problems! We should trade places!"

Instead of insisting that the homeopath take her suffering seriously, Carrie laughed at the joke. She also stopped sharing openly about how powerless she truly felt about her situation. She left the office with a few remedies in her purse, and a subtle feeling of shame for having had the nerve to suffer over her thinness.

While there's certainly a place for humor and humility in our work with clients, it's not always helpful, especially when those we work with are feeling vulnerable. It's even less helpful when we're unconsciously masking an area of our own vulnerability, or trying to avoid vulnerability all together.

The Intrusive Interviewer

Tim had been working with a plethora of alternative coaching techniques for years. He finally found one that really spoke to him. It embraced a basic underpinning, common in positive thought circles: *happiness is a choice.*

This particular technique involved asking a series of questions aimed at helping people see painful experiences or problems in their life from a more positive light. One of the tricks to the technique was to continuously pose the question, "Why do you see that as a problem? Why are you allowing that problem to cause unhappiness?"

This technique has had lots of success, and understandably so. People who have judged themselves and their lives as problematic have realized there are different ways of looking at things. Just because we've experienced a disappointment, set-back, challenge or a loss does not mean that we must be indefinitely miserable about it and resign ourselves to a life of victimization.

It is true that many people tend to make disempowering problems out of potentially growth-inspiring circumstances. An effective way to discover the learning potential in any situation is by seeing it as a potential, not a handicap or tragedy that's written in stone. At its best, techniques like the one Tim found support people in cultivating new more life-enhancing perspectives—bringing them into the here and now, the point of all change. They give people the strength and optimism to transmute tragedies into triumphs. They also demonstrate a basic trust in the fact that we all have the answers we seek, if we are just asked and allowed to discover own deep source of wisdom.

At their worst, these kinds of techniques can be experienced like bulldozers, convincing people to ignore their feelings and superficially change their minds, while sadly ignoring the deeper wisdom which often resides in the body and heart. Let me tell you what I mean.

One day, Tim asked a client if she was willing to be his guinea pig. Tim had just taken an intensive course learning the technique and wanted to practice his new skills. The session started out just fine. He asked her, "What seems to be the problem?"

The client answered, "I do not feel comfortable in my body."

"And why is that a problem?" he asked.

"Because it keeps me from being physically intimate with the one I love."

"And why is that a problem?"

The questions went on and on, as did the answers. Eventually, the answers led to the client revealing a horrifying experience from her past. When she was a child, a group of teenagers tried to rape her and lock her in a basement. She was saved from the actual rape, but the experience had scarred her for many years.

During the session, the client began to cry. Instead of assisting her in exploring and making space for her sadness, Tim kept plodding away with his inquiry, "And why does that make you sad?"

"Why did nearly having been raped make me sad?" the client asked, puzzled.

"Yes, why do you see that as a problem?"

The client had no idea what to say. She was stunned.

Perhaps, if the client had been a person who consistently clung to victim thoughts, such an exploratory process (handled with skill, compassion and a keen sense of timing, *and* used in the context of a safe, established relationship) could have been eye-opening or helpful. This client, however, was both wise and well-versed in New Thought philosophy. She was aware of the power we all have to identify and shift our negative attitudes. For her, this technique felt—and was— cruel. The more Tim asked 'why,' the more she felt interrogated, judged and victimized. Though Tim's aim was to empower his client, he ended up violating her boundaries, acting ironically similarly to the rapists from her past.

'Why' is a fascinating question. It can lead to all sorts of interesting insights. It can also be addictive and lead to a false sense of healing. Just because we understand why we are suffering up in our heads does not mean that we understand in our hearts or our bodies.

Although embracing the thought that we are healed can sow the seeds for true healing, it is important to remember that the mind is not only in the head. Just because we can logically prove to ourselves that we have no reason to be unhappy does not mean that there are no reasons, or that the unhappiness, or deeper feelings and energy resources lying behind our painful emotions cannot be useful or transformative. I have to wonder about the ultimate effectiveness of any technique which does not take the unconscious part of the psyche into consideration, or make compassionate room for the whole being's experience.

Learning how to be in the presence of grief and suffering—without shutting down the heart, checking out from life or explaining things away—is a life-long journey. Sometimes, the most powerful way we can communicate compassion is through slowing down, giving permission, and paying keen attention to what each moment is asking of us. For professional Wisdom Keepers and Seekers-on-the-path, there are few things worthier of cultivating than the art of Timing and the skillful navigation of Transitions.

PART SEVEN: TIMING & TRANSITIONS

No matter how wise, gifted or knowledgeable you are, if your timing stinks, your work will too—whether or not your students or clients notice it.

The Tao of Leadership

"When a sage king rules
his influence is felt everywhere
but he does not seem to be doing anything
His work affects the 10,000 things
but people don't depend on him consciously
No one is aware of him
but he brings happiness to everyone
he stands on that which is not known
and wanders in the land of nowhere."

~ Lao-Tzu

I loved John Heider's *The Tao of Leadership*. This simple yet profound book greatly impacted me and my approach to counseling and teaching. It can be a friend to those who tend to move too quickly or mistrust the natural way of things.

Embracing a similar philosophy in relation to the birth process, Binnie Dansby taught me a great deal about how to support women (and people in general) through a birth—or life transition process. One thing she always said was that the less helpers interfere, the better. Doctors, nurses and midwives can have a difficult time understanding that their presence is sufficient during a birth, that sometimes the best support they can provide a laboring mother is relaxed trust in birth as a natural process. When birth is allowed to unfold without too much prodding, pushing or opinions, when there is enough stillness in the room so that the woman in labor can listen to the signals her own body gives her, chances are things will go a lot more smoothly.

Sometimes our need to be helpful obstructs our ability to help. We think we must do so much that we end up doing too much. Our nurturing smothers. Though our clients and students might feel filled with our knowledge, wisdom and tools, they may also unconsciously feel cheated. If left to their own paces, and filled up a little at a time when they were ready and asked for it, they might feel more satisfied. They would feel like active participants.

When professional Wisdom Keepers can relax, stop trying so hard and trust the natural process of development, their clients and students often end up arriving at the very same destination—but with the added perk of empowerment.

Again, this is about balance. Too much interference is not necessarily helpful, but no feedback or interference at all can be just as destructive. It is up to you to be aware of this dynamic. I only suggest that if you tend to be someone whose overzealous helpfulness can get in the way of your trust in the natural power of presence, then practice doing less and being more. You might be surprised at how effective your very presence can be.

Beware of the Spiritual Salesperson!

There is a fine line between providing encouragement and applying pressure. I have found that some alternative organizations which also are 'big businesses'—especially those run in hierarchical or pyramid-like structures—tend to apply a great deal of pressure on people while selling their spiritual products. I know most employees within such organizations sincerely believe their organizations are good ones, and that their teachings and sales tactics are meant to encourage and support, not to push. I also know that many of these organizations do provide students and Wisdom Keepers-in-training with valuable learning experiences, inspiring material, and life-enhancing philosophies.

At the same time, I have seen how such organizations can create potent atmospheres of pressure, and how these contagious climates wind up manipulating people into buying too much, too soon. Using catchy phrases like, "If not now, when?" and "Don't let your resistance control your life," recruiters play on people's human desire to be included, their longing to be seen as courageously committed, and their need to keep up with the righteous rat race.

When the goal of recruiting and building up an economic empire overshadows the goal of supporting people in making decisions which are right for them in the moment, quantity replaces quality. Though many people benefit from the good in the product sold, many others allow themselves to be blindly swept up by the rush of enthusiasm, forgetting everything about whether the timing or intensity of their participation is appropriate for them.

If you are an alternative professional belonging to such an organization, I ask you to take care. Be honest with yourself about your motives. Why are you really in such a hurry? If you truly trust that the courses you are selling are all that they are cracked up to be, you can afford to be more patient, and less insistent. See how it feels to allow people to sign up voluntarily, happily, and in their own good time. If you sense that the organization disapproves of your decision to let go of your personal investments, then you might want to think twice about the organization.

If, on the other hand, you are a Wisdom Seeker considering joining an organization which has similar traits, all I want to say is:

Don't be afraid to take your time.

If you feel any doubts, do not sign up right away. Give yourself a day or month or year to think it over. The organization is not going to disappear overnight, and will definitely survive your waiting until next spring or fall, or whenever the time feels right for you. It is perfectly OK to say no, even when surrounded by hundreds of people, including your family members or entire social circle saying yes. Whether you sense your wish to decline your first course or your eighteenth, it does not matter. Saying no does not necessarily mean you are unwilling to heal, afraid to take risks, or unable to grow. Perhaps the timing is not right or something even more wonderful is just waiting around the corner.

Even if your supportive coach thinks you are missing out on the opportunity of a lifetime and lets you know how disappointed they are in your decision, be true to yourself anyway. You can always change your mind. Besides, the best coaches in life are non-attached to the results of their actions and feel best when you respect your own boundaries, learning at a pace which feels safe and empowering for you. Be a good coach for yourself by respecting your feelings, your intuition, and your own sense of timing.

Slowing Down

Sometimes professional Wisdom Keepers go too fast. This is not only unavoidable to a certain extent, but can also be a good thing, for part of what we are being paid for as healers, therapists, teachers, astrologers, coaches, or guides is being a few steps ahead of those we serve. We are here to hold the vision of their future fulfillment, while keeping an overview of how they're doing in the now.

Sometimes we can be a hundred steps ahead of our clients and students. Skilled clairvoyant healers might be able to see their clients' auras and futures instantaneously. Similarly, many practitioners who work intuitively, or who have years of experience behind them, often know much more about their clients and students than the clients and students know about themselves—at least on one plane.

The fact that professional Wisdom Keepers can be exceptionally insightful does not mean, and I repeat, does not mean that we should indiscriminately share everything we know and see whenever we feel like it. When we make this mistake, we frequently end up giving those we serve useless advice, needless scares, and empty prophecies.

Occasionally I find it nice, even essential, to let a trusted, wise helper share their objective, intuitive and insightful perspective about me and my life. More often than not, though, I appreciate it when I discover aspects of myself and my path at my own pace. I feel good with the opportunity to develop my own revelations, and to draw my own conclusions.

A wise client of mine once said that all satisfaction comes through effort. In other words, when people do not apply themselves or cannot feel a connection between their own commitment and energy-input and their successes, their capacity for experiencing satisfaction is lessened—so true when it comes to self-help. Having the Truth handed over to us on a silver platter gives less reward than discovering The Truth ourselves.

See if you can allow your clients and students satisfaction by giving them room to discover themselves and gain important insights at their own speeds. Keep your ego in check. Make sure your attempt to share your wise observations isn't just showing off. When you truly feel your clients are ready, feel free to give a hint or plant a seed or two, then let them take the next step.

Prefer to Follow, Not to Lead

Have you ever been to therapists, healers or coaches who ask probing questions—for which it is painfully obvious that they already have the answers? I have, and it doesn't feel great.

Try not to put your clients and students through such a grueling experience. If you have something to say and think they are ready to hear it, then just say it. Don't disguise your opinion by forming it into a question. If you want to demonstrate your non-invasive nature or your openness, then do so by letting them have the option of disagreeing with you and your theory. Say, for example, "I sense you are feeling angry. Is this true?" Don't say, "So, how are you feeling right now?" If you are sure they are angry, they will most likely intuitively sense your sureness of their emotional state. When they sense this, they will either desperately begin to look for the right answer, or shut down—probably getting even more angry. No one likes to be indirectly led, and no one needs performance pressure from their professional Wisdom Keeper.

The Right Help Too Early

Nishan suffered from bulimia. He had struggled with a negative body-image and a painful pattern of binging and purging for many years. Although he had been going to group therapy and the bulimic behavior was under control, he still had a difficult time accepting his body. He set very high standards for himself in relation to diet and exercise. Carrying a history of repeated weight loss failure in his psychological suitcase, he went to a holistic nutritionist filled with new hope.

Though the nutritionist asked Nishan a few questions about emotional eating, they weren't able to see that he was not emotionally ready for their treatment. The eating program they suggested was spiritually and physically sound and specifically designed for his body's needs. It healthfully focused on lifestyle changes as opposed to crash and burn dieting, and it was undoubtedly capable of whipping Nishan's body into great shape.

That did not change one all-important fact: its timing was off. No matter how enthusiastic Nishan seemed, he was still too entangled in his inner body battle to use the nutritionist's methods in a self-loving way. In his jaded psyche, it was just another diet, another way to deprive himself.

Sometimes, as professional Wisdom Keepers, we need to take time to assess our clients' and students' readiness for what we have to offer. The best and most effective methods in the world aren't worth much if given to people who are not ready to receive them. Understanding this truth means that sometimes, in order to serve people in the best way possible, we have to turn people away, refer them to someone else, or tell them to come back when they are ready to receive the valuable gifts that we do have.

Time

In your efforts to honor your clients' and students' right timing, it's important that you don't forget to honor your own time. As a professional Wisdom Keeper, being in charge of whom you see and when you see them does not mean that you're being inflexible. It does mean that, if your client says that they can only arrange a meeting with you at midnight on New Year's Eve, you need not say 'yes'—just because it's the right timing for them, or your feel uncomfortable saying, "That just doesn't work for me. Let's find another time."

I invite you to not only create a container that supports your work, but a schedule that supports your life. Start by not taking more clients in one day (or in one week)—or more students in one workshop—than you have the time and energy to serve. The last thing you need is to have to fight your own clients and students for your own attention.

This particular lesson can be especially difficult for those in the beginning stages of setting up a practice, as well as for those who have achieved great outer success. If you are an alternative professional who is just starting out, you may need to be more flexible with your schedule now than later on, demonstrating your availability as well as your deep commitment to do whatever it takes to manifest your vision. This doesn't mean that you should be overly accommodating out of desperation. Clients can usually smell desperation from miles away, and the skillful ones will have you wrapped around their little pinkies in no time—not to mention resenting them for taking over your life.

If you are already a highly successful professional Wisdom Keeper, with more people flocking to your office or retreat center than you can count, you might want to consider inserting small pauses in between sessions, taking regular vacations, forming a wait list for interested clients, or referring potential new clients to other respected practitioners. I know too many professional Wisdom Keepers who've said 'yes' to working with so many clients that they border on burnout, just trying to keep up. There are only so many hours in a week, and only so many clients and students one person can support well through a deep healing process—without losing a valuable and potentially replenishing chunk of one's life.

I recommend setting realistic goals for yourself. Make sure you have as much time to fill up your tank as you have time to divvy out your delicious goodies. This will help you help those who come to you do the same.

Managing Transitions

I t is not uncommon for professional Wisdom Keepers to make professional transitions—moving from one modality to another, or incorporating new modalities into our present work. Some of us make personal transitions as well—shifting professional relationships with clients and students into more personal or more 'equal' ones. At some point, most clients and students become ready to transition out of their work with us and into their lives. In all of these cases, an awareness of boundaries comes in handy, as well as a dedication to ensuring that we're transitioning healthily and appropriately, honoring the natural and correct timing of things, and preparing ourselves to let go.

From One Modality to Another

Since many professional Wisdom Keepers think and work holistically, we often integrate more than one philosophy, system, technique and modality into our unique rainbow-like service. Our eclectic and organically evolving approach to the healing arts has many advantages. It allows us to meet the varying needs of clients with greater flexibility and specificity. It allows us to work creatively and intuitively, finding the just right method for the right person at the right moment.

Although over all, I'm sure my clients and students have benefited from my eclectic professional explorations, finding a balanced synthesis of the paradoxical methods I've learned hasn't been exactly bump free. I've had to learn some lessons the hard way.

After working intensively as a Rebirther for years, I began studying expressive arts therapy. The particular school I attended was based on Jungian theory and had a more therapeutic and depth psychological bent to it than Binnie Dansby's Rebirthing training.

While both the Rebirthing and expressive arts therapy educations focused on the creative process, they concentrated on different aspects of that process. Acknowledging the immense impact our pre-birth and birth experience had on our lives, decisions and self-concepts, the Rebirthing training made healing separation its deepest intention.

Work on the Rebirthing training was highly intimate. We could spend entire days immersed in warm water, holding and supporting breathers as they surrendered completely. Our job was to support and receive new 'babies' into the world, so a great deal of physical closeness was allowed and encouraged. Our work was deep, soft, and in a way boundary-less by nature. Bonding was highly prioritized. Friends, colleagues, teachers, students, assistants, supervisors, Rebirthers and 'Rebirthees' all blended together—everyone focused on the same goal of healing separation. The boundary-less nature of our work, together with the family-like feeling of our community, made our work as healing, powerful and life-transforming as it was.

The qualities that made our work so effective as breathworkers were the same ones I later found difficult to combine with the more psychotherapeutic methods I learned at The Institute for Art Therapy. Individuation was the focus at the Institute. Vibeke Skov, a licensed psychologist and spiritual pioneer, artist and free thinker in Denmark, was the founder of the education. Her teaching style and professional focus were the opposite of Binnie's. While the Rebirthing training focused on creating an exceptionally warm, safe and supportive environment where group togetherness was encouraged, the expressive arts therapy education focused on creating a free environment where individualism could flourish.

I must admit the Institute looked to me about as loveless and cold as a dead fish at first. It took me some time to see, understand and appreciate Vibeke's way—not only of teaching, but of loving. I was used to Binnie the *Great Mother*—a teacher who made grand entrances, brilliant introductions and who was always there to take care of her students (her children) so carefully. I was used to an atmosphere where each bit of progress was acknowledged, each group process was meticulously monitored and guided, and where people were constantly reminded of their adequacy and lovability. During the first few expressive arts therapy sessions, I understandably found myself doubting whether it was safe to fully surrender. Could I trust Vibeke to hold the high vision for the group and help us keep the peace? Who would look after me if or when I felt vulnerable?

After some time, I started to feel safer. I participated in enough group processes where projections were allowed, expressed and creatively dealt with to realize they were not lethal. I realized that people crying or feeling insecure without being held and affirmed by Binnie the *Great Mother*, were trusted, encouraged and authentically seen by Vibeke, the *Good Father*. No matter how chaotic things seemed, Vibeke continued to trust that our creative explorations would work magic on our psyches and our relationships, eventually causing the shifts each of us needed. She was right.

Eventually, some of Vibeke's Greek column-like trust rubbed off on me. In the middle of the circus, I began to feel increasingly seen, loved and most of all... *free*! I basked in the creative free space I was given at the Institute, relishing the beautiful surroundings, the paints, feathers, clay and the outdoor trampoline. I delighted in the variety of therapies and theories we were exposed to, and found Vibeke's non-attached yet compassionate approach to teaching both fascinating and useful. (Given my childhood and background, it was quite a relief not to worry about having to win the approval of a teacher!) We had many exciting guest teachers from around the world, and I enjoyed many of them. Ironically, I even enjoyed *not* enjoying a guest teacher or two.

In retrospect, I see that the greatest gift those years at the Institute gave me was the freedom to practice my honesty, to explore the shadow, to unfold as I pleased, to test my limits, to express the inexpressible, and to embrace the whole of me and my psyche—without rejecting or judging any of the less than beautiful, 'spiritual,' yet equally important parts.

Artistically speaking, I enjoyed greater freedom as well. I tended to 'paint pretty' before I entered the program, yet a growing part of me longed to explore the forbidden, the dark, the childlike and the ridiculous. I wanted to use blacks and browns. I wanted to scare myself without being labeled 'unspiritual.' Plenty of opportunities arose where I could delve deeply into exactly that—the murky and non-adult worlds within me. Meeting and exploring my shadow was just the beginning of that process.

Eventually, I wanted to incorporate the best of both worlds into my professional service. I wanted to provide clients and students with both a safe, holding environment and an experimental, freeing one, to be both *Motherly* and *Fatherly*. I wanted to create a warm, supportive environment where they could feel deeply and think highly of themselves and their potential. At the same time, I wanted to make a space for them to test their limits, express the forbidden, and discover their own unique style and personal/spiritual path. Finding this sacred balance was easier said than done.

To find that balance, I needed to correct and work through two false impressions. One was the thought I could combine and use everything I had learned with all of my clients all of the time. I quickly discovered that the physical closeness of Rebirthing did not jibe so well with the artistic and psychotherapeutic means of expressive arts therapy. Often, I had to make a choice between the two, depending on what I sensed was best for my clients and students.

The second false impression was this: I felt obligated to give my clients what they asked for. If a person came to me and said they wanted to do Rebirthing with me, I'd do Rebirthing with them—even though I might have intuitively sensed that expressive arts therapy (a more psychological and boundary-conscious approach) would be more appropriate.

In the beginning, I didn't think I had the right to trust and follow my intuition. Now I know I not only have the right, but the responsibility to be in charge of what services I provide to whom, and when. Often clients and students do not know what they are asking for. They may think they need one thing when they actually would benefit much more from something else. I learned to trust myself and what I'd learned from my professional experiences about what would serve people best, but this took time.

I remember once agreeing to do a breathwork session with a new client, without sufficiently researching their past experiences with physical closeness—which turned out to have been pretty traumatic. I felt obliged to give them what they were asking for, and soon realized that Rebirthing was simply too confrontational a method for them. By the time I realized my mistake and began doing some conscious boundary work with them, it was almost too late. Some damage had already been done. It took us quite some time to reestablish a sense of safety and trust between us.

I regret not having had the awareness or the experience I now have. If I did, I would have handled things much differently. Now I am grateful to that client, for they turned out to be a powerful teacher. I learned to be much more aware and respectful of boundary issues as a result of our work together. Today, I take more time to get a sense of clients' and students' boundary systems, before suggesting more intimate modalities.

I am glad to have had two very different, powerful and competent teachers from whom I could learn a great deal. I am also happy to have (at least) two solid foundations of work as opposed to numerous half-foundations. I recommend to all professional Wisdom Keepers that they have at least one fully integrated technique, one area of expertise. Being a good professional requires deep inner trust and conviction. The kind of conviction I speak of is not the kind that comes from taking a weekend workshop or two in some method. It comes from years of personal experience and physically integrated knowledge.

In our Wisdom Seeking world, many people meander about, looking for a quick fix here and there and end up repeatedly disappointed. In the professional Wisdom Keeping world, we can get similarly lost, hopping from modality to modality, plucking out and packing on new techniques and systems, without ever making it through the honeymoon stage into the nitty gritty of any of them. When we do this, our new techniques turn into shiny distractions, for us and those we serve. The more intimately we know our method, the more flexible and creative we can be with it, and the more we can catalyze a deep commitment among our clients and students.

True healing is rarely a quick fix.
It takes time, effort and a willingness to stick with the process
even when it gets sticky.

A method is only as good as the one who uses it.

When Tai Chi masters stand, they plant both of their feet on the ground, keeping their knees bent and flexible, their weight centered in the belly, and their mind and body focused and relaxed at all times. Their mind is sharp and awake, soft and relaxed. They are both giving and receiving, expanding and contracting. Though they are moving continuously, they are deeply centered, invincible. If someone tries to push or pull them off balance, they instantaneously respond by following the energy flow put in motion. This throws off their opponent and allows them to stay peaceful and present at all times.

It follows that if you stand as rigid and stiff as a tree, thinking you are strong, a mere sneeze will be able to knock you over. Flexible and creative strength comes from commitment and depth.

Let's join hands, hearts, minds and spirits with our Wisdom Keeping vocation, like the Tai Chi masters. From that grounded, strong and flexible space, anything we add—any technique, method or source of knowledge—can only enhance our effectiveness.

From Professional Wisdom Keeper to Friend
(or Vice Versa!)

You are not the roles that you play.
But you do play them, and they do have real consequences.

If you are a professional Wisdom Keeper, most of the shifts you'll experience with those you serve can be made and contained within your professional relationship. All you need to do is fine-tune the roles you play and agreements you make as you go, ensuring that your service continues to evolve and appropriately meet your clients' and students' changing needs.

Some shifts may lead you outside of your established professional relationship. I am referring to the (perhaps rare) case when you and your clients or students desire to move from a professional to a personal relationship—whether the personal relationship involves a friendship, romance, business partnership, or all of the above.

When contemplating a personal shift in your present professional relationship, it is useful to keep two things in mind. One is the basic truth that you are not the roles that you play. None of us are. Understanding this truth can help you to see how playing one role in relation to a person at one point can be completely appropriate, while totally inappropriate at another point.

Ram Dass once told a story about his going to a therapist to work through some issues. He managed to come through the crisis beautifully. In fact, he became so healthy that the therapist had to stop treatment, stating, "You've become healthier than me. I'm not able to take you any further in your journey. Actually, if it is OK with you, I'd like to enroll myself in one of your courses on meditation."

This story illustrates beautifully how roles are nothing but convenient structures people agree to accept and play out, as long as the roles are beneficial to both parties, and no longer. This professional Wisdom Keeper understood that just because he played the role of 'therapist' did not mean that he was superior or more evolved than his client. He understood that buying into or identifying with his role and its associated status would actually inhibit his effectiveness as a healer. Ultimately, he knew that status-identification was nothing but an illusion.

May we all be as non-attached to the roles we play as this brave and honest therapist. When we can dis-identify with our roles in such a way, we can recognize when our roles have become outdated and gracefully let them go, acknowledging the change which has taken place. Such an awareness allows us to manage relational shifts with those we serve, with integrity, respect and sensitivity.

Here's another perhaps paradoxical truth to keep in mind. When you take on a role in relation to someone else, certain dynamics come into play whether you like it or not. The more aware you are of these dynamics when making a personal shift or transition, the more you can prepare yourself for the consequences which almost always come from making such a shift, and the more responsibly and respectfully the shift can be enacted.

I do not take shifts from the professional to the personal plane lightly, (or the other way around, for that matter), nor do I underestimate the power of role playing. No matter how much we try to diffuse the roles we play for our clients, or stress our ultimate spiritual equality, or share social settings with those we serve, we cannot help but become parents, beloveds, idols and authority figures for our clients and students. We become whatever our clients need us to be emotionally, in order to work through their personal histories. (This can also happen when we choose to provide professional support to friends we've known for years. Despite our best efforts, power dynamics kick in, and if we're not careful, our friendships can be ruined.)

Even when everyone seems convinced that our clients and students are emotionally and intellectually ready to shift towards a personal relationship, they may not be. (*We* may not be!) It often takes a lot more than a verbal agreement and a shared intention to enter into a truly equal and balanced relationship.

Letting Go

In many ways, professional Wisdom Keepers undertake an archetypal parental journey. From the moment we meet our clients and students, we must prepare ourselves for two distinct and paradoxical processes: one, to bond, care for, nourish and support our clients and students to the best of our ability; and two, to prepare them for the day they no longer need us. We need to be able to let go, no matter how we may be feeling.

While most professional Wisdom Keepers manage to let go despite understandable feelings of sadness and loss, some of us try to postpone the inevitable transition for as long as we can. We keep encouraging our clients and students to come to us for help, even when we know deep down that they're capable of helping themselves, just as they keep turning to us for answers, even when they have the answers within.

Sometimes we avoid change because we don't want to hurt each other. One of the best ways to avoid a need for change is by not acknowledging that the need exists, or, that the change has actually already taken place, as is often the case. When we deny that a change has taken place, things tend to go haywire. Clients find themselves feeling irritated, bored, angry, critical, sad, desperate, lonely, needy or guilty, and they're not sure why. Professional Wisdom Keepers can have similar feelings.

Often, clients and students express their love and appreciation for their helpers by needing what their helpers have to give. When they sense that their need is lessening, they may mistakenly think that their love is too. This can be very confusing for everyone involved, making it equally hard to stay or leave graciously.

Easing Growing Pains

In a natural order of things, children are supposed to individuate from their parents. They are supposed to be the ones who leave when they are ready. When parents or primary caregivers leave their children—whether through death, divorce, mental illness or emotional distance—things often get screwed up.

For children who are left, the natural process of individuation can be delayed or complicated. Many of them turn to professional Wisdom Keepers and alternative communities when they grow up, in order to learn how to complete unfinished business and leave. They recreate new sets of parents who, when at their best, can facilitate this natural leaving process in a healthy way.

Depending on the professionals' comfort levels with the process of letting go, they can either make things easier or harder for their clients and students journeying forth into self-sufficiency. If professional Wisdom Keepers can acknowledge the fact that their students and clients need them less than before, and if they can send the essential message that this is not only OK, but the actual goal of their work together, the individuation process will go much more smoothly.

This does not mean that saying 'goodbye' should be pain-free for counselors and teachers. Feelings of sadness and loss are only natural, especially when the healing relationship has been long-lasting and deep. What matters is that these natural feelings don't get in the way of the professional helper's ability to act in accordance with what is truly needed.

If you are an alternative professional and in the position of having to let go, it may be totally appropriate for you to tell your clients and students that you will miss them, and that they are always welcome, as long as you refrain from subconsciously laying guilt trips on them. Just like children leaving the parental nest, they likely need to know you will survive their leaving. Accepting greater responsibility for their lives is hard enough. They don't need to carry around the additional weight of being responsible for your well-being.

Let's imagine that, for months, you supported a client through a difficult crisis. You held onto the vision of their healing when they couldn't hold it themselves. You provided the safety, clarity and strength needed to get them through. Over time, instead of talking about not being able to get out of bed, they started talking about places they'd like to go and things they'd like to do. The energy in the room, between you, felt different. Your client was emerging from the tumultuous tunnel they'd been in; they were reentering the world.

When such a positive turnabout takes place in a healing relationship, it can be deeply beneficial to verbally acknowledge and explore the shift. You might say something like, "You seem to be in a very different place than you were when you first came to me, a much stronger place. Do you sense this as well?" This gives your client the opportunity to check in and see if they feel the same way. If they do, you might ask, "Now that you're feeling stronger, I wonder what kind of support from me would feel right. Are there any changes in our way of meeting or in the focus of our work together that might feel better, given where you're at now?"

By verbalizing and legalizing the positive shift, you not only give your client the opportunity to acknowledge how far they have come, but to take more responsibility for their own healing and growth process. Together, you can explore their options with the understanding that they are now much more able to assess and meet their own needs.

Your client may want to continue working with you as intensively as before, but with an entirely different focus, like career, creativity or intimacy. They may continue working with you, but less frequently, or only on an as-needed basis. They may decide to stop working with you for a while, so they can test their wings.

Whatever they decide, the fact that they are involved in the decision-making process can leave them feeling empowered, proud of their increasing independence, and better able to make healthy decisions for themselves. They can also learn that 'growing up' is safe, a sign of progress, and that they don't have to lose you or your love (or anyone they care about) just because they need you less or in a different way than before.

The potentially painful transition from childhood to adulthood, from client/student status to autonomous individual status, should be handled as tenderly and lovingly as possible. Like the small child who contemplates jumping into the cold swimming pool by sticking one toe in the water at a time, students and clients may need time to get used to their growing independence. In such cases, professional Wisdom Keepers do them a great service by leaving a door open for them to come back if and when they need it, so they have a place to recharge, refocus, remember and get back on track.

Another important lesson for clients and students can be the realization that there is no actual need to return.

Clients' needs change during different stages of their lives. The more aware professional Wisdom Keepers are of this fact, the better it is for everyone.

The Sacredness of Transitions

For thousands of years, indigenous cultures have used sacred ritual to mark and celebrate passages from one stage of life, or state of being, to another. Unfortunately, many people in present day society find themselves without ritual. Either they've lost touch with, or interest in, the traditions of their ancestors, or they have been unable to find communities and customs which reflect their unique way of connecting with meaning and spirit.

Many of today's therapists, coaches, counselors, healers and spiritual teachers are doing the work of yesterday's shamans, priests, imams, masters, rabbis and gurus, finding meaningful ways to acknowledge growth, honor loss and celebrate change. These are wonderful gifts professional Wisdom Keepers can offer their clients and students, as they move along the path towards wholeness.

Clearly, there are so many ways in which our work as professional Wisdom Keepers can be positively or negatively influenced by our relation to Timing and Transitions. As with most things in life, there are no rules that apply to every situation, and there are far more gray areas than black and white.

Let's now turn our attention to a few of the biggest gray areas I've noticed in Wisdom Keeping and Seeking circles, and see if we can do some discerning together. Let's walk the fine lines between guilt and blame, affirmation and superstition, and intuitive resistance and sabotaging fear.

PART EIGHT:
THE 'GOOD,' THE 'BAD' and
the FINE LINE BETWEEN

The Art of the Deal
Becoming Empowered Consumers at the Shopping Mall of Life

Let's paint a silly scenario. You go to a high-end health store to buy yourself a pair of quality cotton underwear. A salesperson enthusiastically recommends a special aromatherapy-infused brand, brings you a gorgeous box, and swears profusely that you won't regret your purchase. Though you can't see inside the box, the picture on the outside looks great, and the box gives off a delightful scent of rose. Happily, you make your purchase and take it home. To your dismay, when you open the box, you find a single pair of polyester undies, smelling more like a family of skunks than a bouquet of roses.

The ultimate outcome of your shopping adventure will likely depend on your conditioning background and current level of self-esteem. If you've learned to assert yourself and you feel relatively worthy as a human being, you'll likely go back to the store, find the pushy salesperson and ask for a refund. When you take your business elsewhere in the future, you'll be sure to find out what's inside the box.

If you've been conditioned not to make a fuss, you're more likely to either get rid of the underwear, or keep it and never wear it. If you seriously struggle with self-worth, you may force yourself to wear the underwear as a form of punishment. Whether you're punishing yourself for being impossible to satisfy, unable to assert yourself, or for some other reason, you're going to spend too much of your precious time in stinky undies.

If we're willing to entertain a somewhat materialistic 'Western' metaphor, this scenario illuminates something profound. All of us are shoppers at the mall of life. Some of the salespeople we run into will be more trustworthy than others. Some of the spiritual products, packages and programs we purchase will be of higher quality than others. Some of the Wisdom Keeping philosophies and practices we're introduced to will be more healthy, empowering and better fits for us than others. Usually whatever and whomever we encounter along our self-development paths will reflect imperfectly mixed bags.

People who work with Gestalt-inspired therapies use an analogy which links learning with eating. Our early caregivers' beliefs, opinions and worldviews are like food, or meals. When we're little, whether what we're fed is healthy, poisonous, or something in-between, we swallow without chewing. Ideally, as we get older, we learn that we don't have to swallow whole everything that we're given. We can take more 'conscious bites' out of life, as well as take our time chewing. Ultimately, we learn to swallow what's useful, healing and empowering for us, and to easily—without fear or guilt—spit out the rest.

As Wisdom Seekers, one of our most essential tasks is learning what, from whom, how much, and when to take something in. Whenever we encounter a new bit of wisdom, our job will be to practice healthy discernment. Should we take a bite? How long should we chew? How much should we swallow? When is it time to spit something out? Bear in mind: the more we idealize, need, or feel emotionally attached to the person who happens to be feeding us, the harder our discerning job will be.

As professional Wisdom Keepers, one of our sacred roles is to be caring chaperones for our clients and students, escorting them through 'shopping malls' from their past, gently empowering them to return the damaged goods they bought long ago, when they couldn't differentiate between a 'good deal' and a 'bad deal.' When people trust us enough to accompany them on such a tender journey, we need to have their back. This means staying awake to just how vulnerable they can be when *we* are the ones feeding them a new truth, philosophy, system or practice.

In honor of those we serve, let's not be afraid to explore what we're actually feeding them, and why. Let's ask ourselves hard questions.

- Where did the food we're offering come from? Are we serving food that we swallowed whole in the past, when we ourselves were vulnerable and less discerning?
- If someone plopped a familiar food from our past on a plate in front of us today, would *we* still eat it? Should we do a bit more chewing ourselves, before blindly serving this food to others?
- Despite our good intentions, are those who are eating our food actually being nourished? Is it ambrosia for some, but poison for others?
- What happens when our clients and students choose to spit out some—or all—of what we feed them? Do we get defensive, angry or self-critical? Can we stay open and connected? How identified are we with the meals we're serving?

One last thing to keep in mind: chaperoning doesn't mean we do all of the work. Some clients and students will expect us to do precisely that. They'll walk up to us, carrying a giant sack of undigested life experience, and say, "Hey, you! Eat this, chew it up, spit out the parts that aren't meant for me, and hand over the rest." As tempted as we may be to give it a go, there is only so much we can—or should—do for a person. In the end, we are only responsible for what we ourselves eat and offer, and our job is to empower others to do the same.

Guilt and Blame

Most of us would prefer to live our lives completely free of guilt and blame. Wisdom Seekers in particular are taught that such feelings or attitudes are useless at best and damaging at worst. Not wanting 'what we focus on to grow,' we're often encouraged by our Wisdom Keepers to quickly replace these misguided inner states with more spiritually sophisticated and forgiving ones.

I'd like to advocate for a slightly different perspective. While relentlessly beating ourselves up is never a good idea, there are times when making room for guilt can be illuminating and healing. There are also times when consciously experimenting with blame (or acts of projection) can be empowering and educational—as long as we don't get stuck there.

When Wisdom Seekers and Keepers approach forbidden feelings like guilt and blame with a degree of curiosity, appreciation and respect, we find buried treasures.

Here's something interesting. People who tend to consciously identify as 'guilty' have shadows full of blame. Similarly, people who tend to identify as 'innocent victims' have shadows full of guilt. When our aim is to become psychologically whole, balanced and compassionate beings, we must make friends with our most forbidden parts.

When Jung explored the concepts of introversion and extroversion, he found that extroverted people tended to project their own feelings and characteristics out into the world around them. They experienced their unconscious tendencies and qualities in the people who either deeply annoyed them, or inspired them. They found it difficult to tolerate feelings like guilt, and felt more comfortable handing responsibility over to others. Their healing process involved taking projections home and no longer blaming people who were living out their unloved parts. Since there is a conditioning bias towards extroversion in the West, many who are influenced by Western culture tend to have extroverted traits. We learn from an early age to project out, and to differentiate. ("I am this. I am not that.")

Perhaps in response to this Western bias, many wisdom teachings are inspired by Eastern wisdom traditions. They tend to stress internalizing responsibility and honoring interconnectivity. ("You are in me. I am in you. We are each other.") Many professional Wisdom Keepers aim to assist people who are stuck in blame. We encourage them to release themselves from victim consciousness and to take full responsibility for their inner and outer lives. Many Wisdom Seekers, especially the beginners, benefit from such teachings. We learn to stop blaming others whenever something goes wrong in our lives. We become more empowered.

When we realize how much we've blamed others for our suffering, we can also feel very guilty. Suddenly, we see the humanity in people we've despised for years. We see how our own attitudes and expectations have contributed to our problems and brought out the worst in people, ourselves included. Confronted with our imperfections and blind spots, we begin to hold ourselves responsible for our lives and to regret ever having allowed others to carry responsibility for us.

Most professional Wisdom Keepers know that on a spiritual plane, humans are fundamentally innocent. We all do the best we can, given our level of awareness at any given time. Because we know this, we can feel tempted to encourage guilt-ridden clients and students to pre-maturely embrace their spiritual innocence, and they miss out on guilt's psychologically balancing role in their path towards wholeness.

I invite you to see the guilt of a former blamer as a primitive form of responsibility. If compassionately explored, it can give birth to a healthy conscience, a more balanced perspective, and a more realistic understanding of how co-creativity works. Learn to welcome this kind of promising or 'good' guilt, at least for a while. Trust that it comes as a sign that psychological growth is taking place.

Unlike extroverts, introverts tend to avoid projecting their feelings and qualities out into the world. When it comes to guilt, they tend to absorb it. When something goes wrong in their lives or relationships, they quickly take the blame or interpret what's happening from an internally-centered perspective. While extroverts deal with tension by expressing themselves and releasing energy, introverts hold onto physical tension, often forcing it to manifest through disease or blocks.

Experienced Wisdom Seekers (no matter where we started out on the introversion-extroversion continuum) usually end up developing and experiencing introverted philosophical leanings, especially when it comes to guilt and responsibility. It's no wonder we become experts at taking home projections and more than our fair share of responsibility for our lives. We hear the same lessons repeatedly.

- *The world is your mirror.*
- *You can't see anything outside of yourself which doesn't already exist within you.*
- *Blame and guilt are illusionary and disempowering responses to potentially healing situations.*
- *You are fully responsible for what you think, the choices you make, and the way you respond to every situation.*

Many Wisdom Seekers end up taking personal responsibility to the extreme, using spiritual knowledge to perpetuate painfully old (or newly amplified) patterns of self-blame. Instead of taking responsibility for our share of what happens, and allowing others to do the same, we take the entire world on our shoulders. Although our words and attitudes exude 'personal responsibility,' our actions (or lack thereof) can reflect an exaggerated sense of guilt and fear.

Even when taking action or speaking out against an injustice is called for, we can't do it. Unable to acknowledge the truth of co-creation, and dismissive of the possible validity of our observations, we lose our ability to take true responsibility—the *ability to respond.*

If you are a professional Wisdom Keeper, and your client or student has become a guilt vacuum cleaner, it may be time to help them see how their exaggerated sense of personal power is actually disempowering them. See if you can explore and validate at least some of their projections.

*Just because a projection is a projection doesn't mean it is **only** a projection. Sometimes, a willingness to test out our projections is the only way for us to learn what is ours and what is not.*

I knew a Wisdom Seeker named Shana. She had a terrible fear of public speaking. Once she saw a man giving a speech who seemed very uneasy to her. She wanted to approach him after the speech to offer reassurance and compassion. She didn't, because she feared that her observation was a total projection.

While it was possible that her observation revealed more about her fears than his, it was *also* possible that he was just as nervous as she suspected he was. Just because Shana (rather than someone who didn't fear public speaking) was the one making this observation, didn't make her observation any less true. She could have been breaking out in over-empathic sweats and assuming he was in much worse shape than he was, and he still might have been nervous.

Projections often combine subjective assumptions and objective observations. In Shana's case, the man probably *was* nervous, but perhaps not as nervous as she imagined. Because she totally disregarded the potential validity of her observation, and assumed it was a pure projection, she limited her options. If she had trusted her observation, she could have congratulated him on a job well done, or let him know that he was not alone, that she knew how he felt. She could have learned that her observations were keen. She could have made a new friend. She also could have made a fool of herself. Since she didn't dare test out her hunch, none of us will ever know if it was right, or off.

For Wisdom Seekers like Shana, with internalizing tendencies, trusting our observations does not only require courage; it requires a willingness to experience guilt. Just like chronic blamers can feel guilty when they bring projections home, chronic internalizers can feel guilty when we finally allow ourselves to project.

We realize that the people we've defended for years really did screw up. Misfortunes we've experienced weren't solely our fault. Others' attitudes and expectations (no matter how good their intentions) did negatively influence our lives and ability to cope constructively.

When people fall off pedestals and protective illusions break down, chronic internalizers can feel flooded with unfamiliar feelings, like rage and anger. We can also fear being seen by our teachers and friends as unspiritual blamers and victims. This can be quite uncomfortable and scary. Demonstrating the courage to feel fully and see clearly is our first step towards making self-honoring choices, and experiencing healthier, more mutually fulfilling relationships.

Reality-checking our observations and entertaining the validity of our projections can help us discover what needs private healing, and what contains collective relevance—which thus requires constructive and external action.

Just as a healthy dose of guilt can lead an 'ex-blamer' to experience a more highly developed conscience, a little bit of reasonable blame can lead an 'ex-internalizer' to uncover buried feelings, old patterns of protection, and ultimately, to experience greater self-confidence and the ability to take rightful action.

Herman Releases his Guilt

Herman was a sensitive, empathic man who had grown accustomed to his wife's constant criticism. Instead of getting angry, he assumed she was right, and that since she was such a good person, her intentions were always just as good. One day, in the middle of one of her critical rants, Herman had a heart attack. Luckily, he survived. As a part of his treatment plan, he began to see a therapist. When the therapist asked him how he felt about going home from the hospital, he mentioned feeling guilty in relation to his wife. He blamed himself for not listening to her warnings about his unhealthy diet, and he felt guilty that his illness caused her to worry. He feared becoming even more of a burden on her than he'd always been.

Over time, as Herman felt increasingly safe opening up in therapy, he began to realize just how unsafe he felt in his marriage, and how much he longed for more mutual respect, and tenderness. Unfamiliar feelings of powerlessness, inadequacy and anger began to surface, as he saw how his wife's constant put-downs had contributed to his low self-esteem. His habitual guilt towards his wife was slowly replaced by a greater sense of guilt and indebtedness towards himself. For the first time in his life, Herman realized that his wife wasn't perfect and never had been. Though he knew she didn't harm him intentionally, he could no longer deny the emotional hostility to which he'd been exposed, and its impact on his self-image, health and life.

As therapy continued, additional insights and memories emerged about his childhood. Herman's father had a frightening temper. The way Herman stayed safe was by being 'seen and not heard.' His mother pouted, sometimes even cried, if Herman refused to eat her food. Both of his parents constantly reminded him of the hardships they'd endured, as they worked to accommodate his and his seven siblings' demanding needs and all-around selfishness. Herman's only way of fighting back was to reject his mother's attempts to feed him, and to shut down emotionally. He learned to silence his parents by quickly accepting blame, internalizing his anger, and hiding behind a facade of gratitude, quiet and passivity.

No wonder he ended up with a wife who treated him harshly. It was familiar. With his therapist's help, Herman began to see how he was still relying on old survival strategies that now, instead of keeping him safe, were killing and hurting him—clogging his arteries, stressing his heart, and making true intimacy impossible. If he continued to hold back his anger, accept unfair treatment, and avenge himself by refusing his wife's food and shutting down emotionally, his body and relationship would continue to self-destruct.

Learning how to transform a passive self-defense strategy into an empowered self-nourishing one took time, and didn't feel comfortable. Getting in touch with his rage brought up a great deal of shame, guilt and fear for Herman. There were times he wished he could go back to his more oblivious days. However, he knew that to save his marriage and his life, he had to become more honest and direct with himself, and others. He had to learn how to see and respond to his wife as a life partner, not his parent. He had to grow up.

He also had to face and own the tyrant within. Long ago, he'd internalized an inner judge far more brutal than his wife could ever be. By confronting this inner judge, Herman discovered his own ability to think critically and act constructively. Over time, he learned to use his anger as fuel for more honest and assertive conversations. He began to insist on his wife's respect, and he set down some guidelines. If she wanted him to take care of his body, she'd have to stop bossing him around. He loved her very much, but was no longer willing to be criticized and blamed all of the time. It was his job to take responsibility for his own health, not hers.

Surprisingly, his wife didn't angrily explode or emotionally collapse, as he'd expected. This gave him the courage to share his deeper desire for greater intimacy between them. He'd been missing the sweetness of their early years, when they held hands and talked into the night. He suggested they spend more fun time together, going dancing, watching movies, and talking more about their real feelings.

Again, to his surprise, instead of getting angry and defensive, his wife burst into tears. For years, she'd been longing for more intimacy. She'd felt so alone, so cut off from his inner life. She couldn't even tell if he liked her anymore. He'd been so quiet and withdrawn for so long.

Whenever she'd tried to express her love by making him a healthy meal, he rejected it. His deteriorating health exacerbated her feelings of rejection and fear. If he really loved her, he would take better care of himself; he wouldn't give up on his own body. Whenever he ate something unhealthy, she heard, "I don't care enough about you to care about me." It wasn't her intention to scold or humiliate him, only to save the man she loved, and to make him notice her.

As the two shared honestly, tears were shed, anger exposed, fear released and love reborn between them. Of course, this was just a first step. It took time for them to create new habits and heal old wounds, but Herman and his wife wouldn't ever have come as far as they did if he hadn't reclaimed his anger, and tolerated a bit of guilt.

Not all relationships are meant to survive, as Herman's did.

Staying at any Price is too Big a Price!

I knew a woman who was involved in a very abusive relationship with a man. She had read many spiritual books and was absolutely convinced that the reason she was in that relationship was to learn. She believed that she and her unconscious thoughts had 'created' this unfortunate situation, and that her raging partner was mirroring some self-destructive part of herself.

She went to a professional Wisdom Keeper who reconfirmed her beliefs. Together they wrote affirmations until they were blue in the face. Unfortunately, this only added to the black and blue marks already there.

Of course, there is likely some truth to this woman's theory. Her partner probably was mirroring a very self-destructive part of her, but so was her professional helper. Who says that a willingness to learn always implies a willingness to stay? She and her Wisdom Keeper were convinced that if she just loved herself more, the partner's behavior would stop, that she would automatically 'create' something better. They were convinced that she was taking full responsibility for her situation.

I have known other professional Wisdom Keepers who have similarly misunderstood and misused these kinds of spiritual guidelines. In the name of empowerment and a willingness to step out of victim consciousness, Wisdom Seekers have been encouraged to put up with highly destructive relationships and circumstances, becoming even further victimized.

It is true that we are active and influential participants in our lives, and that a willingness to learn from every situation—no matter how painful—can be empowering. Sometimes, if we leave a relationship before we've healed the unhealthy pattern manifested in the relationship, we risk recreating the same problem in our next relationship.

That said, sometimes a true act of self-love, or stepping out of victim consciousness, requires that we step out of a life circumstance. Sometimes the only thing left for us to learn is how to say 'goodbye.' (If there's more to learn, we might as well learn it somewhere where we are physically safe and have the surplus of energy to stick with the healing process.)

Guilt is a Growing Pain

Growth-related guilt appears whether we know it or not, want it or not, and whether our professional Wisdom Keepers like it or not. It usually surfaces when we break free of an old protective pattern or integrate a lost part.

A fear of disappointing others can make it especially hard for us to feel and accept growth-associated guilt. Even when we know a change would make us happy, we repeatedly choose to betray and abandon ourselves. We hold back our feelings, stuff down our needs, stay in abusive relationships, keep unsatisfying jobs, and put up with endless amounts of life-diminishing circumstances—all to avoid feeling guilty or being seen as 'selfish.' Unfortunately, unless we learn to honor the natural pangs of growth, we remain stuck.

As professional Wisdom Keepers, one of the greatest gifts we can offer our self-sacrificing clients and students is the invitation to see their guilt as a *growing pain*.

Helena, the Guilt-Ridden Client

Helena was a super-parent and life partner. For years, she dedicated her entire existence to her family. As her children grew older and more self-reliant, she began to feel pangs of emptiness and longing. So she decided to seek professional help. With her spiritual coach, she shared how in her youth, she'd always wanted to be an artist, but when she had her first child, she put the dream aside and never returned to it. This made her sad. Together with her coach, she explored ways to revive her dream. Ultimately, Helena decided to go back to school as a full-time art major.

The decision felt exhilarating, until she got home and shared it with her family. Their obvious disappointment instantly turned her excitement into guilt-ridden regret. Her partner felt resistant to having to pick up so much domestic slack, and secretly feared Helena's exposure to the outside world would change her, thus their relationship. Despite her kids' increasing independence, they liked the fact that Helena was around whenever they needed her. They certainly weren't looking forward to taking on more household chores.

Helena swallowed her family's reaction like a dream-killing pill and decided to drop the plan. A guilt-ridden mess, she felt awful for having considered abandoning her family, and now for disappointing her coach. Her coach told her not to feel guilty, and then encouraged her to go through with the plan anyway, reassuring her that whether or not her family knew it, what was good for her would be good for them.

Helena did go back to school, and she faithfully followed her Wisdom Keeper's instructions to continue affirming her innocence, no matter what her family said or did. But the guilt didn't go away. In fact, it got bigger, which made her work even harder to get rid of it. As she fought off the guilt, she became increasingly angry, defensive, and even more neglectful of her family than was necessary. She forgot appointments with her kids, snapped at her partner, and yelled at the dogs. She had less and less control over her increasingly prickly behavior. When she couldn't take it anymore, she confessed to her coach that even though she knew she *shouldn't* be feeling guilty, she *was* feeling guilty.

This is a perfect example of how well-meaning Wisdom Keepers can do our clients a disservice by falsely advertising the ease of innocence. Leading clients and students to believe that they can take self-honoring risks without feeling any guilt can make them feel guilty about feeling guilty! A healthier message for Helena to receive might have gone more like this:

"You know what, Helena? Whether you like it or not, you're probably going to feel some guilt about going back to school. Feeling a little guilt right now is actually OK. It doesn't mean that there's something wrong with you, your decision, or that you are unspiritual. All your guilt means is that you're starting to love and appreciate yourself as much as you have loved and appreciated your family for so many years. It makes sense that making a shift towards prioritizing yourself is going to make you feel awkward and uncomfortable, because it's leading you into new and unexplored territory.

The truth is no one knows how your growing commitment to your own happiness is going to affect the people in your life. There are no guarantees in life when we take a leap of faith into greater self-love. One thing for sure is that, just as you're going to need time to adjust to the changes you're making, so will your family. They're used to your prioritizing them and their needs over yourself and your own needs. They will probably not understand or like everything you do—especially in the beginning. They may get angry with you. They may feel really hurt. This doesn't mean that you're doing something wrong or that you don't want the best for them. It also doesn't mean that ultimately your family doesn't want what's best for you.

It's actually because you love each other as much as you do, that you're all feeling some resistance to change. You are all probably much more afraid that the change will cause you to lose each other, than you are afraid of the change itself. The more you can remember this, the better chance you and your family have of managing this shift patiently, lovingly and constructively; and the better chance you will all have of transforming an initially scary and guilt-ridden situation into a growth opportunity for everyone."

Most of the time, guilt arises out of a deep wish to protect the ones we love from suffering. Though our wish to prevent others from feeling pain can inhibit their growth, the basic intention behind our guilt is almost always loving.

Learning to acknowledge the love behind our guilt can make things easier on everyone. When we feel guilty, we can remind ourselves that there are many ways to express our love that don't require self-sacrifice. We can do reality checks, noticing that our self-loving decisions aren't destroying the people we love.

If we can remain true to ourselves, without giving up or getting defensive, we usually discover that our self-honoring has a positive impact on our loved ones. It helps them learn to deal with disappointment. It helps them become more self-reliant. It can inspire them to revive their own neglected dreams. Together, if we can keep our hearts relatively open, we can learn how to resolve conflicts, improve teamwork and communicate more honestly. We can all learn that when we're each true to ourselves, our relationships get even better.

Resistance

In Wisdom Keeping communities, we are encouraged to say 'yes' to life, and 'no' to old limitations, doubts and low-frequency thinking. We hear slogans like: "Do what you fear. Watch it disappear!" "If not now, when?" "Don't let your past determine your future."

No wonder we feel confused when we also hear, "Trust your intuition!" "If in doubt, lean out!" It can take time to discern between the kind of resistance that is worthy of our attention and respect, and the kind that must be breathed through and overthrown.

When healthy resistance knocks on our door, we're hearing the soft, clear voice of our intuition. A master of timing, our intuition can let us know when we're acting too quickly, over-exposing ourselves, or taking too much of a risk. It signals our need to slow down, cultivate a more effective shield, set more realistic goals, and/or bring back balance. If we honor our intuitive resistance, we are stronger and better prepared when the right time for action comes.

When unhealthy resistance grabs us with its hook, we're not hearing intuition. We're hearing the manipulative, deceitful and sabotaging voices of ego-based fear. When these voices speak, we're better off ignoring, outwitting or overcoming them. Each time we manage to avoid the traps of unhealthy resistance, we break free of old patterns and find ourselves doing things we never thought possible. We express our vulnerability in front of an entire community; we walk on burning coals with our bare feet; we throw our inhibitions to the wind.

More often than not, our resistance reflects a conscious and unconscious blend of our bright hopes, dark fears, high expectations and cynical predictions. They're all hurled together into a giant decision-making stew of ambivalence.

When confronted with resistance, just like martial artists, we have the opportunity to transform a clumsy fight into a delicate dance, as long as we're willing to get to know our opponent (in this case, our resistance), and show them some respect. It is important that we remember that behind every resistant voice, there is at least some wisdom.

When professional Wisdom Keepers insist that our clients and students 'do what they fear, no matter what,' without exploring what's coming up for them, we can put them in a bind. They can end up resisting their resistance to such an extent that they unconsciously merge with it. Usually when that happens, the *resistance persists*, in increasingly subtle and twisted ways.

If you are a professional Wisdom Keeper, try encouraging your clients to befriend and dialogue with their resistance. Chances are they'll find an underlying positive, creative and self-protective longing hiding beneath the surface sabotage, and the energy will begin to move.

When Saying No leads to a Yes

In the early nineties, I was invited (quite last minute!) by Vibeke Skov to teach a week-long immersion workshop to the incoming first-year students, called *Jung and Expressive Arts Therapy*. She left the planning of the curriculum entirely up to me. I was honored, excited and terrified all at once. Given how much I had on my plate at that point in my life, revving myself up for such a big teaching gig felt like a giant responsibility and a lot of pressure, especially given the lack of time I'd have to prepare. I was afraid I'd do a bad job if I said 'yes,' and of letting Vibeke (and myself) down if I said 'no.'

My wise sister helped me remember that I had the right to say 'no.' Just because I was honored by the invitation didn't mean I had to accept it. Just because the job seemed to need me didn't mean I needed the job.

My sister then suggested I give myself a day to 'try on' a firm *no*— just to see how it felt. I declared my decision to her and my husband Kim, saying, "I'm not going to do this. It's just not the right timing for me." At first, I felt relief. My breath flowed more freely; my shoulders relaxed. With time, my body could feel that not only would I survive passing this opportunity up, but everyone else would too. It really was OK not to do it.

As the 24-hour 'no period' came to an end, I noticed myself wondering, "Well, if I *had* said 'yes,' how might I have approached the teaching?" Free from pressure and obligation, I found myself naturally exploring creative ideas. The more I thought about what I could give to the students, the less resistance I felt, and the more I could feel genuine excitement. The next thing I knew, I said YES.

Chiara says No

Chiara was a client who had a tendency to give her power away to men. She'd learned from a very young age that women are more powerful when they have a powerful man by their side. As a result of her work with a supportive Wisdom Keeper, she had come to understand that her dependence on men wasn't healthy for her. It tended to distract and hold her back, rather than bring her forward. Fortunately, despite her strong desire for a partner, she was no longer desperate enough to settle for anyone. She was also open to trying something new.

Together with her Wisdom Keeper, she created a list of what she believed 'having a man in her life' would make possible for her. The long list included everything from buying a car, to owning an expensive ring (a gift from him, since he'd make a good living), to feeling proud when she walked into a room, to becoming a member of a scuba-diving club (something she'd always admired, but could never imagine doing on her own).

Holding the vision of her self-emancipation and shadow integration, she and her Wisdom Keeper decided to use this list as a set of literal and symbolic goals for her to work towards. One of the most inspiring list items was her wish to join a scuba-diving club without a man. To her delight, she signed up for a club membership, worked extra hours to afford the monthly fees, and participated fully as a member. She soon discovered that she had a talent for diving. She even managed to resist the pull to lose herself in a romance with any of her attractive diving mates. She remained centered, empowered, reminding herself that she was there for her own sake, not to seduce or impress a man.

As time went on, Chiara noticed that she was losing interest in scuba diving. Whenever she contemplated taking the next logical step—becoming an instructor herself—she felt a lot of resistance. It would require so much of her time, money and energy. At first, her resistance sent her into a tizzy. She couldn't tell whether it represented her fear, or an intuition. Was she terrified she'd fail the test? If so, maybe she should face her fear and prove to herself that she could do it. Or, was she done? Maybe she'd already proven what she'd originally set out to prove. She'd learned what she wanted to learn.

As she came to feel that her resistance was indeed intuition-based (she was done), she found herself thinking about her family and friends. They'd all become so proud of her. She didn't want to disappoint them. Together with her Wisdom Keeper, she explored the healthy, self-honoring undercurrents in her frustrating dilemma. The truth was she wanted what was best for her. She didn't want to get sucked back into old inadequacy or external-approval traps. If she was going to become a diving instructor, it had to be for her own sake. Before Chiara could make a confident decision, she needed to know she'd survive the disappointment of her family and friends. Chiara did some reality-checking with the people in her life, and got to a place where she knew she'd be fine, regardless of what they thought or felt. After that, her decision was easy to make. She said an empowered "No!"

Positive Thinking

The Positively Patronizing Positive Thinker

I will never forget the day I received a phone call from a man with whom I'd been seriously involved for over three years. We'd built a home, a visionary art school and a life together in Denmark. Though there were some *serious* underlying issues (as you'll soon see), we were both happy in the relationship.

While visiting my family in the States for a few weeks, he called daily to let me know how much he loved and missed me—until he stopped calling. A week went by, and then I received the most shocking phone call of my life. In a strangely cold, empty voice, he confessed that he'd fallen in love with someone over the past week, that they were soul mates, that she'd already moved into our home, and that he thought it would be best if I remained in the States and never came back.

As you can imagine, this was quite a traumatic experience, one which catalyzed a deeply healing and empowering journey, which I won't get into. My point in sharing this story here is to illustrate a monstrous misuse of positive thinking.

He could have said something I could understand, or at least partially respect, like, "I'm so very sorry, Rosy. This whole thing comes as a shock to me. I really do care about you. I just don't know how to care about two women at the same time, and I don't think I can deal with the guilt of having to look you in the eye, even when I know that's the very least you deserve from me. I wish I had the strength to do things another way, but I don't." That would have hurt like hell, but at least it would have been honest. I *clearly* had more than a few blind spots at the time, but I know I could have dealt with that kind of honesty.

Instead, he declared with spiritual pride, "I'm innocent. You are innocent. Everyone on the planet is innocent," then hung up.

Please don't get me wrong. I am not saying that he wasn't innocent on some level of existence. I am saying that our ultimate divine innocence doesn't make us any less accountable for our actions here on planet Earth. Sometimes pulling a juicy affirmative apple off the Bullshit Tree is a little too easy.

Unfortunately, he felt too guilty, and I was too busy trying to respond in a perfectly spiritual manner to insist on something other than crystal-coated horse poop. He ended up living peacefully with his new love in our old home, and I spent a lot of time working on forgiveness and taking responsibility for having attracted such a horrible situation to myself. Instead of telling him where he could put his innocence, I wrote many affirmations, and developed a painful ear and throat infection which lasted for about three months.

Now I can think back to that time in my life with clarity, gratitude and humor. I definitely deserved better treatment from him. The experience also helped me grow into the person I am today. To get here, I needed to do more than write affirmations, although my radical gratitude practice of the time did get me through the initial panic. It gave me a positive direction and helped me count blessings when it felt like I was losing everything. It also temporarily spared me from having to face deeper wounds activated by this situation before I was ready to deal with them.

Eventually I needed to deal with my anger. I had to feel it, believe it and express it. I needed to put my high-frequency thinking on hold, so I could hold this man accountable for his actions. I needed to feel in my bones that I deserved better. Over time, I needed to locate parallel yet more subtle experiences of early abandonment in order to understand why this happened to me, how I might have unconsciously participated, and how I could participate in preventing the same thing from happening in the future. I had to deal with what happened from a psychological perspective, not just a spiritual one. I'm actually convinced that I could never have reached the spiritual peace I feel today had I not moved through a very real and painful psychological grief process set in motion by this break-up/breakdown.

As professional Wisdom Keepers, it's not unusual to have clients and students who glaze over guilt, fear and rage with spiritual jargon. I say 'jargon' because that is exactly what words become when they're used to deceive the self and others. Many of us Wisdom Keepers share this tendency.

Whether we are Wisdom Seekers, Keepers or both, for the sake of ourselves, and those we serve, let's stay connected to our gut. Let's listen beneath the words we speak, and the words we hear. If we find dissonance, let's dig a little deeper. We're bound to find a treasure.

When we're truly in touch with our shared innocence, we don't need to fear anything—not our thoughts, not our feelings, not our imperfect interactions. True innocence can look at and learn from everything.

Affirmation or Superstition?

I had a positive-thinking client who suffered from major paranoia. Once this person learned that thoughts were powerful creative tools, their imagination was off to the races. If a self-critical thought drifted into their mind while walking down the street, they worried that a random mugger would pick up on the thought and pounce on them. If they had the thought it might rain the day of their birthday picnic, they feared their mind was literally whipping up a hurricane.

When I suggested that the client write down some of their most negative thoughts and fears, as part of an exploratory exercise, they refused, fearing doing so would be giving their thoughts too much of their energy. Convinced that every negative thought was instantly heard, processed and set in motion by the universe, this poor client was paralyzed not only by fear, but an over-inflated sense of power. This was an extreme case, and the intensity of this person's fear reflected deeper problems. But I've witnessed a similar kind of superstition in Wisdom Keeping communities.

In spiritual learning environments, we can easily misunderstand and overestimate the powers of our thinking, unintentionally turning life-affirming tools into stressful pressures. Even if we'd be better off without a negative thought, that doesn't mean we can make it go away simply by denying its existence or cramming it under an immaculate affirmation.

Any hypnotherapist will tell you that our conscious thoughts represent the tip of the thinking iceberg. It's our subconscious ones that hold the power. When we refuse to see and explore our psyches' favorite 'bottom-dwellers,' we're more likely to run into trouble. (That still doesn't mean our individual subconscious thoughts have the power to whip up a hurricane.)

Before we tell each other to 'just change our minds,' let's remember that we are co-creators here on earth, not sole creators. No matter how much power our thoughts do have, they probably don't have as much as we think. Let's also remember that our Wisdom Keeping tools are here to enhance our lives, not give us control over life. Control is overrated. Better to appeal to a sense of adventure. When we're open to life, even a hurricane can provide us with unexpected opportunities to help our neighbors or take artistic photos.

If you'd still like a few affirmations for yourself or those you serve, here are a few good ones:

It is safe and innocent for me to have negative thoughts every once in a while.
I appreciate myself even when I forget to appreciate myself.
I am actually thinking much higher thoughts than I think I am.
I'm a lovable and beloved human being, even when my mind forgets.

Can Negative Thinking Be Totally Avoided?

Most humans on the planet—whether we've worked on refining our mental powers or not—have a negative thought or two (thousand) sauntering through our mental systems, now and again. This is to be expected. We are human. If we've got a navel, we've had our fair share of traumatic, painful and confusing experiences, all of them influencing the contents of our minds and the tone of our thinking.

We also live in a world filled with physical, political, social and spiritual realities which are, objectively speaking, food for negative thought. We are surrounded by people who've been profoundly influenced by these painful realities. Whether they're our parents, friends, colleagues or strangers walking down the street or on our television sets, we are affected by their thinking, just as they are affected by ours.

Despite the fact that Buddha's personal world was peaceful, luxurious and happy as a boy, he came to understand that as long as someone was suffering in the world, a part of him was suffering too. This is true for all of us, though we may not be as aware of this fact as Buddha was! On the level of collective consciousness, if someone is thinking a negative thought in the world, that thought exists for us too. We share a global brain (and heart). The chances of totally avoiding mental negativity are pretty slim.

Wisdom Keepers wouldn't use the term 'monkey mind' if there weren't some truth to the label. Taming and calming the mind can be a (multi) life-time effort—a noble goal requiring discipline, intention, patience and oh-so-much compassion.

Taking Baby Steps

During my early teenage years, I kept a journal. It was a true New Age nightmare. I probably wrote a hundred negative thoughts about myself per day. It wasn't uncommon for me to write, "I hate myself." At some point, I began to write, "I hate myself for hating myself."

I knew nothing about affirmations at the time, but I did have common sense. I figured, if I hated myself for hating myself, that probably meant there was a part of me that thought I deserved better than self-hate. Without any techniques or books to guide me, I began to write primitive forms of affirmations: "I appreciate myself for hating myself for hating myself." It was a start. If I'd judged myself for my word choice then, I might have stayed stuck in self-hate longer than necessary. Somehow it was easier for me to make the bridge from, "I love myself for hating my self-hate," to "I love myself." By honoring where I was, and by taking a self-affirming step that didn't feel too threatening or overwhelming, I allowed myself to safely begin a lifetime journey towards authentic self-appreciation.

Seeing Negative Thoughts as Creative Adjustments

Unless we can begin to see the caring intention behind our judgments,
our affirmations will only take us half of the way.

Even our most self-destructive thoughts start out as self-protective drives, or 'creative adjustments' to difficult or dangerous situations. Let's say you're a professional Wisdom Keeper, and one of your clients is an intelligent, beautiful woman who is constantly hiding her gifts. In her mind, she's convinced she is ugly and unintelligent—actually not that unusual a scenario. If she's had a bit of 'positivity training,' she probably blames herself for being stupid enough to think she's stupid.

Before affirming her beauty and intelligence, you might want to take some time to explore those negative thoughts. What positive or protective function might they have provided her in the past? Perhaps one of her parents believed they were stupid. Perhaps the other was threatened by her beauty. If this was the case, hiding and devaluing herself in this particular way would have been a wise protective strategy for her. By not posing a threat, she did what was necessary to win the love and attention she needed from the people she depended on. In a way, putting herself down was a way of caring for herself.

When we look at our negative thoughts without judgment or superstition, we realize that they're not 'bad,' they're just outdated. Learning to think more kindly towards ourselves feels more natural and less foreign, once we understand this.

Now that our discernment muscles are all warmed up, let's move on to one of the most important subjects of all for professional Wisdom Keepers: Boundaries and Roles. Without discernment in this arena, we can do the most damage. With it, we can facilitate the deepest healing.

Learning to work with boundaries consciously, take on roles responsibly, and navigate transitions graciously, is not always a priority in Wisdom Keeping learning environments. We may learn incredible healing tools, but many of us are left to our own devices when it comes to understanding and skillfully navigating the multitude of boundary systems that exist between us and those around us. Let's shine a light on some of the complexities we can encounter on our Wisdom Keeping and Seeking paths.

PART NINE:
BOUNDARIES & ROLES

As professional Wisdom Keepers (and humans), we deal with boundaries every day—personal boundaries, professional boundaries, cross-cultural boundaries, social boundaries, physical boundaries, time boundaries, sexual boundaries, spiritual boundaries, and many more. The more awareness we have of the various boundary dynamics taking place in our interactions with clients and students, the better our service will be.

A Basic Definition of Boundaries Inspired by Gestalt

The word 'boundaries' refers to a system of limit-setting which is meant to enhance our sense of self, and our ability to manage the impact 'reality' has on us and others. By 'reality,' I mean *that which we experience through our physical body, thoughts, feelings, actions and behavior in general.*

According to Gestalt theorists, we each have at least four different sets of boundary systems: *External Physical Boundaries, Sexual Boundaries, Internal Boundaries and Spiritual Boundaries.* All of our boundary systems serve one essential function—to help us 'contain' and protect our experience of reality.

Broadly, our *external boundary* system of limit-setting helps us to protect our bodies, to be in charge of the physical distance which exists between us and others, and to control whom we touch, who touches us, how, when and where. Our *internal boundary* system allows us to protect our thinking, feelings and behavior. It acts like a block or a filter, letting some things in and others out, keeping some things in and others out.

When Boundaries are Intact

A boundary system is 'intact' or healthy when it provides us with the amount of protection we need to have a sense of self, and, the openness and flexibility we need to interact safely, creatively and effectively with our surroundings.

When we have *intact external physical* boundaries, we are aware of our differing needs for physical distance and/or touch, depending on whom we're with. We're able to negotiate and exert control over how much distance exists, and how much touching takes place, between ourselves and others. We're also able to allow others to do the same. In other words, we let others negotiate distance and touch in relation to us, according to their own needs.

Our *intact external sexual* boundaries make it possible for us to be in charge of our sexual activities. We get to decide with whom we want to enter a sexual encounter. We get to actively participate in choosing where, when, and how it happens. We easily allow others to do the same. We respect others' rights to be in charge of their own sexual needs, desires, decisions and eventual activities.

As a general rule, when we have an *intact internal* boundary, we don't blame too much. Instead, when presented with a 'reality'— whether it be a bodily experience, a thought, a feeling or an action initiated by ourselves or someone else—we are able to discern between what is true about the reality, what is not true, and what is uncertain. In other words, when we have intact *internal* boundaries, we're good shoppers at the mall of life. If we're confronted with another person's negative opinion, we're able to determine whether or not we want to accept it as true, or take some time to consider its possible relevance and allow space for questioning.

Further, when we have *intact internal* boundaries, and we share ourselves or relate to other people, we understand we are responsible for influencing (not controlling) our own reality. We can also be intimate and share ourselves with others without having to do anything that doesn't feel right to us, or to be anything other than who we are. We feel safe letting others know who we are inside, how we think and feel.

When we have *intact spiritual* boundary systems, we are able to be intimate with other human beings—on a physical, sexual, intellectual and emotional level. Whenever two people are being physically, sexually, intellectually or emotionally intimate with each other, and when they simultaneously use their own *external* and *internal* boundary systems in a healthy way, they experience what can be called an intact *spiritual* boundary.

Whether we join together with another person (as a romantic couple, a Wisdom Keeper and Seeker, or as two close friends, etc.), if we can feel close to each other while simultaneously feeling a grounded sense of self, we are experiencing what Gestalt therapists describe as a genuinely spiritual connection. It is through entering this kind of intimate space with another that we connect with our own spirituality.

When Boundaries are Violated

When our *internal* and/or *external* boundaries are violated, our ability to interact in a healthy way with our environment can become undermined. We may have *no boundaries* at all, *no protection*. Or, we can *build up walls* around us, *complete protection*. Or, we might have what could be called *damaged* boundaries, *partial protection*.

Depending on our personal history, and on the type, frequency and intensity of the boundary violations we experienced growing up, our boundary systems can range from none at all to excessively strong.

Our *external* boundaries can be violated if, for example, others try to touch us or stand too close to us without asking for our permission, if they go through our personal things without asking our permission, or if they don't allow us the physical privacy we need.

Our *internal* boundaries can be violated if we are yelled at, teased, ridiculed, criticized, lied to, patronized, emotionally manipulated, controlled in a negative way, or treated with sarcasm.

When we have *no external physical* boundaries, we can't negotiate physical distance or touch with others. It may not even occur to us that we are not taking charge of who touches us, and who we touch, much less bother us. Another possibility is that we *build walls* around ourselves, never reaching out to touch others, or allowing others to touch us. We physically isolate ourselves from the world. Many of us fall somewhere in between the two extremes. With *partially damaged* boundaries, most of us can protect ourselves, control and negotiate who comes close to or touches us, at least some, but not all, of the time.

When we have *no external sexual* boundaries, we can't control the circumstances around our sexual activities. We can't make healthy decisions about who our partners are, or when, where and how our sexual encounters take place. Some of us construct *walls* around ourselves and become completely self-protected. We can't reach out to anyone sexually, and no one can reach out to us. Whether we have *no sexual boundaries* or are *totally walled off*, we have trouble negotiating our sexual experiences. When we have *damaged sexual* boundaries, we have a certain amount of protection. Some of the time, we can healthfully manage the circumstances around our sexual activities, and some of the time, we struggle.

When we have *no internal boundaries*, we have no internal protection. Feeling unprotected, we are more likely to engage in blaming, holding others responsible for who we are, or holding ourselves responsible for who others are. When we build up *internal walls*, on the other hand, we pay no attention to others. We don't listen to them or show any interest in getting to know them as individuals, nor do we share ourselves with them. When we have *damaged internal* boundaries and encounter information, we can discern whether the information is true, untrue or questionable, some of the time, but not all of the time.

The Double-edged Sword of Seduction

Laura had very poor boundaries as well as a long history of sex and love addiction. Though she'd been in a committed monogamous relationship with Nigel for the past eight years, she continued to have affairs. No matter how sorry she felt about her actions after the fact, she couldn't control her self-sabotaging and hurtful behavior. Despite his better judgment, Nigel—a classic codependent—continued to take her back as soon as her temporary infatuations wore off.

Along with poor boundaries, Laura had a great deal of personal charm. Her charisma controlled her life instead of enhancing it. It also controlled Nigel, and many of the others she attracted into her life. She could convince anyone of practically anything she wanted them to believe—or anything she wanted to believe herself. Much of her infatuation addiction was sourced in a history of abuse and a resultantly exaggerated dependency on external validation.

One day, she met and fell in love with yet another lover. In the heat of romance, she agreed to run off with them. Returning to her patient and habitually wounded partner, she declared that she was going to leave him for someone else, and that this time, it was for good. Her partner was devastated.

Feeling excited about her new life, but also sad for Nigel, she made an appointment with a tarot practitioner, seeking guidance. Just as she'd hoped, the tarot spread affirmed that she'd found her true soul mate. After the Reading, Laura confidently went off to pursue her newest infatuation. She was relieved of guilt and any sense of responsibility she'd felt for the mess she was leaving behind.

Even if Laura had met her spiritual match, this did not mean that impulsively following her whims, or continuing to seduce people with her charisma (at the expense of her most intimate relationships), was healthy for her or fair to the people she loved. Running off would not help to repair her damaged boundary systems; nor would it change the likelihood that the way she left her old relationship would impact the foundation of her new one.

Although there was no way for the tarot practitioner to fully understand the extent of Laura's wounding, they had been given enough information to see that Laura would benefit from more time to digest and implement her big decision. They could have provided Laura with a soul perspective, while still appealing to her human conscience. Unfortunately, they were too focused on the cards in front of them to notice Laura's self-destructive patterns at work.

This story reveals a double-edged sword of seduction—one blade belonging to the client, and the other to the professional Wisdom Keeper. Despite the good intentions of each party, the client seduced the practitioner into believing she was doing the right thing, and the practitioner seduced the client into giving away her power.

Working with Boundaries as a Professional Wisdom Keeper

When our clients or students walk through our door, they arrive with their own set of boundary systems—each in its uniquely *intact, non-existent, walled-off* or *partially damaged* state. The state of someone's boundary systems is rarely advertised in flashing lights on their foreheads, so it can take time to get a good sense of how healthy or damaged their boundary systems are.

It's often through a violation of boundaries that we discover their existence. When our work includes relatively 'boundary-less' techniques, where emotional and physical closeness are encouraged, it's important to remember that the bigger the violation, regardless of intentionality, the harder it is for clients and students to recover, and the longer it can take to repair the damage and earn back trust.

While some professional violations are too big to remedy, others can be catalysts for healing. If clients and students feel safe enough to risk sharing their discomfort with us when we unintentionally cross their boundaries, and when can meet them with self-awareness, honesty and compassion, uncomfortable interactions can become blessings in disguise, deepening the trust between us.

Whether we work consciously or instinctively with boundaries as professional Wisdom Keepers, our ability to manage the invisible space between ourselves and others influences all of our interactions. Our capacity to respond constructively to boundary-related challenges arising at work will reflect the state of our own boundaries just as much as our clients' and students'.

Many professional Wisdom Keepers have been trained to see people, not as purely psychological beings, but as physical and spiritual beings as well. Our work is often as multi-faceted as the people we serve. Our approaches usually involve more than talking or traditional psychotherapy, as we weave together a variety of techniques—many of which involve the body.

As transformative as our synthesizing approaches can be, they can also be confusing. Being massaged, touched, healed or 'read' by the same person one relates to on a deeply emotional, relational and psychological level can blur all sorts of lines. The more muddied boundaries get between us and those we serve, the more awake we need to be as teachers, therapists, coaches and healers. Because professional Wisdom Keepers are in the business of spiritual healing (where healthy *spiritual* boundaries are dependent on the general health of *physical* and *internal* boundary systems), we have the potential to do as much damage as we do profound work.

Being Connected Does Not Mean Having No Boundaries

In alternative communities that focus on healing separation, it is important that we don't mistake healthy boundaries for the ego's unhealthy devotion to the illusion of spiritual separateness. As we acknowledge our interconnectedness, let's not be afraid to discover, explore and respect our own and others' boundaries. Doing so won't make us any less spiritual.

Cultivating healthy boundaries can enhance your spiritual journey.
It can prepare you for the day when you are ready to dissolve into the All.

If you are a professional Wisdom Keeper, remember that everyone is different. What might be safely appropriate to do with one person might be damaging to another. What's needed is not always obvious. Outwardly bold people may have a history of being too open. They may need you to help them learn how to better protect themselves. If you immediately buy into their openness and assume they can handle yours too, you may do more harm than good.

I know of a handsome, single, heterosexual man who was a highly skilled massage therapist. One day, an enthusiastic female client came into his office. She was articulate, beautiful, intelligent, highly conscious of spirit, and seemed very much in tune with him and his philosophical orientation. He felt attracted to her immediately. She wanted to purchase a series of sessions because she knew that healing massage would be good for her and he came well-recommended. He felt flattered.

As she prepared herself to lie down on the massage table, she gave very clear signs that she was interested in him sexually. Allowing himself to be seduced by clients was not his usual practice, but this time things felt different. Her self-assurance and their instant chemistry were so alluring that he couldn't help himself. Convinced he'd met his soul mate, he gave her the erotic massage she openly desired and obviously enjoyed. Over the coming weeks, the erotic sessions continued, and the two became officially involved in a romantic relationship. Both were happy.

About three months after their initial encounter, the woman disappeared. The man was shocked and didn't understand why she left—since she'd never given any signs of unhappiness. Months later, he received a letter from a woman looking for his long-lost lover. This woman turned out to be her sister. In the letter, she shared the sad and shocking story of her sister's life, and he was left feeling horrible.

It turned out that the attractive, intelligent woman with whom he fell in love had a tragic personal history filled with severe sexual violations. He'd become one of a series of therapists and healers with whom she'd been involved. Each time, she left the relationship without warning.

As the man read the letter, he was filled with regret. He had no way of helping the sister find this woman, nor could he change what had happened. Suddenly he could see that for this woman, seducing and physically merging with men in 'helping' roles was the familiar. Her external boundary system was so severely damaged that she had no idea that what she, or they, had been doing was inappropriate.

No doubt, with years of experience, this woman was highly skilled at the art of seduction. Some very capable professionals had fallen into her tragic trap. This does not excuse their behavior. It also doesn't change the fact that this healer ended up betraying the woman he'd come to love, her opportunity for healing, as well as his professional integrity.

We don't have to cross sexual boundaries to cause trouble. Other boundary crossings of a less severe nature can have their own consequences.

Take someone like me. Because of my personal background, I've tended to feel responsible for people in helping positions. In the past, when I came to someone for help, and they casually launched into a self-disclosing share, I'd quietly shut down and move into listening, supportive mode—whether I wanted to or not. Repeating my childhood survival strategy, I 'parented the parent.' Assuming the role of supporter felt familiar and comfortable to me, and I was good at it. It was also deeply disappointing. When my helpers gave me what I unconsciously expected, not what I actually needed, I felt unsafe, hopeless and alone.

It's not uncommon that the patterns we come to professional Wisdom Keepers to heal are the very patterns that sabotage the healing process. In my case, my resistance to having needs, taking space, and receiving support reflected my deeper longing to learn how to be a client—not just a 'good client' who was courteous, deferential and protective of the healer, but one who dared to receive, challenge, frustrate and be 'difficult.'

Though I've gotten much better at embracing and expressing my humanness in a variety of arenas, I still look for professional Wisdom Keepers who know how to keep me from wiggling out of the spotlight. I do best with helpers who have clear boundaries, take good care of themselves, and share personal information with me only when it reflects or somehow illuminates my process.

Many Wisdom Seekers tend to be caretaking clients like me. Others have the opposite problem; they have no trouble taking up space or becoming absorbed in their own worlds. If you're a professional Wisdom Keeper, some people will need your help in discovering their inner worlds; others will need your help in connecting with the outer world. Many won't have a clue about what they need, and will be counting on you to help them figure it out. To the best of your ability, it's so beneficial to pay close attention to arising interpersonal dynamics, and resist the pull of the boundary dance that brought them to you in the first place.

The Time Boundary

As previously mentioned, my first in-depth introduction to working professionally in an alternative environment was through a specific form of breathwork. One of our most important jobs as 'Rebirthers' was to assist people in healing their own births, both physically and emotionally. Our approach resembled the work of a midwife more than it did a therapist. Each session was like facilitating a birth experience, as unique and unpredictable as the birth process itself.

During sessions, people were gently guided through a profound experience which involved the entire body. Often old memories and emotions surfaced, causing a great deal of energy and sometimes intense sensations to move through the body. To help people let go and surrender, to experience a more gentle, loving entry into this world, we focused on safety above all else. We made sure clients and students felt welcome and received, and that they knew that they had all the time they needed to move through and integrate their experiences. At the end of sessions, they often felt like newborn babies—open, soft and vulnerable.

If we did our work strictly by the clock, we'd be doing our clients and students a great disservice. Cutting off a breathwork session midstream would be like kicking laboring mothers out of a birthing room before the placenta (or the baby!) had a chance to come out. We could actually risk re-triggering original birth traumas. There are many modalities and approaches, similar to breathwork, that require a certain amount of flexibility and spaciousness around time. It can also make sense to soften and relax around time boundaries when working with clients, modalities and in settings that aren't dominated by Western cultural norms, where relationships tend to be compartmentalized and life is dictated by the clock.

In some healing contexts, however, letting sessions drag on and on can be problematic. When I went to traditional therapy many years ago, I was surprised by how strictly my therapist managed our time. In the fifty-five minutes we had together, I could sit as still as a pebble, cry my heart out, or talk at the speed of lightning, but when that secondhand reached its destination, my time was up.

Before working with her, I was accustomed to hearing the gentle, patient voices of breathworkers, reassuring me that I had 'all the time in the world.' The abrupt endings of our therapy sessions shocked me.

I felt hurried and nervous. The fact that I generally had trouble relaxing into 'client mode' only amplified my anxiety. After a while, I grew to feel increasingly familiar and safe with the container. Those fifty-five minutes were mine—all mine. Now, given the nature of the work we did together, I can see my therapist's commitment to adhere to a time schedule as a strength. She respected her own boundaries as well as mine. Our time together became precious and effective, and I always knew I could count on her full attention.

A later experience with a professional Wisdom Keeper made me especially appreciative of my therapist's boundaried relationship with time. During our first session, the healer spent about ten minutes listening to me, and the rest of the session telling me all about his life, broken heart and buried rage. I could barely get a word in. Ultimately, I was the one who had to end the session. By the time we stood at the door, I wasn't sure whether I should pay him or send him a bill!

Learning to respect time boundaries as a professional counselor has been perhaps the most difficult one for me to learn. Thankfully, I've had conscientious clients who over time have helped me see that often, when I worked overtime, I was doing them no favor.

A while back, a lovely client came for a one-hour session, but I allowed our session to continue significantly beyond the one-hour point. When she realized we'd gone over time, she felt as though she'd misused me, and was upset that I let it happen.

Fortunately, our relationship was strong enough for her to share her feelings with me. Her illuminating feedback taught me how confusing and guilt-inducing it can be for clients when I don't set and honor proper time limits.

There are certainly professionals who easily bring sessions to a close. If you are like me, however, you may find guiding people out the door awkward, challenging or guilt-inducing. You might fear that your clients and students will feel rejected, cut off or incomplete. You may even panic at the thought of sending someone home without feeling *totally* healed, relieved or released.

If you tend to struggle with endings, consider this: your willingness to honor your time agreements is a way to provide clients and students with an experience of safety. It's a way to let them know that they can count on you to honor your agreements with yourself and them. For clients who struggle with boundary-setting themselves, honoring your own boundaries makes you an inspiring role model. It also allows you to communicate non-verbally that not everything needs to be solved immediately for them to be OK; that it's safe to be 'in process,' to practice patience, and to trust in life. They—and your relationship—can survive uncomfortable feelings and unfinished interactions without falling apart. If your work requires a certain amount of time flexibility, make that clear from the onset.

If you tend to go overtime because you easily move into social mode, remember that most of the time your clients come to you for help, not a friendly chat. Even if they are looking for a friend in you, you may not want to be their friend. Even if you want to be their friend, becoming friends may not be in their best interest.

Crossing the Line:
The Gossiping Astrologer

Shen had a great reputation as an astrologer, and he was indeed quite knowledgeable. For the entire hour-and-a-half session with his new client Ivanna, he provided a thoroughly professional and enlightening Reading of her present and progressive horoscope.

Ivanna was an attractive and intelligent woman. Shen liked her so much that he worked overtime, and then invited her for a cup of tea and casual chat after the Reading. The chat included additional feedback about Ivanna's horoscope as well as all sorts of general topics.

Ivanna found his company delightful, until he let his professional wall fall down. He began to talk about his other clients in a not-so-flattering way. Finally, when he harshly criticized a client he had seen the previous week, revealing personal information about them, Ivanna took her last sip of tea and walked out the door.

This story not only makes a good argument for a strict policy of confidentiality and honoring time limits; it also shows how a person's insecurity, lack of boundaries, and shadow can get in the way of what otherwise would be a fine service. It's hard to feel safe with a professional who talks badly or disrespectfully about their other clients.

A Place for Processing

While honoring time boundaries is an important part of being a professional Wisdom Keeper, it's equally important that we pay special attention to *how we structure our time* with clients and students—especially when we work with emotionally powerful modalities. It is one thing to allow sessions or workshops to end without everyone feeling completely healed and complete; it's another to leave clients and students feeling open, raw and disoriented.

The more fully we understand the nature of our work and the needs of the people we work with, the better we'll be at designing the right container for our work. Ending on time becomes useful once we've figured out how long each session/workshop should be, how to pace ourselves, and how much time should be devoted to creating safety, imparting information, facilitating an experience, and ensuring integration.

Many Wisdom Keepers do very deep work. In a way, we practice open heart surgery. Just as a surgeon would never leave a patient on the operating table with their chest cranked open, we don't want to leave our clients and students feeling helpless and vulnerable after working with us.

Over the years, I've witnessed many professional Wisdom Keepers make the mistake of devoting all of their time and energy to opening people up, and forgetting the importance of integration and closure. Others make the mistake of focusing on the yang-like aspects of their work, at the expense of the yin. They prioritize doing over being, dynamic self-expression over receptive silence.

One Wisdom Keeper tried to cram the contents of a weekend workshop into one day. The participants got a powerful taste of the emotionally evocative technique, but they were given way too little time to digest their experience. With no follow-up support, many suffered from spiritual indigestion, to say it mildly. Another Wisdom Keeper I know was so infatuated with the exciting aspects of their work that their students were bombarded with so much action that they left the training feeling overwhelmed, overstimulated and under-resourced.

If I had to make a mistake, I'd rather give people too much time to integrate their experiences than too many experiences to integrate. So often I've found that leaving lots of empty space to be, feel and metabolize an experience leads to some of the deepest insights and most profound sharings to surface.

Honor the exhale.
Enjoy the silence.
Make space for the sharing.
Do less. Be more.

Cross-Cultural & Social Boundaries

All humans carry within us the tendency to categorize people, to put them into recognizable (often culturally agreed upon) groups based on a certain set of characteristics or descriptors. Within the first few moments of meeting someone, our minds are already hard at work—identifying areas of sameness and difference, determining potentials for inclusion or exclusion, and assessing levels of status. Our cultural conditioning amplifies this inborn tendency, contributing to a complex social fabric which usually consists of an uneven distribution of resources, power and privilege.

The fact that we are professional Wisdom Keepers puts us in a position of power. We may be sure we've had lifetimes of experience as members of an oppressed people or a marginalized social group. We may embrace the ultimate truth that we are all One. If, however, we belong to the dominant culture, gender, age, class, sexual orientation, neurological style, etc. in *this* life time, the power dynamics in our professional relationships can be exacerbated by any social, political, institutional or economic realities that either unite, or separate, our and our clients'/students' experiences of reality. The more we can hold this paradox with empathy, sensitivity and humility, the better.

Let's take 'culture' as an example. There are very few homogeneous cultures left on our planet. The age of information, increase in travel accessibility, growth of big cosmopolitan cities, as well as the breaking down of borders have all served to speed up a cultural blending process which has been impacting and transforming our world for decades. Today, all kinds of people are moving across the globe, creating families, work forces, and neighborhoods composed of different cultural backgrounds. As we all hop into the mosaic of our planet, our self-definitions, values, belief systems and worldviews are constantly influenced and challenged.

The coming together of peoples clearly has had positive consequences for all of us. With each opportunity we have to share our cultures, perspectives and creativity with each other, we discover what it truly means to be planetary citizens, to be joined in our ultimate humanness.

Some consequences of our coming together have been and remain more complicated. The innocent desire to explore, honor and connect with others was not the prime motivator for many of our original 'cultural bridge-builders.' Material greed, ignorance and arrogance drove the majority of world travelers across the oceans. Unbearably cruel acts of violence and cultural violations permeated their journeys. The sad consequences of colonialism, crusading and slavery have left their scars on all of us, leaving our collective *external* and *internal* boundary systems severely damaged. There are many shadows for all of us to integrate, numerous cultural wounds to be recognized and healed, and many lessons to be learned. Different strategies will apply to different situations at different times.

As we engage consciously in our collective spiritual transformation—from the many to the One people—we also need to acknowledge, honor and celebrate our differences. Many Wisdom Seekers (and Keepers!) belong to peoples who have been so oppressed and culturally disempowered that they need support in reclaiming the unique gifts of their lineage. They need to honor their spiritual roots, nurture their cultural heritage, and define themselves as autonomous and sovereign.

It follows that when we're working with those who come to us, or integrating another wisdom culture's practices into our way of working, an awareness of personal boundaries is not enough. We need to remember the existence of collective cultural boundaries as well as the social (or symbolic) boundaries that emerge within any given culture.

When we live in modern, democratic societies where respect and equality are publicly valued, it can also be easy to assume that social stereotyping and forms of oppression (such as sexism and racism) are much smaller problems now than they used to be. Unfortunately, this is far from the truth.

Take sexism. Despite the fact that women and girls have more educational and career opportunities than ever before, they are often treated differently than boys and men. In the majority of political, religious and working environments, they are still contending with glass ceilings, low pay and sexual harassment.

In 'modern society,' there is still a widespread tendency to reward certain approaches to leadership, styles of decision-making and types of 'intelligence' (e.g. linear thinking, factual logic and intellectual analysis)—all typically associated with the *masculine* or maleness.

The damaging and insidious way that modern media depicts women—as objects to be desired, judged, violated and used, as opposed to honored, accepted, respected and partnered with—are impossible to ignore. It is no wonder that record numbers of young girls are suffering from eating disorders and depression, and that the wisest of women still find themselves struggling to live up to cultural definitions of beauty and to step fully into their power.

In many Wisdom Keeping communities, sexism (and related forms of oppression) can be harder to detect, thus correct. Though this is by no means always the case, in many spiritual communities, heterosexual men are more likely to rise into positions of power and leadership. Male voices are often given more weight and authority than the voices of women. Binary gender identities, hetero-sexual orientations and monogamous relationship structures are often assumed by Wisdom Keeping cultures, and reflected in the language used and roles played by community members.

Much of the time, acts of discrimination are subtle, unintentional and operate outside of individuals' and the community's awareness. More often than not, they are the result of people's unexamined privilege and a general lack of understanding of their impact. Sometimes, oppressive acts are not so subtle. Power is abused, sexual boundaries are crossed, and people get hurt. (Soon I'll be sharing an example of this.)

Of course, sexism is far from the only 'ism' that is alive and well in our world today. While it is beyond the scope of this book to address the need for every social movement that exists, we can look at how most social movements overlap, and how our identities are impacted by *intersectionality*—a concept developed by the sociologist Beatrice Potter Webb, and a term later coined by a feminist and civil rights advocate, Kimberlé Williams Crenshaw. The theory of intersectionality helps us to see that gender, sexual orientation, race, class and disability don't exist in vacuums. They are deeply interconnected. We can't fully understand the human condition without acknowledging that each of us is a unique, intricately woven tapestry—a complex and beautiful wholeness—not a collection of separate parts.

A Native American lesbian woman, for example, might be recognized by the Native American community for her indigenous background, by the LGBTQIA community for her 'gayness,' and by the feminist community for her 'femaleness.' She, on the other hand, would experience herself as a whole human being. It would not only be impossible for her to reduce, compartmentalize or split off different aspects of herself. Attempting to do so would be down-right oppressive.

Just as the differing aspects of our identities can overlap, so can the systems of oppressions that impact them. Much research has been done on the interconnectedness between racism, sexism, homophobia and class oppression, just to name a few. When we look at any system of justice or social movement in isolation, we run the risk of missing out on important understandings and healing opportunities.

What I'm addressing here is a vast field of study, and not all professional Wisdom Keepers are meant to become experts on cultural and social boundaries. However, a growing awareness of these complex dynamics can allow us to see just how many of our assumptions about psychological and spiritual health are determined by our limited experiences and conditioning backgrounds. Whether our internalized assumptions are based on racist, sexist, heterosexist, ageist, classist, 'able-ist,' 'Westernist' or other paradigms, we want to be sure that they're not sabotaging our ability to see and serve the people with whom we work.

Often cultural and social biases are the most difficult to detect, because they go so deep and are rarely questioned, especially when we tend to surround ourselves with people with similar backgrounds, styles and orientations to our own. When we project our own social and cultural conditioning onto clients and students, we end up teaching non-self-acceptance, which is the last thing we want to do, since most of us consciously embrace a universal, inclusive, respectful and open-minded worldview.

Though none of us are free of prejudice, with time, honesty and commitment to mutual learning, this can change. Many of us would benefit from genuinely exploring our deeply ingrained prejudices and belief systems, and how we may be—albeit unconsciously or unintentionally—contributing to (and benefiting from) systemic oppression, cultural appropriation and unhealthy power dynamics in society, and in our professional relationships.

Personally, I recommend that all professional Wisdom Keepers participate in consciousness raising work where we are not only exposed to concepts like multi-culturalism and *intersectionality*, but are supported in examining our own internalized prejudices and assumptions, as well as our areas of privilege. The more actively and continuously we do this essential work, the more we can wake up to and break through our biases, and the more our clients and students can enlighten, teach and inspire us to meet their needs in ever more appropriate ways.

In some cases, we may find that our socio-cultural glasses are too foggy to see our clients and students clearly. If or when this happens, the most professionally responsible act we can take is to refer them to another Wisdom Keeper who is better prepared to meet them where they are, and as they are.

The Perfect Storm in a Spiritual Community
Sex, Power, Love & Confusion

Years ago, I was part of a spiritual community and training environment. Gloria, a powerful teacher and inspiring role model, welcomed me warmly into the community, provided me with much needed encouragement and introduced me to beautiful spiritual principles. For quite some time, I dedicated myself to this community. I promoted the training, supported its members, and provided my services wherever and whenever needed. The training became one of my professional homes, and family.

I met Mario the day I met Gloria. We became fast friends. Aside from being one of Gloria's most devoted students, he was a successful healer, counselor, course leader, organizer and spokesperson for her training, as well as a knowledgeable, caring and good-natured person. Unfortunately, as I learned over time, he was also the seducer of many of the women who were (had been, or would become) his clients, assistants, course participants and Gloria's training members. Several of these women eventually came to me (and other more seasoned community members) for help in working through their feelings of infatuation, confusion, vulnerability, misuse, and in some cases, psychological violation.

Struggling with conflicting loyalties as his friend and professional colleague, it took me a long time to figure out how to deal with the situation, and to realize how serious it was. Mario's problems didn't always interfere with his work. He had several intimate relationships during the time I knew him, and periods when he seemed more self-aware, receptive to feedback and in control of his actions, (which I knew were sourced in a painful childhood wound for which I had compassion). Eventually, I realized that he had an addiction that was beyond his control, and much more outside of his conscious awareness than I had believed and hoped.

Several times, I considered directly confronting Gloria with his actions, but I feared the consequences. If I exposed Mario's lack of professional integrity, I'd be challenging hers too. She was a perceptive woman, and his charisma was undeniably good for business. It was also hard to locate the 'un-crossable' lines (e.g. between teachers and students, seasoned training members and newer training members, etc.) in this alternative community. We weren't doing 'therapy,' but what we did went every bit as deep. The fact that most of us were playing quintuple roles in relation to each other further complicated matters. I felt bound by my oaths of confidentiality to my clients, as well as to my community friends and colleagues whose clients were in similar situations with Mario.

Despite my public attempts to raise awareness around boundaries in the community, and private efforts to encourage women to speak out about what was happening behind the scenes, almost no one did. They were either too in love with Mario, too worried about their own futures as professionals in the community, or too busy staying out of victim consciousness to consider blaming anyone else for their woes. Some did share their experiences with older training members, but were often handed catchy 'New Age' phrases—holding them even more responsible for attracting their unfortunate circumstances.

Few people seemed to question Mario's lack of professionalism, abuse of power, or the severe and damaging consequences of his actions. Few fully grasped what their silence meant for the women who had been through his addiction machine, or for everyone being trained in the community as a professional, or for the profession as a whole.

While I was disturbed to see so many wise, loving people victimizing themselves (and others), all in the name of rising out of victim consciousness, I was even more disturbed by how deeply I'd fallen into the same trap. Coming from a family where mental illness wasn't acknowledged, I knew the painful consequences of pretending everything was OK when it wasn't.

Eventually I gathered up the courage to confront Gloria about Mario's abuses. By then I understood that I wasn't only confronting his sex addiction and her complicity. I was confronting my own complicit codependence. I was facing my own shame and breaking through my own denial.

Unfortunately, my actions didn't lead to a positive resolution. I ultimately chose to withdraw from the community. It was a painful, yet important decision.

Looking back, I can see how much I learned from this experience. I came to see how Mario, Gloria and I (all unintentionally) illuminated our community's shadow, each playing our part. We acted out three of the largest-looming problems that the entire community shared—poor boundaries, a dependency on love and approval, and a deep fear of conflict.

There are many people like Mario, Gloria and myself in this world of ours, all deserving compassion. Our shared story exemplifies to a frightening degree what can happen in any community, organization, or professional field when someone with Mario's particular wounding pattern rises to a position of power, when the community consists of people with codependent, conflict-avoidant and/or 'over-owning' tendencies, and when the community leader and/or culture fails to empower its members to act from a place of courage and integrity.

Now that we've shined a light on the many complexities we face when dealing with boundaries and playing roles in relation to each other, let's turn our attention to Wisdom Keeping communities. There are, of course, so many wonderful advantages to living, working, serving and growing within a spiritual or alternative community. There are also plenty of challenges, such as the ones illuminated in this last story. The better we understand these challenges, the more we can benefit from all of the blessings.

PART TEN:
LEARNING & WORKING IN WISDOM KEEPING COMMUNITIES

Light and Shadow

Learning, growing and blossoming within a Wisdom Keeping community can be deeply fulfilling. In the company of kindred spirits, we're given countless opportunities to encounter, embrace and express our whole selves—the beauty of our Light and the potentials hidden in our Shadow. Inspiring learning environments enable us to gain invaluable insights, gather transformative tools and make life-long friends. While engaging in professional alternative communities can make our lives infinitely better, it can also be challenging.

Groups Enhance Whatever You've Got Going
Egos Beware!

Whatever may be going on inside of us, if we're in a group, it'll likely get amplified. If we're experiencing a genuine moment of self-love, and are being held and supported by a spiritual community, our experience will sweeten and deepen. If we're on a massive ego trip, and are surrounded by admirers, the group energy can act as a powerful drug. When we become addicted to the spiritual high, we can end up thinking we're full of God, when we're actually full of something else!

Role Juggling in Communities

When you enter an alternative training or community, you walk in as yourself—an eager, open-minded person who is ready to be inspired by your new environment. Within a very short period of time, you may find yourself being asked to (or volunteering to) play a myriad of roles. Aside from student or participant, you might play the role of assistant, organizer, helper, exchange partner, colleague, group leader, supervisor, coach, friend, lover, etc. You may find yourself performing several of these functions within the span of a single weekend or course session.

We all play a variety of roles in our daily lives. Playing multiple roles in a Wisdom Keeping community can be both doable and rewarding. It can also get complicated. If you find yourself getting dizzy or losing your center because you are playing too many roles at once in your community, please don't be hard on yourself. There is nothing wrong with you.

I've found that the more roles we are asked to play in relation to each other, the harder it can be to know what to do or say…when, where, and with whom to do it…and why. To move from surviving in community to thriving in community, many of us must learn the delicate art of role juggling. This is nothing short of a spiritual practice, requiring that we become present to each moment and allow the specific circumstances (and our intuition) to guide us in graciously navigating each situation. To do this well, we must become very awake. If we doze off for too long, we may have to kiss our peace of mind and our personal/professional integrity goodbye.

As you work towards achieving perfect presence, I recommend that you cultivate patience and prioritize simplicity. If you're exhausted or overstimulated, you might consider cutting down on a role or two. If you're confused, you might want to set some clear guidelines for yourself about what role you want to play and with whom. This can make things easier for you, especially in the beginning.

When beginning musicians play a new piece,
they must first learn the basic melody.
Taking one note at a time and practicing through repetition,
their song becomes imprinted
on their mind and in their body.
Once the melody is a part of them,
they are free to improvise.
Improvising too soon is possible, but it's not always pretty!

Some of the decisions you make regarding role playing will be easier than others. Depending on who you are and your level of expertise, you will probably have some clear preferences. You'll want to relate to some community members as friends, and others as friendly acquaintances, colleagues, mentors, students or clients. The more you are aware of your own needs and wishes, the easier it will be for you to make these kinds of decisions from the start.

Other decisions you make won't necessarily be based on what you want, but on your ability to sense what is needed from you. As a group leader, for instance, you may be tempted to bring out your flirtatious, seductive self, even though the participants need you to play a purely professional, supportive role. If you give in to your temptation, you may confuse matters and do a disservice to your group. If you are willing to put your inner seducer on hold, however, you'll establish more safety in the group.

Please don't be afraid to be honest with yourself. Most often, if you tap into your integrity compass, you'll know what to do, when and with whom. (Or at least you'll know what not to do, and where to go for help if you're having a hard time resisting.)

Pay attention to your impact. Notice how the roles you play are affecting you and the people around you. Give yourself regular role check-ups. Make sure you're not over-extending yourself. Explore your thoughts, feelings and concerns with community members you trust. Ask others playing multiple roles how they do it. Together explore what's working, and what isn't. Make role juggling—and refining—a topic of conversation in the community.

The Art of De-Roling

I recommend finding simple ways to acknowledge and symbolize the switching of roles. Drama therapists have a term for this. It's called *de-roling*. Any time you're moving from one role to another—from supervisor to colleague, group leader to assistant, teacher to friend, a mini-ritual marking the transition can come in handy.

Let's say you've been working as a Wisdom Keeper all day long. Now you're on your way home to be alone. Or, perhaps you're going out to meet some friends. Take a moment to de-role. Sometimes I literally sweep the energy off my body with my hands, saying, "I am no longer a counselor. I'm just Rosy, a totally regular person." Or, if I've had a pretty intense day, I get my husband Kim or a good friend to do it for me. It's fun, and it helps.

If we don't have simple ways of releasing ourselves from the roles we play, we risk lugging them around with us everywhere we go—into our other relationships, our beds and places they don't belong. If we aren't careful, we can end up walking around like Wisdom Keeping zombies. Taking regular 'role vacations' makes it easier for us to return to our roles with the right combination of clarity, care and non-attachment.

You might also find it helpful to practice a simple ritual whenever you're about to take on a role. Before you begin your work day, you might want to light a candle, draw an oracle card, take a walk around the block, recite a poem or prayer, or sing a song. While walking to my counseling office, I used to think up a custom-designed prayer for the day, where I acknowledged each of my clients and my desire to serve them, opened myself to inspiration and released any attachments I had to outcome.

The Hazards of Hierarchy

The Popularity Contest

Few Wisdom Keeping trainings and communities manage to escape the potential hazards of *hierarchy*. Whenever people with differing levels of experience, expertise and charisma gather together to form a group, 'in' groups, 'out' groups, 'up' groups and 'down' groups burst through the fertile community soil and ultimately bum a lot of people out. Unless community leaders and members work consciously to foster an atmosphere of inclusion, and unless they're willing to look at how exclusion is inevitably (sometimes subtly) showing up in the community culture, everyone ends up watering a popularity contest with their human nature.

Of course, appropriate respect and influence should be given to community members who have demonstrated commitment, competence and long-term involvement in the community. This doesn't mean, however, that they are better, more valuable or more desirable human beings than someone who is new to the community.

If you are a Wisdom Seeker and you've recently joined a spiritual learning community, remember that you've had a whole life before you ever stepped foot in this place. Personally, I hope that you *still* have a life of your own outside of this community—even if it is smaller, simplified or somewhat changed. If you've dropped everything and everyone for your new spiritual family, I gently caution you.

Whenever you embark on a new path of self-development, you are going to reevaluate your life and relationships. It is only natural that the inner changes you go through will bring about outer changes. Still, if possible, keep a good old friend who knows you and your roots, hire a counselor who is super grounded, or maintain relationships with people who are 'normal' planetary citizens. During trying times in your community, these are the people you're going to need to keep your life and community in the proper perspective.

If you find yourself getting sucked into the community pool of teenage insecurity,
remember your other life, if nothing else.
If you forgot, dumped or lost your other life, reclaim the best bits of it.

Social cliquing in alternative communities can activate old and painful memories—throwing community members into the jaws of adolescence, disempowering them both personally and professionally. Even if they are fully grown adults and functioned just fine in their pre-community life, they can suddenly find themselves asking, "Do they like me? Will I be invited to this? Why wasn't I invited to that? Am I *in* with the *in crowd?*"

If you find yourself asking questions like these, remember your worth. Breathe deeply. Include yourself if you can. If you can't, find an ally in the community, or somewhere else where your strengths and passions just naturally come out. To the best of your ability, try not to get too caught up in the social popularity game. It is likely an ego trip, and definitely a waste of your precious time. If it helps, remind yourself that it can be lonely at the top.

"There is No Justice in this World"

Spiritual communities like ours have so much potential to do good.
Let's not let our collective potential
be overshadowed by a collective ego trip!

I come from a long line of social activists and lawyers, many who spent their lives working for justice. Unfortunately, my idealistic ancestors were often proven wrong, which is why my Grandma Nettie used to repeat with merciless candor, to everyone's chagrin, "There's no justice in this world."

Justice has been something I've valued and fought for as early as I can remember. Once I went on strike in my third-grade gym class. I thought the team-picking system was so cruel and unfair that I refused to participate. You probably recognize it. The teacher chose two captains, who would then take turns picking their team members, going from the most 'desirable' classmate to the biggest loser. It was a humiliating process, especially for the kids who were always left sitting alone on the gym floor, staring at the ground and feeling awful. While I managed to change the way we picked teams in that particular gym class, many of my other justice-seeking efforts were less successful.

Justice is a relatively new concept for Homo sapiens. We may have had an enlightened civilization or two in our past, but much of the time, the people with power and control over resources have made out like bandits, while the rest of us have either been left out in the cold, or to take care of each other. For thousands of years, our 'human community' has been riddled with war, manipulation and power grabs. One pseudo-spiritual justice system after the other has been erected to rationalize and promote persecution, discrimination, colonialism, slavery and death.

During especially disillusioning times, I've found solace in alternative perspectives on justice, usually provided by Wisdom Keepers. Many of these wise beings spoke of a higher form of justice— one which operated on another plane, beyond time, space and the specificity of a single life, act or earthly experience. This broadened, more mystical perspective helped me to release my despair, return to center, and live with the seemingly senseless world around me. Somehow, these Wisdom Keepers managed to make our terribly flawed justice system seem less all-powerful or all-determining (at least on a soul level). For that, I am eternally grateful.

I wish I could say that all of the Wisdom Keeping communities I've participated in have been just and fair, and that all members were treated with equal amounts of respect. But I can't. Despite the idealistic values that were consciously embraced in my communities, our earthly practices were often embarrassingly lacking. Social cliques easily turned into professional power cliques.

I've seen this happen in so many alternative trainings, with the best of intentions. The *in* groups don't only decide who to invite to the most intimate gatherings, but who to promote professionally. They rarely do so transparently. Even when the decisions that are made are wise, and the people who end up in leadership roles do a wonderful job, if the decisions are made behind closed doors, the decision-making process itself causes hurt feelings and paranoia to ripple out into the field. Transparency around decision-making is a key characteristic in healthy Wisdom Keeping communities. People tend to thrive when community systems, structures and processes *are* fair, and *feel* fair.

As my community grows and evolves, its needs change.
I am an essential part of my community, also growing and evolving.
My needs and ideas matter and can make a positive difference.

An Invitation to Speak Out
Against Community Injustice

At some point, our inner work will lead to outer action.

Many Wisdom Keeping communities become successful because of their ability to grow, transform and learn over time. As a community member, one of your responsibilities is to help your community evolve to its highest potential in whatever way you can. If you have a suggestion which could foster an atmosphere of greater equality and respect in your community, yet you choose to withhold it, you do your community a great disservice.

Many Wisdom Seekers believe that voicing dissatisfaction is synonymous with being a victim. We equate saying 'no' with complaining, blaming and projecting. We tell ourselves if we can only think at higher frequencies, we'll attract something better, or will realize that everything has been perfect all along. We keep ourselves busy judging ourselves any time our minds get judgmental. We work diligently to find happiness within the status quo.

Here's the thing though. A status quo is a status quo, even if it's in a spiritual community. Whether most of the people in your community are wise or dense, the majority will continue to set the norms until you do something about it. Ironically, the dissatisfied are often the majority. When no one speaks out, this fact is rarely discovered.

I don't mean to deny the importance of doing your inner work. If you are constantly feeling unloved and unwanted, you will have a hard time honoring your truth and speaking out. To speak up for yourself effectively, you must know that you have the right to be here, and to have your own perspective. If low self-esteem is preventing you from bringing essential issues to the light, then certainly empower yourself using any techniques you're drawn to. Affirm yourself. Learn self-love. Fine-tune your thoughts. Work on feeling included and valued regardless of circumstance. Take the time you need. This inner work is crucial.

That said, if you get so wrapped up in your inner work that you forget all about the outer, it is a pity—for you and for your community.

The most positive social-spiritual-political changes ever made were initiated by heroes who dared speak out for what they believed. Many faced disapproving mobs, risking their lives, but that did not stop them. Being a victim is settling for what you don't want because you don't think you can get or deserve something better. If you want something better for your community and humanity, then dare to want.

I invite you to act as soon as you feel empowered. Don't wait too long. When you feel empowered, you will see the people and conditions of your community much more clearly. You will be able to discern between the fair and unfair. When you know your own worth, you can take the appropriate steps to restore justice and equality, and people will thank you for it.

The Serenity Prayer

God (Goddess), grant me the courage to change what can be changed,
the strength to accept what cannot be changed,
and the wisdom to know the difference.

Speaking out takes courage. I believe it is worth every bead of sweat and pitter patter of the heart it invokes. If you never try, if you never go out on that limb, you will never know what was possible. Think what would have happened if Rosa Parks spent all of her days writing affirmations, forgiving her parents, and learning to see the perfection of all things, without ever daring to refuse the bus driver's orders to give up her seat to a white passenger.

Who knows? Maybe your entire community will rejoice in your words and become a city of gold, illustrating for the world how earthly and spiritual systems of justice can work cooperatively and synergistically, promoting everyone's good. Or, maybe it won't. Worst case scenario, you discover your community is beyond help. If this is true, at least you will know that you've done your best, and can walk out the door with your self-respect intact, and peace in your heart.

Overpopulation, A Potential Growth-Stunter

Thriving Wisdom Keeping and alternative learning communities can experience an increase in population, and consequently, a more multi-leveled organizational structure. Based on experience and longevity, community members are given increasing amounts of responsibility and more public roles.

This can be wonderful for incoming Seekers. There's nothing like having an abundance of competent role models to learn from. Watching—even imitating—seasoned Wisdom Keepers can be inspiring and empowering for newer community members. When

Wisdom Seekers act like their mentors, they get to have an embodied experience, a visceral taste of what it's like to actually be that person, to know what that person knows, to do what that person does. Ideally, of course, this is just a phase of the learning process. Students integrate their leader's qualities and wisdom, taking their projections home.

At some point, students must find their own styles. To do this, they need ample opportunities to learn *through experience* how to trust in their own authority and follow their creative intuition. Alternative training communities can serve their members well by encouraging younger members to take risks, follow their instincts, and learn from the consequences of their actions. There are few things more empowering than getting to test one's wings in the context of an encouraging, supportive community.

When a community is experiencing over-population, students who feel ready to engage in more bold experiments may feel cramped for space. Even if they've been in the community for years and become quite skilled, they may still feel energetically held back. This can confuse them. They long for greater freedom, and everyone around them seems supportive, but they can't embody it. They may suspect it's a self-esteem problem, but feeling and expressing one's full authority is objectively hard to do when surrounded by too many role models.

If you resonate with what I'm describing, you may be suffering from community over-population. Instead of being hard on yourself and insisting that you learn how to assert yourself within your community, consider using your skills *outside* of the community—at least for a period of time.

When I was a kid, my sister was always the social one. Our huge Jewish family would come over for some big holiday, and she'd graciously connect with all of the guests and make it look so easy. I barely got by. An introvert, being social and small talk never came easily to me. I often wished I could disappear into a cave.

When my sister left home to go to college, something curious happened. My shyness diminished. Though at the time, I was baffled by the shift, I now understand that the shyness had to disappear. I no longer had my 'other half' living out my inner socialite. When my relatives came over, I was the only Aronson daughter present at the party. I had to sink or swim. I learned to swim.

Sometimes it's hard to learn to swim when you are surrounded by Olympic free-style champions. When you are a second-year student, and you are doing your best to give a brilliant healing session to a first-year student, and then a group of fifth-year students walks into the room, you might easily think, "Why bother? They're all better than me anyway." In a way, you would be right since they have more experience.

I was once one of the first fifteen participants to sign up for an alternative healing training. We all started together. There was no hierarchy to speak of. We were all pioneers. I was a group participant in the first year, an assistant in the second, a group leader in the third, a supervisor in the fourth, a super-supervisor in my fifth, etc. If I were still a training participant today, I'd be a super-duper-pooper-scoopervisor.

There was something exciting—and—easy about being one of the very first to join the training community. It was a bit like showing up to a family party without my sister. I simply had to rise to the occasion.

I'll never forget the first time the teacher left me alone in the bodywork room with a group of first-year students. (During our first year, the teacher personally used the healing technique on each and every one of us, showing incredible stamina and care. He never left us alone.) As I watched him walk out of the room, I felt nervous. I was afraid I wouldn't be good enough, that I wouldn't know what to do without him—especially if things got intense, or complicated—which they often did.

Thankfully, I moved through my fear, showed up for the students and held the container. I did this over and over again until I mastered the process. I am grateful to this teacher for trusting me so much that he was willing to leave the room. I have no doubt that if he had stayed, he would have done a better job. At the same time, if he'd stayed, none of his older students would have blossomed into professional healers as much as we did. We were given plenty of opportunities to sink or swim. We made plenty of mistakes, but there was nobody around to compare ourselves with. It was easier for us to forgive ourselves.

This particular training has changed a lot since those early days. It certainly grew in size. While I'm sure many lessons have been learned and improvements have been made, I am grateful that I was able to learn about leadership through trial and error, to know that no matter how much I might have screwed up, I was still one of the best practitioners around (because no one else was around!).

It may be impossible to turn back the clock in more established communities, but extra space can still be made for the newcomers. If you're at the top of the hierarchy in your community, step out of the way every once in a while. Give the new people a chance. You wouldn't be where you are today if someone hadn't risked trusting you.

A Special Note to the Old-Timers: Don't Let Your Success Keep You from Growing

Professional Wisdom Keepers should celebrate our developmental triumphs and acknowledge how far we've come. This is important, as long as we see these moments of celebration as temporary resting places, as preparation grounds for further development—as opposed to our final destination.

Some outwardly successful Wisdom Keepers make the mistake of thinking we've learned all we need to learn, and know all we need to know. When we continue to surround ourselves with the same kinds of students and clients, the people who need what we already know how to give, we can easily forget that our spiritual journey has just begun. Our success blinds us to the great mystery awaiting us. We may look impressive to the world, but we may be nothing more than dried-up snake skin, watching our soulful essence slithering off into the distance.

If you are a seasoned Wisdom Keeper, you're most likely very good at what you do. Many people probably look up to you and appreciate the quality of your work as well as your wisdom. You've likely earned your place in your community and deserve to reap the benefits of your efforts. You also have the possibility to continue expanding and deepening your own journey, to keep growing personally, spiritually as well as professionally.

Stagnation has little to do with an outer form or method; it has to do with an inner mindset, a way of being. If someone manages to keep their mind open, intuitive, curious, humble and flexible, they could work in a factory for their entire life and learn something new every day. Problems arise when our minds become fixed and rigid, when we get caught in a success groove, and we are rarely challenged with new ideas or feedback from others.

Sometimes a chosen—ideally stretching—change in our outer life can facilitate inner growth. If you are a professional Wisdom Keeper who is accustomed to listening and reflecting, for instance, try teaching. If you've been a teacher for years, try writing, or going back to school. If you are used to working on your own, try working with a partner, or vice versa. Do something completely different, or do whatever you've been doing, but in a new setting. Changing environments, even cultures, can also be a powerful way to challenge everyday assumptions and grow professionally. The riskier your chosen change feels, the greater impact it can have on you, your life, and ultimately your service.

Leaving our comfort zone requires that we actually feel uncomfortable. If we make a change, but the stakes are too low, we're just pretending.

Overcoming the Fear of Separation
Graduation Can Feel Like Separation

I'd like to address the tender issue of graduating, that moment when we leave our Wisdom Keeping community or training environment, at any time, for any reason. When our place of learning is also our social and spiritual home, graduating or leaving can be difficult. The more wonderful the community, the more friends we've made there, the harder it can be to leave—even if we know in our hearts that the time has come.

One day you may find yourself wondering whether your time to leave a Wisdom Keeping community has come. Perhaps you are longing to unfold your professional wings and fly. You may want to go out into the world on your own and test all that you've learned, in a new, untouched territory. You may feel ready to release the training wheels that your community has provided, and walk on your own. Only you can know when a community that was meant to be your launching pad has turned into a set of outdated crutches.

Given the painful nature of leaving, you may want to be gentle with yourself and take things slowly. Maybe you start by skipping a training day, session or module, just to see you can survive. You might take a year-long sabbatical, giving yourself time to digest all that you've learned, with permission to return to the community should that feel right. You might also want to take the plunge and throw yourself a graduation party, inviting all of your community friends to celebrate you.

Whatever you do and however you do it, you really need to be the source of your own approval. Sometimes it is difficult to be that source when you are surrounded by external sources who you've come to rely on to provide that function for you.

Alternative communities are exceptional sources of approval.
This is what makes them wonderful, effective, and hard to leave!

Speaking Out Can Feel Like Separation

Most humans share the fear of separation. We long to be included, and we are afraid of being kicked out of the tribe. This fear is wired into us. It can also be experienced especially strongly in Wisdom Keeping communities, where harmony is valued. Being true to ourselves, when we're not in agreement with the community's status quo, can feel very risky. Though we've probably been taught that being true to ourselves is a good thing, our social bodies tell us otherwise.

Sometimes being true to ourselves involves speaking out or refusing to keep a secret. Secrets exist and grow in most communities. It doesn't matter if the community considers itself highly evolved. Because most of us fear losing the people we love if we expose their mistakes or vulnerabilities, we learn to look the other way, bite our tongues, and keep toxic truths inside our bellies. Ironically, our attempts to protect each other by keeping secrets is what ultimately separates us.

When we speak the unspeakable, when we dare to 'betray' family or community secrets by speaking out in appropriate places, in compassionate but truthful ways, we can free ourselves, and ultimately those around us.

As it is said, the secret to freedom is to have no secrets!
We are as sick as we are secretive.

Wisdom Keeping communities, just like families, develop family secrets. Community members can loyally defend some of the most unprofessional, even violating acts, and they do so in the name of love, spirituality and devotion.

Usually, when someone longs for spiritual community, they carry a deep wish that the community will provide them with what their own family, or a previous group experience, couldn't. Whether they lacked a feeling of belonging, a sense of the divine, or permission to be who they are, they now turn to the alternative community to fill the gap. The less functional their familial history, the more attracted they'll be to the apparent 'high-functioning' role of their desired community. Consciously, they'll expect their new community to provide them with the stability, safety and support they longed for when growing up. Unconsciously, they'll expect the community to help them complete the developmental stages that were left incomplete within their own family context.

Many Wisdom Keeping communities live up to this important task. Many spiritually sound communities also have their areas of dysfunction. Wisdom Keeping guides, teachers, mentors, leaders, gurus, coaches and counselors are also human beings. Many of them were born into semi- (or majorly) dysfunctional families themselves.

Most people who dedicate their lives to helping people heal old wounds have had their share of wounds and life challenges. The majority of them are as inspiring, wise and compassionate as they are *because* of the pain they've experienced and worked through. This doesn't mean that professional Wisdom Keepers have healed, or are even conscious of all of their wounds, or how they may be playing out in their relationships. This is why community members should keep their eyes open and feet on the ground.

The Teacher's Special Role in Letting Go

Separation can be an essential part of the developmental process. I'm not referring to spiritual separation, which is impossible, but psychological, professional and sometimes physical separation.

Think of the time in a child's life when they need to test, explore and express their own autonomy, or the time in a community member's or student's process when they are ready to test their own strength and knowledge. They need to stick their toes in worldly waters and do things their own way—even if their way is less than perfect.

Students also need to practice saying 'no.' It's healthy for them to sometimes disagree and engage in lively dialogues with teachers and fellow students. This essential part of the growth process is not every alternative Wisdom Keeper's focus nor should it be. In Rebirthing, for example, the focus is to help people heal their own births and the short-yet-highly-impactful period which follows. When working with pregnancy, birth and infancy, fostering an environment based on safety, connection and physical closeness is key. As a Rebirther, it would make no sense to do otherwise, since one of our main goals was to heal the traumatic separation which often occurs during the birth experience.

At the same time, if teachers do their work well—whatever their main focus is—the inevitable and positive conclusion will be that their students are going to grow up and become competent enough to want more freedom. In other words, whether teachers' professional foci are on the individuation process or not, they will inevitably be met with a longing among their students to speak out, participate more actively in decision-making processes and/or move on. How teachers meet this longing in the context of their Wisdom Keeping community can either facilitate this positive and natural process, or make it complicated and guilt-ridden.

Ideally, teachers see their students' eagerness to expand as a tribute to their good work. They thus give students the message that speaking out and moving on are not only OK, but healthy.

Some teachers fear conflict, letting go, being outgrown or rejected. They may subtly, or not so subtly, give their students a discouraging message—communicating that their students' need for greater independence is hurtful, unspiritual or unnecessary. Unlike cult leaders, few alternative teachers blatantly forbid their students from leaving their communities, or from growing up and speaking their minds. If they do discourage growth, their way is often hidden, or at least hard to decipher and pinpoint. Most of the time, Wisdom Keepers have no idea that they're discouraging their students from becoming the free thinkers and doers that they believe they want them to be.

Wisdom Keepers, teachers and leaders can unintentionally stunt their students' growth in a number of ways. They can seem disappointed or disapproving whenever students show signs of growing independence. They can consciously and unconsciously withdraw their support or attention when students disagree with them, spend less time with them, or express a desire to leave the community. They can subtly sabotage their students' attempts to stand on their own by demanding credit and compensation for all of their students' endeavors. (Although it is important that teachers are properly acknowledged, they can sometimes cling to credit more out of fear than out of appropriateness.)

Instead of celebrating students' growing independence, and creating rituals to acknowledge important milestones, teachers can overlook students' accomplishments, or make them feel wrong about their needs and wishes to disagree or leave. They can distort spiritual truths so that signs of individuality are equated with the ego's work, or their students' unhealthy insistence on clinging to illusions of separateness and difference.

Some teachers make it hard for students to leave their communities or trainings by continuing to create new roles, duties, jobs and status positions for graduates. Although many students can and do benefit from evolving training possibilities, others who would benefit from leaving can end up feeling guilty about shirking on their (continuously mounting) responsibilities, or sad about missing out on the fun experienced by their peers who stay. Finally, some teachers discourage their students' individuation processes by showing little or no interest in any new aspects of the students' personal and professional lives.

No matter how teachers discourage their students' growth, their actions or lack thereof tend to produce guilt. If a student must constantly worry about giving credit to the teacher, or about betraying or not prioritizing the teacher, they can lose touch with their more important job of becoming independent, sovereign beings. All of their energy goes towards proving their loyalty and devotion to the teacher and the community.

A teacher's positive or negative approach to legalizing 'separation' can either create a peaceful aura around the community, the kind every alternative teacher wants, or an agonizing one. Whether we are Wisdom Seekers or Wisdom Keepers, as long as we are community members, let's keep this in mind. Let's do our best to support each other's growth and liberation.

Now that we've thoroughly explored the Light and Shadow aspects of living, learning and serving within an alternative healing arts community, let's take a deep dive into some of the most common traps professional Wisdom Keepers and Seekers can fall into: *The Self-Absorption Trap*; *The Peaceful-Loving-Kindness Trap*; *The Martyr Trap*; *The Money Trap*; *The Love, Attention and Approval Trap*; *The Charisma Trap*; *The Forgiveness Trap* and lastly, *The Perfection Trap*.

PART ELEVEN: COMMON TRAPS

The Self-Absorption Trap

A certain amount of belly button picking is to be expected in the beginning of any personal development process. If people who have been living unexamined lives decide to embark on a journey towards wisdom, they often need some time to get acquainted with their inner worlds. This is good. As has often been said in many Wisdom Keeping cultures, one cannot love, understand or give to anyone else, if one cannot first love, understand and give to oneself.

With this said, I can safely state that at some point the belly button becomes spick and span. The lint is out, and continued picking accomplishes nothing but agitation of the skin. If you have clients and students whose belly buttons are as clean as whistles, the time has probably come for such soul-searching pupils to turn their gazes outward and shift their orientation towards creativity and service.

Many of the Wisdom Seekers you work with will automatically feel their readiness to broaden their horizons. Like butterflies, they'll voluntarily leave their contemplative cocoons, eager to explore and give back to the vast world around them. Others might need some friendly coaxing. They'll need you to help them see that flying free can be just as fulfilling as digging for gold.

Interestingly, for newer Wisdom Seekers (with extroverted leanings), learning to be introspective can be a drag at first. Their brains and hearts hurt from so much inward-looking. Everything they do, say, feel and think is suddenly put under a magnifying glass. Nothing is taken for granted anymore, and there's no going back to the burden-free aspects of an unexamined life.

Overwhelmed Seekers who come to you for support may need you to encourage them to hang in there, and to let them know that inner work—though uncomfortable at times—is safe, gets easier and is worth the effort. If they trust in your guidance, they eventually surrender to the richness and value of their inner world. They let go of their earlier emphasis on outer achievement. They dive deep into their psyches; journal mysterious dreams; explore early wounds; excavate past lives; and analyze powerful feelings. As they do so, their memories sharpen, inner visions crystalize, sensitivities peak, and their psycho-spiritual vocabularies become impressively nuanced.

Over time, they can detect and dissect every emotional shift, skillfully interpret every relational dynamic and pull apart every troubling pattern. Few things escape their penetrating gaze. While their introspective journeys are irresistibly filled with meaning, they aren't always fun. In fact, if you ask a dedicated Wisdom Seeker how they're doing, they'll often share that they're still working through their deepest wounds and releasing their oldest patterns.

What they say may very well be true. Yet for Seekers who've been working hard and deep in the cave, for a long *long* time, inviting them to leave the processing behind may be the best way to support their process. This is especially true for Seekers who tend to equate all growth with pain and struggle, and to have perfectionistic tendencies. These Seekers are especially vulnerable to falling into The Self-Absorption Trap. They may be hanging onto familiar painful material in order to avoid taking the next natural step towards greater autonomy and wholeness.

If you suspect your clients or students have fallen into such a trap, do your best to stay awake, listen carefully and keep your heart open. Eventually, you'll sense whether they are truly working through essential issues, or whether they are getting sidetracked, stalling or falling into a trap.

If and when it feels appropriate, let them know that the inner journey never ends, and that none of us have to be perfectly healed in order to take our passions seriously, turn our focus outward, and make a meaningful contribution. Help them appreciate the wisdom and resources they've gathered along their journey. Encourage them to share what they've learned with others, practice generosity, and take risks in service of their authentic dreams and growing inner authority.

Some Wisdom Seekers will have become so accustomed to the safe, cozy and contemplative nest they've shared with you, that they may feel sad, misunderstood, rejected or frightened by your suggestions. They may feel cast out of Eden. This too is worthy of exploration. Make space for their concerns, and speak honestly about how the shift you're suggesting may impact your relationship, as well as their lives. But don't get lost in this exploration. At some point, they must rise up from the cozy couch of introspection and walk bravely out the door, even if it's scary.

When it comes to the Self-Absorption Trap, I appeal to your sense of balance and your highest respect for timing. This is not about pushing people before they are ready. It's about sensing their readiness and not being afraid to give a gentle nudge in the right direction.

Breaking Free of the Golden Cage

Keysha came to a professional Wisdom Keeper feeling stuck and unfulfilled. She had been working as a corporate lawyer for years, had plenty of money and material comforts, but she wanted to do something more meaningful with her life. She just didn't know what that would be.

It took time for Keysha and her Wisdom Keeper to uncover her deep—and surprising—desire to work as a hands-on healer. Though as a child she knew she had healing gifts, she had drifted so far from her true nature and spiritual roots as an adult, that it felt entirely impossible to embrace such a fringe vocation.

Together with her Wisdom Keeper, Keysha identified and worked through one fear after the other: the fear of losing financial security; of compromising her professional status; of disappointing her parents; of losing her friends; of becoming a beginner again; of being seen as 'woo woo'; of failing; of succeeding, etc.

As she became increasingly aware of the fears that stood between her and the manifestation of her dream, she started to understand how deeply they were connected to her parents' fears, and *their* parents' fears. In addition to her primary Wisdom Keeper, she sought out other alternative professionals to supplement her uncovering process. She found a healer to help her release the pain of her ancestors; a past life regressionist to uncover her soul's wounds; an urban shaman to facilitate powerful soul retrievals; and an Indian Astrologist to reveal her future through the Akashic Records. Each Wisdom Keeping encounter led to new insights, exciting breakthroughs, and even more questions.

Whenever her original Wisdom Keeper gently suggested that she enroll in a hands-on healing training, Keysha resisted. She always felt there was more to discover, unravel or work through. It didn't matter how deep and wide her wisdom was, or how far she'd come along her multi-dimensional journey. If there was an ancestral story in need of understanding, an old fear in need of conquering, or a deep wound in need of healing, she had to heed its call. Until she did, she was convinced she was not ready to put her dream into practice.

One day, after listening to Keysha describe her latest revelation—and complain about her corporate job—for the ten trillionth time, her Wisdom Keeper finally gave her the loving-yet-swift kick in the practicality pants that she needed. Her *wisdom seeking* had become her new Golden Cage. It was time to stop 'seeking' and to start leaping!

The Peaceful-Loving-Kindness Trap

Many Wisdom Keepers and Seekers embrace expansive, transpersonal definitions of Love, such as: *Compassion, Oneness, Is-ness, a field of consciousness, the All, the Mystery, the Great Creator, Grandmother/Goddess, the intelligence of the universe, that sacred point where all are connected, everything other than fear,* etc. We also set high standards for ourselves when it comes to embodying a more personal kind of love.

Most Wisdom Keepers and Seekers drawn to the healing arts are kind-hearted, sensitive and compassionate people. We tend to feel best when things are harmonious. Because life is rarely harmonious, many of us learn from an early age not only to be peace-seekers, but peace-makers.

Without inner and outer peace-makers, we'd all be in deep trouble. We need peace-makers to help us build bridges, get along, communicate better, understand and forgive each other, so that we can all live in harmony. Peace-makers only run into problems when our deep desire for peace is driven by an even deeper fear of conflict—often sourced in an even deeper fear of anger. Because I've noticed a larger degree of conflict/anger-phobia than peace-phobia in professional Wisdom Keeping communities, let's take a look at The Peaceful-Loving-Kindness Trap.

I used to think if I was just peaceful, loving and kind enough, things would work out. I was wrong. Although it is wonderful when being nice is enough to create a desired result, being a 'good guy' isn't always enough. At some point, we must face a tough yet essential truth:

Sometimes in life, even nice guys have to be bad guys.

Many Wisdom Seekers learn that we can manifest our harmonious wishes without ever having to lift a finger (especially not the middle one!). There is certainly some truth to that. Love, faith and forgiveness do heal. High-frequency attitudes do attract positive experiences and people into our lives. Releasing struggle can melt concrete conflicts into soft puddles. Those who trust can afford to be patient.

That said, envisioning 'the desirable' doesn't always cut it, especially when being non-desirable is experienced as taboo.

If we spend too much energy refusing to be the bad guy, we'll inevitably attract bad guys to us, since bad guys love to annoy good guys. If we continue to cling to our goodness, using harmony-loving philosophies to justify passivity and an unwillingness to stand up for ourselves and our core values, we fuel the fire. The bigger the fire gets, the bigger the bad guy gets, and the bigger a hose we'll need to put it out. Unfortunately, when we also buy into the thought that only bad guys use hoses, we dig ourselves a deeper hole. Next thing you know, we find ourselves sitting in a life-threatening situation, with only two options. We can save our goodness, or our lives.

Many of us Wisdom Seekers choose our goodness. We simply can't bear the idea of anyone seeing us grabbing a bulky hose, straddling it like a horse and blowing out the raging fire with an equal amount of fury. We'd rather be consumed by fire than stoop so low. Ironically, when we stick with 'goodness' at all costs, we end up merging with 'badness,' becoming one with the fire.

The Day Monique Learned that Being a Good Person was Not Enough to Make her Life Worth Living

For years, Monique, a successful Wisdom Keeper, had never forgotten an appointment with a client. She took great pride in her professional accountability as well as her loving and accommodating nature. Once she forgot an appointment with a new client. Horrified by her mistake, she called the client up, apologized profusely and offered another session, free of charge.

Instead of expressing a bit of understandable disappointment and accepting Monique's kind offer, the new client became enraged—accusing her of being insensitive, selfish and unprofessional. Relying on a lifetime of 'goodness training,' Monique kept her heart open and worked towards a peaceful, constructive resolution. Patiently and persistently, she empathized with the client's upset, acknowledged her mistake, and offered an even sweeter deal…two free sessions.

The client responded to her kindness and generosity with more vicious and humiliating attacks. "I should have listened to *all* of the people who recommended that I see someone else. You're clearly insecure, under-qualified and desperate for new clients. I wouldn't work with you if you paid me. Now I'm going to make sure that everyone in this city knows how unprofessional you are!" Then the client hung up.

If Monique hadn't already fallen so deeply into *The Peaceful-Loving-Kindness Trap*, she would have probably been relieved to have lost a client with extreme narcissistic and abusive tendencies. But she was too attached to maintaining a self-image of utter decency and goodness. All she could think about was how badly she'd failed, and how terrified she was that this person was now going to ruin her reputation, and her life. Instead of letting herself off the hook (and getting better at screening new clients), she became even more determined to avoid mistake-making. From this point forward, she would always be kind, loving, nurturing, generous, forgiving and accommodating—no matter how badly she was treated.

Ironically, the nicer Monique got, the more nastiness she encountered at work, and in the world around her. Wherever she went, she was met with an uncanny amount of rudeness and harsh criticism—in the supermarket, on the train, around the dinner table. It was as if a 'doormat' sign was plastered on her forehead.

Finally, Monique reached out for professional support. Her compassionate Wisdom Keeper helped her see how, throughout her entire life, at some very deep level, she had been convinced that she did not have the right to exist unless she was a 'good person,' unless her presence uplifted everyone she came into contact with, unless she was peaceful, loving and kind.

The more Monique felt the immensity of this life-long pressure to be 'good,' the more she realized it had to end. If goodness was the only thing she was living for, what was the point?

After her revelation, she set out on a personal mission to stretch herself. She didn't commit any crimes, but she did do things she ordinarily considered taboo. One day, while waiting in line for a train ticket, a group of obnoxious teenage kids barged in line ahead of her. To her own surprise, she heard herself saying, "Hey, I was here first!" She didn't smile politely. She didn't go out of her way to give the kids the loveliest human encounter they'd ever had. She took back her place in line, got her ticket and walked away—laughing!

Monique could hardly recognize herself. She actually got a kick out of being perceived as an uptight lady. Her goodness was no longer two-dimensional. It was no longer a prison preventing her from discovering and expressing her power and sense of agency. Over time, Monique's effectiveness as a healer grew along with her self-respect, and courage. The world is much better for it.

If you're a Wisdom Keeper or Seeker, and you strongly identify as one of the good guys, you might want to make some room for your inner 'bad guy.' I've found that things have worked out once I demonstrated a willingness to be perceived as something other than angelic. Like Monique, I've needed to show that I could advocate for myself or a core value, when necessary.

I'm not talking about being mean in order to be mean. I'm talking about doing what is required in order to be true to yourself, a virtue or a collective need which is valid. Sometimes lobbyists have to be pushy in order to get a good law passed. Similarly, very nice people sometimes have to be stubborn, determined, loud, annoying, confronting or frustrating in order to get through to those around them, in order to manifest their essentially nice ideas. This is true even in spiritual communities. (More on this later!)

Whoever said that being spiritual meant having to be
nice and accommodating all of the time?

An Affirmation:

I can survive my badness. So can everyone else.
Thus, my goodness is free to increase in authenticity by 100%.

Creating a Safe Space for Conflict

Invitation #1: *Make peace with your own anger and learn to deal with conflicts.*

Even the most evolved beings can get pissed off and feel hurt. When this happens to professional Wisdom Keepers, we can judge ourselves harshly. Like the ego, anger has gotten a bad rap in Wisdom Keeping communities. Given anger's essential role in just about every human and animal rights movement, it can't be all bad. Anger becomes most dangerous when we believe it is dangerous, thus push it underground.

When I'm feeling really angry now, (or when there's lots of 'life energy' streaming through my body), I do my best to channel it creatively. I dance like a maniac, write a raging poem or paint a fierce painting. As the energy is allowed to move, something new emerges. I'm more able to get beneath the reactivity and discover hidden gems.

When professional Wisdom Keepers learn how to respect, use and channel our anger (without slapping a high-frequency thought on top of it, or feeling guilty or like bad people), we empower ourselves to make important discernments in our work with clients and students.

When we find ourselves angry at a client or student, we may need to withdraw for a while in order to contain, explore and transform our feelings. The worst thing we can do is deny that we have them. When we deny our more 'base' feelings, we teach our students and clients that such feelings are unacceptable, or we send confusing messages, which can be worse. If clients feel too ashamed of their feelings to reveal them to us, how can they heal their wounds in our presence?

Invitation #2: *Let your clients and students know that it's OK for them to feel angry. Demonstrate your faith in their ability to solve conflicts by letting them have conflicts in the first place.*

Most Wisdom Seekers embark on self-development journeys to learn how to deal with difficult feelings. As mentioned, many Wisdom Seekers also tend to be peace-makers, often to survive less-than-peaceful family circumstances. Our clients and students can also easily fall into the trap of repressing their needs and difficult feelings, in order to avoid conflict.

They can use common spiritual teachings to justify this repression. They may equate expressing anger with being a 'victim,' not taking responsibility, or engaging in unfair projecting. They can find themselves recycling old survival strategies. Just as they did growing up in dysfunctional families and communities, adult peace-makers end up sacrificing their feelings and needs for the sake of their professional Wisdom Keepers and their spiritual communities.

More than anything, our peace-keeping clients need us to lessen the shame and affirm our shared experience. They have the right to feel what they feel, and need what they need. They are not alone, and we're right there with them, swimming around in the imperfectly perfect soup of our humanness.

For Wisdom Keepers:

*By welcoming all of my feelings, I make space for the feelings of others.
My ability to contain, accept and value anger—mine or someone else's—impacts
the quality of my work and the depth of healing
which can take place in my presence.*

For Wisdom Seekers:

*I am a human being. All human beings feel powerless and angry sometimes.
I deserve a professional Wisdom Keeper who feels safe
with my anger, pain and fear as well as their own.*

The Martyr Trap

Those of us with peaceful-loving-kindness tendencies can easily fall into *The Martyr Trap*. Because Wisdom Keepers tend to want the very best for our clients and students, we can end up over-giving and turning sacrifice into full-fledged martyrdom.

When our hearts overextend themselves, and are met with little or nothing in return, we can experience a deep loneliness. When this happens, we can unintentionally send out a message like, "After everything I have done for you! Is this all you've got for me?" When deep in *The Martyr Trap*, we consciously cling to our good intentions and push our feelings of resentment, anger and loneliness underground. This closes us off to potentially valuable transference and counter-transference material which would otherwise be useful in our healing work; for it is in the alchemical space between connected yet distinct beings that true healing takes place.

Cancelation Policies and Such

Some professional Wisdom Keepers, in our attempts to be kind, understanding and accommodating, continually put up with situations that in the end aren't sustainable or good for anyone.

Our clients come and go, cancel last-minute, or constantly reschedule, and we twist ourselves into pretzels trying to meet them on their terms. Even if we do manage to establish a limit, like a cancelation policy, we can't bring ourselves to enforce it. I've definitely been one of those people.

Amir and Kava Learn Together

Several years ago, Amir, a professional Wisdom Keeping colleague of mine (and exceptionally understanding person), had a really bad week. Clients were calling left and right to cancel last minute or reschedule.

Prior to that week, a client would cancel a session five minutes before they were supposed to arrive, and Amir would say, "No problem. You get that haircut. I know how hard it is to get a time with your stylist." Though he said it wasn't a problem, it *was* a problem. He'd set time aside for them, which he could have given to someone else if he'd known earlier about their hairdressing plans. It was hard to admit, but Amir felt taken for granted. (He, of course, understood that this was not a good thing for a professional Wisdom Keeper to make a habit of feeling. But that didn't make learning to honor his time any easier.)

At the end of that week, he received an extra gift from the universe, a huge flood in his office. As he waded in water up to his ankles, Kava, his first client of the day walked through the door, almost an hour later than they had agreed upon. (He hadn't been able to reach Kava on the phone to tell her about the flood. He had managed to reschedule the rest of his appointments.)

This was one of those rare and unsolvable appointment mysteries. Amir was sure that Kava was late, and Kava was sure she was on time. Though Kava was willing to stay for the rest of the ninety-minute session, Amir was not up for it, considering the sorry state of his office. He was willing to talk for a few minutes that day, but would need to reschedule. Since he was already up to his ankles with frustration, he asked Kava to pay for the part of the session they had missed.

This was the first time Amir had ever asked a client to pay him for time when they were not with him. It was an important experience for him to have. Even though he worried that Kava might feel disappointed or unfairly treated, he needed to stick to his guns—at least for a while. He needed to know he could value his time and energy, even if his decision made someone he cared about feel uncomfortable or upset.

Ironically, Kava had similar martyrly tendencies. Being experienced as needy, difficult or a burden was a big taboo for her. As a client, Kava was cooperative and accommodating. Always empathizing with others, she rarely if ever challenged professional Wisdom Keepers or outer authorities (even when that would have been appropriate). She always insisted on paying Amir's full fee, even though this caused her great financial hardship. Kava felt so indebted to Amir for all of his support that it felt impossible to remind him about her impeccable track record when it came to being on time, that *Amir* was the one canceling the session, and that it could have just as easily been his scheduling mistake. Instead, Kava accepted Amir's decision without saying a word.

Once the floods were gone, and Amir gained a certain amount of trust in himself regarding this type of situation, he decided to return Kava's money. He had learned what he needed to learn, and when he thought about Kava, he could see just how responsible and conscientious she was. The appointment confusion was likely his mistake, given all that was going on that day. Kava had also been perfectly willing to stay for the duration of their session. *He* was the one swimming around in a deluge, feeling fed up with a lifetime of self-sacrifice, and telling her to come back another day.

Amir's decision to refund Kava's money and his genuine desire to understand her experience opened up a door to great healing. For the first time in her life, Kava was able to express disappointment and anger for having been treated unfairly, and to let Amir know just how afraid she was of asking him for what she needed, and deserved.

Today Kava knows that being a 'good client' doesn't require total obedience, self-sacrifice or agreeability, and that everyone is served when she is willing to advocate for herself and her needs. Amir now has a general policy where he asks clients to pay for sessions if they don't call to cancel or reschedule within a certain amount of time, and if he can't reschedule them within the same week of their session. Because he has learned to value his time and energy, he can be more flexible and generous with clients like Kava. Together, Amir and Kava released themselves from *The Martyr Trap*.

Most professional Wisdom Keepers can greatly benefit from knowing that it's safe to have and express our 'selves' in our working relationships. Being selfless and overly-flexible more often than not sabotages our ability to genuinely connect with those who come to us. It can also get in the way of our capacity to see our clients' and students' needs clearly, and to realize that they may not need us anywhere near as much as we believe they do (or need them to)!

*One of our most important jobs as professional Wisdom Keepers is
to model for our clients and students what it means to truly love oneself.
In order to love ourselves, there must be a self to love.*

The Money Trap

Money makes a good servant, but a lousy master.

Even the most generous and well-intentioned Wisdom Keepers can get trapped in the desire for and addiction to money. I'm not talking about the need or wish to make a good living. I am a big supporter of prosperity in all its forms. That's completely different from professional Wisdom Keepers selling our souls for money, because everyone loses when we do, especially our clients and students.

If you are a professional Wisdom Keeper and want to live and work with integrity, consider this scenario. All sixty of your clients and three-hundred of your course participants come to you one day and say, "We're healed now! Thanks for the ride! Ta ta!" If you need to go to therapy to deal with the major life transition set in motion, as well as to affirm your faith in miracles, then you are pretty normal. If the thought of being client- and student-less terrifies you so much that you start convincing your clients and students that they're not really healed and that they'll suffer tremendously without you and your help, you've probably fallen deeply into *The Money Trap*.

Although this hypothetical situation is unlikely, it makes a point. When professionals try to convince our clients and students to stay longer than necessary in order to stay in business or keep the revenue rolling in, we are bound to do some damage. We not only perpetuate an unhealthy dependency, we damage our own sense of integrity, and ultimately, our ability to serve. Money for a job well done is a wondrous thing, but money at any price isn't. Let's not fall into *The Money Trap*.

(Don't) Show Me the Money

Although generally speaking, people who invest in their healing journeys tend to get more out of them, this isn't always true when it comes to money. Some time ago, a woman walked into a professional Wisdom Keeper's office with a large check in her hands. Before the two of them even sat down, she presented the Wisdom Keeper with a massive sum of money, declaring she wanted to pay in advance for a series of sessions. Despite her willingness to invest money, she showed almost no commitment to the work itself.

The professional Wisdom Keeper felt a responsibility to hold the highest vision for their clients, and to gently push clients when they lost steam, felt afraid, or resisted the process. The Wisdom Keeper also knew that it wasn't their job to take full and complete responsibility for their clients' lives or do the bulk of their work for them. As soon as it became clear that this is what the client was paying for (and what she'd paid countless others to do in the past), the Wisdom Keeper handed her back the check and escorted her kindly out the door.

This particular Wisdom Keeper could have definitely used the money. They could easily have found ways to fill up a series of sessions with fascinating material. But they also knew that saying 'yes' to the client's unconscious 'no,' in order to enhance their income, would have been bad for both parties.

I highly recommend refusing money when appropriate. It is wonderful to confirm that we really do care more about the well-being of our clients and our integrity than about material things. While we don't always get to reap the economic benefits of our noble actions, we benefit in other ways.

For those of us who have learned to equate our intrinsic value with our workload, refusing money can also help us embrace our true worth. Regardless of how many clients or students we have, or how filled up our calendars are, we have value. Realizing this can be profoundly freeing.

For many of us who have fallen into *The Martyr Trap*, it's equally important to know we can receive money! Many professional Wisdom Keepers, especially when they're starting their own businesses, have a genuinely hard time asking for and receiving money for their services. They can feel awkward and guilty. When I first opened my private practice, I certainly felt that way. I'd become so accustomed to listening and helping people free of charge over the years that it felt highly uncomfortable to ask for compensation. I made the common mistake of dramatically undercharging, which of course wasn't good for anyone.

When we invest time, energy and money into extensive training and we do our best to provide a valuable service, charging too little (or willingly bartering for chickens when we're vegan and could use the money to pay rent) sets us up to either resent our clients and students, or our work.

If you are starting a practice or business, and you have bend-over-backwards tendencies (like Amir with the flooded office), you may need to be a little more rigid in the beginning than you will need to be later.

When you work professionally with people, it is crucial that both you and your clients feel free and unbounded in relation to each other. By allowing clients to pay you, by setting up policies and practices that sustain your life, you help your clients feel entitled to your attention. You also give them an opportunity to demonstrate their willingness to actively participate in your relationship, and symbolically express how much they value your work together. Do not dishonor them by giving away all your goodies, and then resenting them for it later.

Resentment can be subtle. It can pop up when we least expect it. Even if we're good at convincing ourselves that we can survive on good will alone, when deep down we feel like we're giving more than we're receiving, we end up subtly sending out a martyr-like message,

"You owe me one!" It's rare that people are empowered through a relationship riddled with debt.

Healing occurs when there is an energetic balance between people. Each person involved in a healing or teaching exchange may give or receive something different. What matters is that the exchange leaves both parties feeling nourished and enlivened, not depleted and resentful.

The Love, Attention and Approval Trap

In a world where most people are starved for love, attention and approval, a professional Wisdom Keeper's love, attention and approval becomes a great power, best used wisely and with a high level of awareness. If your lifelong journey has led you down a Wisdom Keeping path, you probably know what it's like to need love and acknowledgement. You are no different than everyone else on the planet who shares these fundamental human needs. You, however, have consciously chosen to spend a large portion of your time and resources learning and teaching the arts of self-love and other-love.

As a professional Wisdom Keeper, you're likely quite gifted at offering your attention and acknowledgement. You know what people need to hear, and are able to meet their needs with radiant compassion. You can convey your love and approval to others as convincingly as you do because you know what it feels like to be starved for this kind of support, and how marvelous it feels when someone truly sees you and recognizes your worth.

Many Wisdom Seekers will be willing to pay the highest price for your love and approval. If you are not careful, one of your greatest strengths as a healer can turn into a professional weakness. You can fall into *The Love, Attention and Approval Trap*.

When professional Wisdom Keepers don't keep our own need for admiration and acknowledgement in check, when we don't have other places (aside from our relationships with clients and students) where we can go to receive the love and acknowledgement we need, we can find ourselves totally and hopelessly dependent on our clients' and students' admiration. One of the main reasons people choose to enter therapeutic, healing or self-help settings is to heal their relationships to the forbidden, hidden and judged parts of themselves. Clients and students, both consciously and unconsciously, seek a place of safety to reveal and explore their least lovable parts with someone who is 'tough enough' for the job, someone who won't judge them and will love them anyway. Supporting people in befriending their entire selves, so they can become the unique, creative and whole people they are meant to be, is an essential goal for most self-development journeys. Professional Wisdom Keepers must be more aware of this goal than our clients and students. If we forget the goal, our clients and students most certainly will.

Sometimes, to support wholeness in those we serve, we must let go of what feels easy and most familiar to us. We must choose between our own desire to be liked, admired and harmoniously connected with everyone always, and our ultimate commitment to service. When we subtly give and withhold our approval, our sensitive clients and students inevitably pick up on our selective signals. Sensing that we love them more when they are 'good' clients, when they are high-frequency thinkers and eternally grateful to us, they quickly learn to be who and what they sense we want them to be.

If this pressure to become our perfect pupils continues to go undiscovered, they will either have to stop being real, or stop being our students and clients. Though on the surface, they may seem to be making tremendous progress, they won't be. They'll simply be perfecting their ability to live up to others' (in this case, our) expectations. They'll lose their power to do and feel what is authentically right for them. Winning our love will supersede winning their own.

There are many ways to fill up the holes inside of us, and to repress less-than-utopian feelings, like anger, fear and disappointment. Being loved, liked and approved of can be as powerful a 'hole-filling substance' as drugs and alcohol. If we find ourselves unable to deal with situations when our students and clients disagree with us, feel angry at or hurt by us, feel dissatisfied with us, or simply aren't constantly affirming, imitating or uplifting us, it may be time for us to reach out for support. Until we free ourselves from *The Love, Attention and Approval Trap*, we can't free our clients from it.

Believe me. This is going to be one of the most important gifts you can give your clients and students. I know very few people who don't need to develop the ability to love and appreciate themselves, regardless of how others perceive them.

If you tend to do a lot of affirming, reassuring and uplifting in your work, here are a few little experiments for you to try with your clients and students:

- See how much sadness you can contain.
- See how much anger, complaining or 'negativity' you can hear without immediately attempting to make people feel better or think higher.
- See how much silence you can allow.
- See if you can get through a session or a course without dishing out hugs.
- See if you can relax your shoulders, breathe deeply and listen without defensiveness when a frustrated client or student is speaking their mind.
- Check yourself when you feel an impulse to encourage your clients and students to choose higher-frequency thoughts, or consciously choose more joyful and loving feelings. Be sure you're not trying to manipulate them into being happy, nice or pleasant for your sake.
- Notice when you give compliments. Honestly examine why you express your admiration when you do.

Without realizing it, we can use compliments to disarm clients and students who are showing signs of individuation.

From Outer to Inner Authority

After much consideration, a dedicated and thoughtful Wisdom Seeker in an alternative learning environment decided to write a loving yet honest letter to their teacher. This student valued the training a great deal and cared deeply about their teacher, but there were aspects of the teacher/student relationship, the teacher's way of working, and some dynamics arising in the training which were troubling to the student. Because this Wisdom Seeker admired the teacher and feared confrontation, it felt quite risky for them to reach out in this way.

In the letter, the student asked for an honest, open dialogue with the teacher. Instead of responding to the content of what the Wisdom Seeker wrote, the teacher complimented their writing style. The teacher was so impressed, in fact, that they invited the student to use their wonderful writing gifts to help improve the marketing material for the training.

At first, the student felt flattered and fell right into *The Love, Attention and Approval Trap*. Eventually, they regained their center and insisted on a real response to their initial reach out.

Unfortunately, the teacher was not able to meet them in the way they had hoped. Although seeing the limitations of their teacher was painful and disillusioning, it was also empowering. For the first time in their life, the student found themselves asking a very different (and much more important) question: Was their teacher worthy of *their* unconditional love, attention and approval? This seemingly simple 'flip of focus' helped the student shift a lifelong pattern of seeking approval from outer authority figures, to seeking out and honoring their own inner authority.

When professional Wisdom Keepers use uplifting words and positive attention to avoid real contact or diffuse uncomfortable situations, our (otherwise truthful) compliments can turn into subtle or disempowering bribes. Our clients and students can feel flattered, grateful, stunned, confused and condescended to all at the same time. Such a mix of feelings can be paralyzing.

If we as professional Wisdom Keepers don't have our own need for love and approval sufficiently satisfied somewhere else, we ourselves may wind up overly dependent on our clients and students, and way too easy to manipulate. Although in this scenario, we may look or feel like the losers, our clients and students will ultimately be scraping the bottom of the barrel.

Usually when our clients or students take control of our shared relationship, the part of them holding the reins will not be the healthiest part. They can get us to smile and laugh when they really need us to take them seriously. They can get us to pretend everything is OK when they really need us to confront them honestly with their pain. They can get us to keep them under our Wisdom Keeping wings much longer than they need to be. They can get us to cross all sorts of physical and emotional boundaries better left uncrossed. Basically, they can inadvertently get us to deepen the wounds they originally came to us for help in healing.

Do not drown your clients with so much love, attention and approval
that they have to spend the rest of their lives doggie paddling
around in your love pool. Make sure you can survive without their admiration,
and empower them to survive without yours!

The Charisma Trap

Leaders don't become leaders without a certain amount of charisma. To lead, we must be able to attract followers, and to attract followers, we must have a sufficient degree of personal magnetism.

Whenever people engage fully in a self-development process, their level of charisma grows automatically. Whether or not they consciously want to become leaders, they often become leaders or role models anyway, simply because they've cultivated qualities that so many people need and want. People naturally look to self-assured individuals for wisdom and guidance. They gravitate towards those who seem larger than life in order to find and feel the 'largeness' in themselves.

A universal law commonly taught in Wisdom Keeping communities says that what we focus on grows. This is especially true when it comes to charisma. The more people align their energy, behavior and thinking, the more they take care of their bodies, and the more they focus on Spirit, the more attractive and magnetic they become. The planet certainly needs such people. When charismatic leaders use their power wisely, responsibly and with integrity, and when their humility is as great as their self-esteem, their power to attract allows them to positively influence many more people than they otherwise could.

Unfortunately, being responsible, having integrity and knowing how to use power wisely are not prerequisites for joining the Charisma Club. Hitler, Charles Manson and Jim Jones all had an abundance of personal charm, but no integrity.

A good definition of integrity is the ability to *integrate* all of one's parts. In other words, to have integrity, we must be willing and able to see and own our seemingly dark, painful, and fearful parts as well as our light, happy and loving ones.

I say 'seemingly' because our parts aren't always as they seem. Just as the ancient yin-yang symbol illustrates, there is shadow in light, and light in shadow. Most manifestations of 'shadow' take on destructive, distorted or primitive forms because they've been forbidden to us, not because the essential energy they reflect or express is bad. Most bad things that have ever happened on our planet were caused by people taking something that was internally forbidden for them and projecting it out onto others. One could easily say that the externalization of the unowned shadow is the root of all 'evil.' This tragic phenomenon, sourced in a core belief in separateness, is the cause of war, divisiveness, oppression and all forms of 'us vs. them' thinking.

The Dark Magician

Once a charismatic spiritual master came to Denmark. She was highly learned in esoteric spirituality. She knew how the entire universe was structured. She could answer any question about the seven heavenly masters, the seven layers of consciousness, the seven personality structures, the seven types of angels, and the seven just about everythings. Many people were taken in by her immense knowledge, her warmth and her ability to recognize their own spiritual potential.

For some time, everyone loved her and she loved everyone. She made a special point of letting her students know that they belonged to a spiritually elite group of beings, here to do the work of 'white magicians,' spreading light around the world, and protecting others from dark magicians.

She began to spend more of her time warning people against dark magicians, energy suckers and evil beings. She named people she considered dark magicians, warning her students against their own therapists, counselors, even some of their friends and family. The students had already given her so much authority in their lives that it was hard for them to resist the power of her warnings. Some of them cut off connections to people they'd known and loved for years in order to stay true to the light, as defined by this teacher.

Over time, their worldview began to match hers; it was split in two. There were glorious light beings and dangerous dark ones. As mistrust grew in their hearts, they felt increasingly grateful for her discerning guidance.

To those of us observing from the outside, this person looked disturbingly paranoid. Yet she was magnetic and charismatic enough to pull off what turned out to be a frighteningly massive and paranoid ego trip. This teacher began to show signs of bizarre behavior that even her most devoted disciples couldn't ignore.

Whenever someone did anything less than idealize her, they moved down an esoteric notch or two in her spiritual book. One poor student who dared question something the teacher said was told that she was the devil itself. It took her quite a while to regain faith in her own goodness.

At one point, the teacher fell madly in love with another disciple who happened to be married. When her love went unrequited, she blurted out the 'truth' for everyone to hear. She was indeed the Virgin Mary, and her student was Jesus Christ. Together, they were destined to reunite and save the world from sin and doom.

As her sad paranoid state was increasingly exposed, her spiritual empire began to crumble. She ended up teaching her students that *she* was the dark magician she'd been warning them against all along. She went on to other countries, gathering disciples and spreading her twisted word. What's perhaps most frightening about this story is that those who followed her were not stupid or particularly gullible people. This teacher had real charisma.

At its worst, charisma can temporarily blind even the clearest seeing person. It took a long time for many of her disciples to regain self-trust. Her greatest teaching was showing her students the dangers of giving their power away to an outer spiritual authority.

Over the years, I've encountered many leaders in the Wisdom Keeping world who have had varying degrees, kinds and combinations of integrity. Some had great personal, professional and spiritual integrity. Some had great spiritual integrity, but no professional integrity. Some had personal and professional integrity, but no spiritual integrity. Some had no integrity whatsoever.

They *all* had charisma, however, and lots of it. In many cases, the more charismatic the leader, the less integrity the leader had. Un-integrated yet magnetic leaders are found throughout the world. They work in every area of human existence. A particular type of integrity-deficit can easily arise in religious or Wisdom Keeping communities where very high spiritual standards are set for the members, and where even higher, almost super-human standards are set for the leaders.

Being a spiritual leader comes with a great deal of responsibility, and a whole lot of pressure. It is rarely enough to be a relatively decent human being. Leaders must live up to a long list of spiritual principles, to 'live in the Truth' as the Jehovah Witnesses say. Each spiritual community has its own set of Truths and standards for righteous living. Although communities vary, their norms usually share one characteristic: they are lofty.

Community members are encouraged to think *high* thoughts, have *high* visions, to look *up* to the heavens, to worship the *light*, to spread the *light*, and to '*light*en up.' Community leaders must not only motivate their followers to strive towards spiritual en-*light*-enment, they must be a source of *light* themselves, modeling for others what it means to be totally and completely committed to and enveloped in the communal Truth. Their inner conviction must be impeccable.

Sometimes a Wisdom Keeper's exaggerated outer conviction is compensating for inner insecurity. The pressure to dwell on positivity that many spiritual leaders feel is often fueled by an intense need to deny negativity. When leaders turn their back on the shadow, in themselves and others, they force essential aspects of their humanness underground. The qualities which could have led to unveiled strengths if embraced, take on twisted and distorted forms. They become servants of the deprived and identified ego.

As Wisdom Keeping leaders, we must learn to cultivate a deep appreciation for the less saintly qualities in ourselves, and in all human beings. It is only when we can embrace and own *all* that we are, when we can reclaim our lost and rejected parts, that we become able to transform them into conscious resources. Trustworthy leaders rest peacefully and humbly in their humanness. They radiate light because they do not reject that which is not light, or that which may be still in a primitive stage of wisdom. They see all people and their inner parts as part of the cosmic whole. They help people accept all of themselves, by walking their talk, and modeling what it means to be human.

The Gorgeous Guru

There was a Western-born guru who also happened to be a very attractive man. He had a big following in Europe. I'm sure that he could meditate as skillfully as the best of them. I'm also sure he spent much more time climbing the Himalayas than controlling his hormones.

A woman went to hear this gorgeous guru speak at his ashram during a particularly difficult time in her life. She was experiencing sexual abuse flashbacks from her childhood. Longing for help, she visited the guru during his office hours. Trusting him, she shared openly about her past trauma. After listening with compassion, he looked deep into her eyes, grabbed her hands, and started kissing and hugging her. He told her that what she needed more than anything was to surrender to the beauty and healing potential of the here and now.

Because she looked up to him, and because he was charismatic, she surrendered. It was only afterwards that she began to wonder what had happened, and why. She noticed that many of his disciples were young women like herself, and that they all were quite physically affectionate with him. This made her confused about their previous passionate encounter. She decided to call him up to express her concerns. The guru reassured her that the two of them were deeply connected on a soul level.

His words calmed her down and confirmed her feeling that they shared something special. There was a deep spiritual reason why she was falling in love with him. To her delight, the guru asked her to accompany him on a sacred journey to India. She was so thrilled and honored that she bought a ticket, packed her bags and was ready to go within a week's time. As her excitement about their adventure grew, her original reason for seeking out his help disappeared into the distance.

Though it was common knowledge that this guru was married, he managed to convince this woman that his marriage was an open one. His wife understood the spiritual truth that no one owned anyone else. She respected his unique and energetically sensitive way of working with his followers.

It wasn't until this student was 20,000 feet up in the air that she saw that the guru's gaze had already fallen on the next young, full-breasted enthusiast on his disciple list. To her added dismay, she also realized that his wife, who was also on the plane, was nowhere near as embracing of her husband's sexual escapades as he had made it seem.

This Wisdom Seeker learned a painful lesson. Just because a spiritual teacher looks, sounds and feels good does not mean they can be trusted.

When students come to a spiritual master, they come with a great deal of trust and a willingness to put their lives in their teacher's hands. If the teacher's hands are more interested in unbuttoning their shirts than providing true healing, damage can occur. Perhaps it is possible for some gurus or spiritual masters to heal through the act of sex, by merging their highly-developed energy systems with those of their students. But the ones who can truly do this are undoubtedly in the minority.

While there is truth to the statement, "What we focus on grows," there is also truth to the statement, "What we repress grows." If you are in a spiritual community, I invite you to pay as much attention to what the spiritual leaders are denying about themselves, as you do to what they're obsessing over (sexuality in this case). Whatever they're denying will likely take up just as much shadowy space in the teaching and community. The more intense the denial, the more powerful the shadow.

If the leader forbids sexuality, for example, chances are pretty high that shadowy forms of sexuality will find expression in the community. Keep in mind that there's a difference between consciously choosing a path of celibacy (while acknowledging and accepting one's human sexual desires and impulses), and rejecting it from a place of shame and judgment. Follow the charge. The more charge, the more shadow.

The 'Geisha Girl'

In my late teens, I participated in a weekend workshop, designed to introduce New Age philosophies to relative newbies. Though I was in Europe, the teacher was a handsome, charming American with a great deal of personal power and spiritual know-how. In many ways, he was an effective, inspiring and irreverent teacher. He had a way of getting his participants to take risks, to do all sorts of wild things they had never dared do before. Most of the custom-made challenges he assigned to his students were fun and appropriate. However, one specific challenge he gave a course participant felt very shadowy, on more than one plane.

The participant was a beautiful young woman to whom he was clearly attracted. He openly flirted with her throughout the weekend. Instead of asking her to participate in the course like everyone else, he gave her a special role to play. Sensing she needed a 'humbling' experience, he made her dress up like a Geisha and be his pleasure slave for the weekend. She washed his feet, gave him massages, fanned his face, the works. At the end of the course, she was rewarded with an opportunity to dance like a butterfly in front of the rest of the group, which she did dutifully and beautifully.

Let's first acknowledge the blatantly racist implications of what he did, and the disturbing fact that no one called him on it. A whole book could be written on that subject. For the purposes of illustrating *The Charisma Trap*, I'm going to focus on another form of violation I saw taking place.

For the sake of argument, let's give the teacher at least one benefit of the doubt, and say his intuition was correct about this woman. Perhaps the ideal lesson for her was to be of service to another person for a weekend. Maybe she needed a humbling experience to compensate for an overinflated sense of self, or for some other reason. If this was true, then why she did she have to be *his* pleasure slave? He was a creative person. I'm sure he could have found a way to impart this same lesson without playing on the sexual and power dynamics that inevitably existed between him and his students. Instead, he designed a task that was perfectly suited to gratify his ego, not to serve her yearning soul.

What is most concerning about situations like this one is the free reign spiritual leaders are often granted. As it's happened for centuries in countless settings, this teacher was given total authority. No one had the outer permission or inner authority to keep his motivations in check, to call him out when he was being racist, sexist and misusing his power. In fact, we couldn't even participate without first agreeing to a list of rules established by him. If we broke a rule, we were asked to stand up and admit it in front of the whole group. Some of us were subjected to humiliation and ridicule, though we were told it was all in jest and in service of our ultimate emancipation.

To further complicate matters, the teacher claimed to be clairvoyant. If anyone was tempted to stand up to him, that temptation vanished once he pulled out the clairvoyant card. It's hard to argue with someone who has a direct line to Spirit. Someone can speak out, declaring that something smells fishy. He can respond by revealing their past life as a mean-spirited fisherman, doomed in this life to smell non-existent fish.

Some people do benefit from authoritative teachers who've mastered the art of tough love and won't let them get away with their usual bologna. Setting guidelines for a workshop intended to create an atmosphere of safety and commitment amongst participants can be important. When a leader has charisma, unchecked authority, and a questionable level of integrity, we run into trouble.

Because spiritual leaders can be highly skilled at presenting a perfected persona, choosing a healthy and integrated spiritual teacher can be challenging for Wisdom Seekers. It takes great discernment to avoid falling into *The Charisma Trap*. Just as you'd do when looking for a used car, look beyond the fresh paint and the new seat-covers. Open up the hood. Take a look at the engine. Bring someone along with you, someone you trust who knows more about cars than you do. Go for a few test drives before signing any papers. Be compassionate with yourself too. Even if you take all of the necessary precautions before you buy the car, there are still no guarantees that the car will live up to your expectations.

If things don't go so well, that's OK. We live and we learn. Some of our lessons are more painful than others. Much of the time, we manage to receive as much or more good from our spiritual teachers than bad. When we can allow our imperfect experiences to refine our intuition and help us make better choices in the future, even the worst experiences become valuable grist for the growth mill.

This very book is my attempt at taking lots of imperfect experiences in Wisdom Keeping communities, and turning them into something helpful. The process of reviewing and examining the challenges from my diverse experiences has provided me with invaluable insights, honed my discerning abilities and increased my self-trust (as well as self- and other-compassion).

The Forgiveness Trap

In most Wisdom Keeping cultures, we are encouraged to take full responsibility for our lives, and to take charge of what we think, focus on and attract. We learn that blame is never appropriate; that no one can make us feel or think anything without our permission or our agreement. We learn about moving out of victim consciousness and becoming the creators of our lives, definers of our realities. We are asked to take charge of our responses to every situation, and to forgive those who have hurt us. We are told that if and when we withhold love from anyone else, we withhold love from ourselves. We learn that all pain is caused by withheld love.

We are often taught that we've chosen our parents or primary caregivers to heal and grow. Even if our early experiences were traumatic, we chose them in order to reactivate past-life patterns and learn the lessons our souls want us to learn. We are urged to understand and love everyone, to see that the people from our past always did their best. If they could have done better, they would have. Not only that, but we would never be who we are today if they hadn't done what they did, exactly how they did it. We should not only be forgiving, but grateful.

In some Wisdom Keeping communities, if someone acknowledges that they hold their parents (or anyone) at least partially responsible for some of their hang ups, they'd better run for cover. In the blink of an eye, they'll be surrounded by a mob of forgivers, coaxing them towards changing their mind and setting themselves and their parents free. To these well-intentioned helpers, there is no difference between holding others accountable for their actions and buying into the ego's illusory world of separation by refusing to forgive. In some spiritual circles, anything remotely resembling blame is considered forbidden territory.

Understandably, many Wisdom Seekers fear calling spades, spades. Constantly told that love, praise and gratitude are the only real remedies for healing past pain, and instant forgiveness is the only path towards freedom, they come to fear a bit of psychological reality as if it were the plague. It makes sense that many end up taking the short cut on the road to forgiveness and miss out on the heart of the matter.

While most of our parents and caregivers did the best they could, given their circumstances and inner and outer resources, this does not mean their best was good enough. Acknowledging this fact does not mean we burn imperfect parents at the stake. (If we did so, there would be no one left on the planet.) Nor does it mean we should set aside forgiveness and compassion as our ultimate goals. It does mean, however, that there is value in exploring what went wrong in our childhoods, what needs were not met, and what consequences our early experiences have had on our inner and outer lives.

True forgiveness happens only when we have forgiven ourselves. Self-forgiveness often begins when we look back at our own past and see ourselves with compassion. If we do not at least temporarily allow ourselves to see our parents' or caregivers' weaknesses, if we constantly hold onto our intellectual understanding of their good intentions, or the fact that our souls chose our biological families, we may never be able to truly understand the experiences we had as children.

Finding the familial roots for some of our most destructive, habitual thoughts can help us in our healing journeys. It allows us to sort through our feelings and thoughts later on in life, as we discover which ones truly do belong to us, and which ones are better left with our great-great-great grandparents.

I am certainly not a blame advocate, and am very aware of the destruction and isolation blame can cause—especially when held onto forever. At the same time, I do not want us to blame ourselves or each other for occasionally holding someone else partially responsible for a shared experience.

It is also imperative that, in our noble attempts to avoid blame, we don't turn to *denial*. I've witnessed too many Wisdom Seekers and Keepers fall into *The Forgiveness Trap*. They treat their past experiences as if they were apples on the Tree of Knowledge—refusing to take a bite into their past with critical, analytical teeth for fear of being thrown out of paradise.

At least blame is expressible and can be consciously explored. It can be used as a tool to discover more healthy resources which almost always lie beneath. Denial is a tough nut to crack. When denial flourishes, family (and community) secrets take hold and spread. The family says, "Mommy is sick." But mommy is crazy.

The Pain of Denial

Laila's father came home from the war physically wounded and emotionally traumatized. Instead of receiving the medical and therapeutic care he needed, he turned to opioids and alcohol to alleviate the tremendous pain he was in.

Over time, Laila watched her loving, good-natured father become increasingly anxious, depressed and unable to sleep because of relentless night terrors. He worked during the day and stayed out all night drinking. When he came home, he collapsed on the couch and passed out.

This happened night after night, until he could no longer hold down a job. His behavior became more erratic as his mood swings intensified. While at first he showed remorse for being tired, absent or moody, he stopped seeming to care…or even to remember what had happened the day, or hour before.

Laila's mother coped with the mounting stress by pouring all of her energy into providing for the family and protecting its reputation. She made sure no one on the outside knew what was happening behind closed doors. Laila begged her mother to do something about the situation. Instead of validating her daughter's feelings and accurate perceptions of what was happening, and seeking help for the family, Laila's mother made excuses. "Your dad is just stressed out." "He needs more time to adjust to life at home." She asked Laila to be more understanding, patient and to not make a fuss. Laila's 'super-sensitivity' and complaints were only adding to his stress.

Laila's older brother had a strong need to admire their father and protect their mother. Most of the time he managed to avoid being around to see what was happening. During the few times Laila turned to him for support, he expressed annoyance. "You're such a drama queen. Mom works so hard to give you everything, and think of what Dad has sacrificed for our family and country. Give them a break." His comments made Laila feel guilty for being critical, ashamed of her sensitivity, and jealous of her brother's seemingly untainted relationship to their parents.

One day, despite her usual attempts to be quiet, Laila accidentally dropped a glass in the kitchen when the father was sleeping on the couch nearby. He became so enraged at her for waking him up that he lunged at her, screaming at the top of his lungs. He threw the television across the room and punched a hole in the wall. Laila was understandably terrified.

Instead of comforting Laila and acknowledging how out-of-control things had become, her mother's response was, again, to normalize the father's behavior and hold Laila responsible for his actions. "Of course, he's upset. You know how hard it is for him to sleep. You should have been more careful. What's wrong with you?" Her brother was nowhere to be seen during the incident, but when he got home, he didn't believe Laila's story, insisting she was exaggerating. Not even a smashed television and hole in the wall were enough to shake his idealized perception of their father.

Though this story may seem extreme, it is not uncommon. Many Wisdom Seekers and Keepers grow up in families like Laila's, where denial is a main coping strategy for pain and suffering. Instead of seeing and dealing with what is actually happening, their families cultivate—and then rigorously protect—family secrets. They do this by 're-writing' actual events, excusing disturbing behaviors and normalizing unmanageable (even dangerous) situations.

When sensitive and observant people like Laila grow up in such a family, they can end up feeling ashamed, confused, afraid, enraged, crazy and guilt-ridden—all at the same time. If they never receive validation for their understandable feelings, they learn to doubt (and eventually deny) them. Professional Wisdom Keepers who immediately encourage these people to 'forgive and let go' run the risk of fortifying their clients' and students' guilt and denial, instead of liberating them from the pain of their past.

Family secrets, such as the one in the above story, are profoundly painful and confusing. They can leave life-long scars with serious relational consequences. When people deny a truth about themselves or loved ones, they not only contribute to systemic dysfunction, they become hard to connect with, thus isolated. The loneliness of denial is exceptionally painful, and difficult to alleviate. To experience—and facilitate—true healing, we need to know and touch the source of our pain. Otherwise, we can only apply bandages.

Some professional Wisdom Keepers do not only avoid focusing on the past; they believe that looking at the past from a psychological perspective is unimportant, a waste of time, or a mere distraction from what really matters—forgiveness and healing in the present moment. Perhaps there are some of us who can fly straight into the arms of forgiveness. In my experience, many of us can't, and when asked to forgive before we're ready, we feel either greater guilt or nothing at all. We say we've forgiven, but our words are empty.

Forgiveness is one of the final stages of development and becoming whole. There is nothing more miraculous than true forgiveness. Forgiveness has the power to melt constricted hearts, heal unhealable wounds and free imprisoned spirits. It can ignite the divine spark of our creativity, and reveal the ultimate truth of our interconnectedness. Forgiveness is one of the worthiest goals we can embrace and work towards in our lifetimes. My concern is not that there is too much focus on forgiveness, but that there is a tendency to move too quickly towards the goal. A slower, deeper and more honest path can give better results.

The Perfection Trap

As John Lennon so wisely wrote, sometimes "Life is what happens while you are busy making other plans." Wisdom Seekers and Keepers tend to forget this every now and then, especially when we're busy trying to be perfect. Most of us are already dealing with mainstream pressures to look, perform and relate to others according to ridiculous standards. As if that weren't enough, in our Wisdom Keeping communities, we're also held responsible for creating (or at least co-creating) our lives. As touched on in previous chapters, we've got to think perfect thoughts, feel perfect feelings, make perfect choices, have perfect births, breathe perfect breath, and Lord knows what else. It's so easy to fall into *The Perfection Trap*.

Having to be a constant and perfect role model, even when we're alone with ourselves, can be a real pain. Being spiritually perfect requires a level of self-monitoring and inner censorship that can really put a drain on what would otherwise be relaxing life moments. At some point, no matter how skilled we are at writing affirmations, no matter how rightly we choose our life experiences, we need to confront one essential fact. We are human beings, and there is nothing we can do about it. Nor is there anything we *SHOULD* do about it. I speak on behalf of all human beings, as well as Virgos like myself dedicated to healing their perplexingly perfectionistic predicaments.

IT IS ABSOLUTELY OK TO BE A HUMAN BEING!

It is OK to make mistakes; OK to be goofy; OK to be forgetful, naïve, confused, quirky, moody, cranky, nerdy, silly, sick; and it is OK to put your foot in your mouth every once in a while. You are going to do it anyway, so you might as well accept it right from the start.

Being the Perfect Counselor
Allergies and Bra-Straps

I once had a client who made my Virgoic perfectionism look mild. Cloe was convinced that if she just thought positively, meditated and soul-searched enough, she'd heal all of her wounds, would never get sick, and would be happy and successful for the rest of her life.

As you can imagine, much of our work together focused on helping her accept her own humanity and learn self-love, even when she wasn't living up to her perfect standards. We were making great progress, and she was beginning to develop a true appreciation for herself as she was.

Just because she was becoming more patient and compassionate with herself didn't mean that she'd let go of the idea that total perfection was indeed possible. Nor did it mean that she'd let go of the idea that *I* was somehow meant to embody that unrealistic ideal!

Despite my very human behavior, Cloe needed to idealize me for quite some time. I did my best to respect her need, while resisting the pull to identify with her projections. Because the co-transference was strong, I needed to keep close check on my own perfectionistic tendencies, in order to prepare myself for the inevitable day when I would come crashing off the pedestal. My job was to move us closer to when she could realize that I was nowhere near as flawless as she thought I was. I knew that her readiness to see the humanness in me would reflect her own increasing self-confidence and independence. It would mean she was integrating the positive qualities she had needed me to hold for her, until she was ready to own them herself.

Although I had internally prepared myself for that day, when it actually arrived, I had to hold onto my Wisdom Keeping suspenders. That day certainly proved the spiritual principle that everything is indeed perfect—even when it doesn't feel that way! About five minutes before Cloe walked into my office, I came down with an enormous allergy attack. I'd actually been feeling great during my previous sessions, with clients who were obviously working on other issues. It was only after I mentally noted that Cloe would be my next client that I started sneezing like crazy.

My first thought was, "Oh no! Why must I have allergies with Cloe—of all clients!" Luckily, I'd practiced enough self-introspection to realize my own issues were being triggered. I was feeling pressured to live up to certain standards. Cloe still had the thought that truly spiritual and fully healed people didn't get sick or have allergies, a thought I'd had myself on more than one occasion. I feared she'd feel disappointed and disillusioned by my congested state. Reminding myself that I didn't need to be perfect to be of real service, and that perhaps my snotty state was exactly what she (we!) needed, I opened the door, let her in, and prepared myself for letting her down.

The moment she sat down, her eyes zoomed in on the clump of wet Kleenex gracing my lap. They meandered upwards, until they spotted my bra strap peeking out from under my sweater. (Knowing me, it probably had a hole in it too.) The sacred combination of bra strap and red nose was enough to initiate my crash into the land of utter humanity. As I felt myself free-fall in her eyes, I blew my nose, took a deep breath, and did my best to stay centered. I asked her to share her thoughts and feelings with me. (One of Cloe's greatest strengths was her honesty.)

We explored the sadness she felt, discovering that I wasn't perfect. If *I* could get sick and wear hole-filled underwear, and I had done even more work on myself than she had, what did that mean about her, her potential and her future? My imperfection meant she might never achieve perfection as she'd hoped. She might get sick. She might feel lonely. Her relationships might never look like they do in the movies. She might never be 'cured' of her fears and insecurities. She might never encounter a perfect person who could solve all of her problems. Though we'd talked about this before, Cloe realized at an even deeper level that she could receive support and inspiration from others, but ultimately, she was responsible for her own healing, and life.

Over time, as we let the veils of idealizations—and illusions— drop to our feet, a new relationship was born between us, and within each of us. Cloe discovered that being human was a lot more fun than she'd ever imagined. Mistake-making wasn't such a big deal, whether she was making them, or someone else was. Though she still occasionally wished someone or something would come from the outside and solve all of her problems, she mostly enjoyed the challenge of relying on her own inner resources, wisdom and instincts.

I, too, became more accepting of my humanness—allergies, exposed bra-straps and all. When clients and students bring my imperfections and blind spots to my attention, I do my best to take their feedback seriously and to acknowledge my mistakes. I've come to appreciate how stifling perfectionism can be to intimacy, spontaneity, creativity and true dialogue. We are all in this human boat together.

People who've experienced a certain degree of success in the Wisdom Keeping world can easily feel ashamed and embarrassed when their humanness is exposed. To avoid these uncomfortable feelings, we subtly hide our humanness. One price we pay for maintaining a perfect image is our chance to experience true intimacy.

True intimacy requires that we down our masks and let it all hang loose. We all need at least one place or relationship where we can be spiritually incorrect. Ideally our 'partners in imperfect crime' are people who share our deepest values and know us really well. They trust in our innate goodness, even when we're taking a little break from being so damned honorable all of the time. When we can let ourselves be loved even when we're feeling or acting in ways we've judged as unlovable, we're in pretty good shape.

If you tend to drag your perfectly polished and positive self with you wherever you go, I invite you to try a change of pace. Make a bit more room for a refreshing degree of normalcy in your life. Try going to a party and not breathing deeply or gazing intimately into the eyes of everyone you meet. Resist the temptation to help Aunt Mildred understand how her favorite self-berating jokes aren't helping her self-esteem. Share a humbling story with someone. See how not having to be 'on' all the time feels, and notice how everyone survives.

There's nothing wrong with sharing our wisdom jewels wherever we go. But at some point, if we want to have a life where we can breathe easy—in the symbolic sense of the word—it's good to create some safe havens for our humanness.

I wholly accept my humanness.
I am perfect in my imperfection.
I am totally lovable even when I don't think so.
I surround myself with people who see my lovability even when I can't.

CONCLUSION:
KEEPIN' IT ALL IN PERSPECTIVE

Ring the bells that still can ring
Forget your perfect offering
There is a crack, a crack in everything
That's how the light gets in

~ Leonard Cohen

Humility, Humiliation & Giggle Fits

I firmly believe that making a complete fool of oneself is one of the most powerful and transformative spiritual practices there is. So, in the spirit of embracing our shared humanity and recognizing how easily we can fall into these traps, I'd like to share with you an exceptionally embarrassing story from my life. Here goes.

My immediate family was not religious, but my mother always worked hard to keep Jewish culture alive in our home, and to breathe humanistic meaning into customs and traditions. During Passover, one of the bigger holidays, Jews around the world remember the times when they and other peoples were (and still are) in bondage. They celebrate freedom from slavery and the alleviation of suffering and oppression for all beings. In addition to giving up foods like bread, pasta and Sarah Lee brownies, practicing Jews take time to count their blessings and ask themselves profound questions about how to make the world a more just and peaceful place. The social, political and philosophical aspects of the holiday were especially emphasized in my family—especially by my mother, the closet politician.

Passover was always hosted at our house, with my dad's side of the family. Though not religious, this was an ethnically diverse, intense and socially conscious bunch. At the time of this particular Passover, I was living and working in Europe. It had been years since I'd participated in a holiday like this, so it meant a great deal to my parents that I was there. My mom had taken the preparations to a new Jewish high. The sounds of 'Havah Nagilah' filled the Chicago suburban air, as fifty guests poured in through the door—a large percentage of whom were *not* Jewish, I might add, and most of them relatives I hadn't seen for years.

Even my father—the very man who conspired with his daughters to bring a Rubik's Cube to synagogue, the man who joined us in accusing our poor mother of using family ceremonies to impose her liberal political agenda on helpless familial audiences, the man who fought for the right to a short and swift service—was feeling the pressure to offer his family a particularly meaningful ceremony.

The scene was exciting, terrifying and surreal all at once. Flooded with scented memories of family get-togethers from the past, I felt an intense rush of emotional overwhelm running through my highly-sensitive and introverted veins. I found myself helplessly merging with my mother's stressed out state, as all of us worked to manage the plethora of practical and energetic details of such a big and important occasion.

Earlier that day, my father gave me a heads-up about a special passage I'd be reading during the service—his way of honoring my presence after so many years away. At one point, he handed me the passage to look over. I quickly skimmed it, looking for difficult-to-pronounce words, and handed it back to him. (There is nothing worse than reading out loud in front of a large group of people and stumbling on a word like 'schtichinchalacktunatoven.' Well, perhaps there is something worse, but I am getting ahead of myself.)

By the time we all sat down for the service, I was exhausted and beyond overstimulated. All I wanted was to relax and observe from a safe, relatively hidden place. I chose an obscure spot at the edge of the giant table. My relative (a highly-respected social activist) sat beside me, and my beloved sister sat in front of me. Shortly after everyone quieted down, my father opened the ceremony. He then immediately reintroduced me to the family, asking me to share the special passage. Caught completely off-guard, I received the long passage from my father, and became very aware of the sea of intense, expectant eyes pointed in my direction.

Now, thinking back, I can see why this particular moment was such an anxiety-provoking one for me. At the time, however, all I knew was that I was beyond butterflies. I was in the danger zone. The last time I remembered feeling this way was when I was twelve, sitting in Mr. Bernstein's science classroom, on the verge of an uncontrollable giggle fit.

At first I read normally, gliding from word to word, pausing in the appropriate places. It wasn't until I began paying attention to the actual words I uttered that my inner nut began to crack. What I was reading was *excruciatingly* serious. In fact, by the time I was through with the fifth sentence, I had already graphically described the horrors and tragedies of Hiroshima, the gas chambers of the Holocaust, African-American slavery, the deterioration of the ozone layer, animal extinction, and nuclear annihilation.

If I were to read this passage any other day than the one in question, it might have moved me to tears. The universe had other plans for me that day. That day, as I sat in front of countless family members who hadn't seen me for years, and who knew I made a living as a *therapist*, the reading seemed so grim, so disturbing, so utterly tragic...that it struck me as...funny.

I bulldozed my way through the next batch of sentences—which were even more horrific than the previous batch. I kept reading, thinking that no passage could possibly *continue* to be as mercilessly heartbreaking as this one had been. I found no relief. Horror story after horror story left my lips, while thoughts of my mother and her life-long attempts to rescue sufferers world-wide tickled me in the strangest and most powerful of ways.

Suddenly, the immensity of my mother's and my own inherited ambitions to save the world burst in front of me like a cartoon bubble. The whole thing—our lives, our over-inflated senses of self and power—seemed so ridiculous to me, so absurd, that, despite my most desperate attempts to resist, I let out a few tee-hees. Terrified of losing it completely, I glanced at my sister (the psychologist), looking for comfort and reassurance. She, of course, knew me better than anyone. Though she did her best to avoid co-plunging into my preadolescent pool of hysterics, it didn't work. She started giggling too.

Any chance I had of making it through the paragraph with even a shred of dignity was thrown to the wind. I surrendered to my totally inappropriate, horrifying, but deliriously satisfying response to an impossible situation. I burst into a fit of hee-haws that would have made Mr. Bernstein reminisce, and handed the paragraph over to my older cousin, the well-known activist, begging him to take over. I caught a few looks from relatives and felt shame and embarrassment. My poor father looked at me with deep disappointment. Even the children were silent as lambs. It was more than I could bear. Again, like a twelve-year-old, I watched my finger point towards my innocent sister, and I heard words I hadn't spoken since I was eleven-years-old leave my mouth, "**She** did it! She made me laugh!"

That was it. The regression was complete. For a person like me, who considered herself to be mature, sensitive, compassionate and pretty good at dealing with anxiety, it took me a while to get over this experience. I couldn't have imagined sinking any lower. I not only laughed in the face of the world's greatest tragedies, but blamed it on my sister! How unenlightened can you get?!

The best part about this story is that I survived it. So did everybody else. I wasn't shunned, thrown out or punished. Even my mother—whom I would have expected to be destroyed—seemed surprisingly at ease with what happened. Who knows? Maybe my unabashed release calmed her frazzled nerves.

Though it took me (about 6 days) longer to relax than it took the rest of the gang, the humiliation eventually wore off, and I was left with a strange and exhilarating sense of relief. I had proven, in public, without a shadow of a doubt, that I am utterly and unmistakably human—as silly and inappropriate as anyone. Hallelujah!

FINAL WORDS

I truly hope that you have found some gems in *Walking a Fine Line*. As mentioned in the Author's Note at the beginning, this book was written more than two decades ago, from the bottom of my heart. It was intended to act as a loving resource and gentle guide for people who, like me, are navigating their way through Wisdom Keeping terrains that are full of Light and Shadow.

After all of these years (and two graduate degrees), I could add about a thousand more stories and a few more sophisticated theories and perspectives to the mix, but I don't think that's necessary. The themes are universal, and more than ever, our culture (both mainstream and alternative) is calling out for an honest exploration of Shadow. We're all being asked to *walk a fine line*.

If you've made it this far, it's been an honor to walk this line with you. I want to thank you for your courage, willingness and self-honesty. Thank you for your commitment to becoming the best Wisdom Seeker and Keeper you can be. This world needs people like you. In fact, we all need each other to learn how to truly embody creativity, compassion, balance and integrity in our lives and work. We need support as we learn to stretch our minds and hearts, increase our questioning capacity, and catalyze a continuing process of self-discovery and professional maturation.

Whether you consider yourself to be a Wisdom Seeker, a seasoned professional Wisdom Keeper, both, or something in-between, I'd like to end this exploration with a few invitations:

Feel free to pick and choose

Whenever we focus on universal truths, we risk diminishing the importance of individual truths. Though the term 'professional Wisdom Keeper' refers to a vast, diverse group of people who don't deserve to be lumped together into one entity, I've chosen to sacrifice some specificity in the hopes of bringing out the common themes faced by so many of us who work within the human potential movement and healing arts fields. Therefore, as you digest what's been presented here, I encourage you to honor your specific work and life experience by picking and choosing from what is written here, keeping what applies to your situation and letting go of the rest.

If you are a successful leader, teacher or practitioner whose Wisdom Keeping work has already significantly contributed to the field of healing arts, use this book as a place to receive inspiration, support and an occasional tune-up. If you're not a professional Wisdom Keeper, but you've actively explored the healing arts for years, belong to a spiritual community, participate in awareness-raising workshops or alternative trainings, or regularly seek the help of Wisdom Keeping professionals, I invite you to allow this book to support you in cultivating healthy boundaries and a more discerning mind, so that you can get the most out of your present day pursuits, and find the Wisdom Keepers, learning and healing environments which best suit your needs.

If you're someone who has watched others journey down self-improvement paths and feel ready to explore your own potential, but you're not sure where or with whom to start, *Walking a Fine Line* is here to help you know what to look for, and what to look out for! This book can support you in assessing your needs, clarifying your wants and improving your ability to find the quality support you deserve.

Take the time you need

To *walk a fine line* well, we must stay awake on so many levels. Just as the tightrope walker moves slowly, carefully weighing each step, making sure each move is balanced, we do best when we move slowly through this multi-faceted discerning process. Our paths may look more cyclical or zig-zaggy, than linear. Mine certainly has!

Remember to take your time. You are not here to learn a simple technique or theory and then universally apply it to all challenges you encounter. You're here to facilitate a highly subtle, inner awakening process which may lead you into unknown and uncomfortable territories. Self-awareness, flexibility and interpersonal tools will all come in handy.

Consider finding a teacher, mentor or supervisor

Many professional Wisdom Keepers I respect believe that to ignite, discover and cultivate their own inner guru and to keep their spiritual and professional work on track, they need an outer manifestation of the inner guru.

Many others do not believe all people must have outer gurus to be spiritually responsible. Instead, they believe more and more of us are becoming self-initiates. If we follow our hearts and intuition, choosing to surround ourselves with good teachers, mentors and enlightening environments, we'll be led to the light within us and find our own unique ways of experiencing, expressing and encouraging spirit to grow in ourselves and others.

Other professionals are especially weary of the disempowering and/or cult-like dynamics arising in many organized religious and spiritual communities. They have seen too many gurus and disciples fall into *The Charisma Trap* as explored earlier. I tend to understand and agree with all three perspectives, which probably explains why instead of having one guru, I have enjoyed countless teachers over the years and the act of uncovering the unifying thread that connects all of their teachings. (If I did have a guru, they would have to be pretty eclectic, embracing a rainbow-like human celebration of spirit.)

The fact that I've thrived from exploring many paths and having many teachers does not mean I don't have deep respect for the depths reached by those on a singular devotional path. Still, if I have learned something, it is that one cannot force an outer guru into being. One can do one's best to make oneself easy to find; one can extend a heart-felt invitation; and one can trust that the right teacher or community will show up at the right time if it is meant to be.

Whether you are an alternative professional who has found your guru, has not needed a guru, or has hand-picked a bunch of part-time teachers, it can be useful to remember that the spiritual solution you have found is not necessarily the solution for those who come to you for spiritual guidance. As we all are connected, each is unique. The roads we take towards the 'One' are unique as well. An ability to see beyond your spiritual path can be infinitely valuable as you strive towards providing appropriate and custom-designed spiritual support for those you serve.

As your students/clients grapple with the big guru question, it can be helpful to support them in finding good earthly teachers and genuine role models—well-adjusted, noble and balanced people who can mirror them at their stage of development and inspire them to take their next step, whatever that step may be.

Generally speaking, being in the presence of Wisdom Keeping role models tends to reduce reactivity and polarized thinking, increase compassion and relaxation, and make it easier to swim in paradoxical waters.

When and if your clients, students or friends express curiosity and readiness to explore their spirituality in more concrete ways, you can help them discover spiritual practices which complement their personalities and psyches. Some practices are best done alone, others, not. Many activities can be used as spiritual practices. Meditation, dancing, moving, painting, writing, sculpting, drumming, walking, gardening, running, listening, serving, parenting, tea drinking, love-making and much more can all be highly effective ways for people to connect with their spiritual core.

Take this path with others

Whether or not you find a teacher, mentor or supervisor, please consider learning to *walk a fine line* with others. If you are a professional Wisdom Keeper, you might want to gather together with a group of trusted peers or colleagues. Support each other as you face common challenges and find greater balance in your work.

If you are an active Wisdom Seeker, consider establishing a support group where you and fellow journeyers can freely discuss and learn from each other's experiences. You don't have to be drawn to the same professional Wisdom Keepers, communities or environments in order to become awakened, empowered and creative life-travelers together. Groups that encourage a variety of experiences can be especially empowering and illuminating.

If joining a group doesn't appeal to you, try choosing a partner, counselor, friend or colleague who is committed to supporting you through this learning process. Exploring *fine-lined* terrains with others will motivate, inspire and help you gain even greater insights than you could on your own.

Finally, I invite those of you who are leaders, teachers or influential members of Wisdom Keeping communities, to introduce the relevant aspects of this material to the people you serve. The themes addressed in *Walking a Fine Line* are relevant to any alternative learning environment and spiritual community. When you can encourage people to participate in honest, transparent dialogues around challenging-yet-utterly-human dynamics, you can raise the quality and integrity of your own work and inspire everyone around you to do the same.

In the Appendices that follow, I will be sharing some creative explorations from my own life. My intention in doing so is to inspire you along your path. As a fellow human being, I want to offer you full permission to uncover your own story through honest, courageous and self-expressive experimentation.

In Appendix I, I'll share about a deeply personal and creative process which helped me encounter (and heal my relationship to) my own inner child. In Appendix II, you'll have the chance to see how a Jungian model of the psyche can work in practice, when explored through an expressive arts journey. In Appendix III, I'll share *A Guideline for Parenting Professionals*, where you'll have the opportunity to use the five-phased theory presented at the beginning of this book as a means of exploring your own strengths and challenges as a 'professional parent.' I hope you find yourself inspired and encouraged to dive deep and take risks, in whichever way works best for you.

APPENDIX I

Discovering My Inner Child

In the Beginning ...

A child awaited me, an inner child who had felt isolated and abandoned, whose cries for my attention had often gone unheard and ignored. This child had learned very early on that it was not safe to be here, that her self-expression was dangerous to herself and to those she loved, and that she needed to adapt to an unfriendly and conditionally loving world in order to survive.

This child would be difficult to reach, for she was used to hiding. She carried with her painful memories. But she also held the key to my freedom. Somewhere in my gut, I knew that if I wished to liberate my joyous, creative and playful self, I must first listen to, make space for, and understand the child within who had been so deeply wounded.

The Split

The day I received a thick envelope from the Institute of Art Therapy in Denmark, I remember opening it enthusiastically and skimming through the material. My strongest immediate reaction was to the week entitled *The Inner Child*...for good reason.

On the first day of the *Inner Child* course, all participants were asked to take out two sheets of paper and put them up on the wall, side by side. We were then instructed to paint two separate paintings: one of the 'archetypal child' within us (the unique child representing our pure, original, untainted, child-like spirit); the other of the feelings, memories and responses activated by the process of painting this archetypal child.

While the first painting was meant to connect us with our inner child's divine potential, the second painting was to provide us with an opportunity to explore our emotional response to this original child, likely reflecting our more 'realistic' experiences of childhood. We were encouraged to vacillate between the two paintings as we saw fit.

Starting with the first painting, I imagined my archetypal inner child. Certain elements of the picture became clear to me immediately. I knew, for instance, that this child would stand in a very open and joyous body position. She would be smiling, feeling intrinsically welcome and capable of shining.

With these basic ingredients in mind, I began to paint her. I planted her feet—literally—on top of the world, where she stood and radiated like the sun. I painted her happy and full of joy. She *took up lots of space.*

It was this last observation which stirred emotional rumblings in my belly. "Danger!" the rumblings said. "Taking up all that space is *definitely* not OK."

Following the arising emotional thread, I turned my attention to the other blank sheet of paper. My brush began to vigorously fling giant black squiggles onto the canvas. As I unleashed one oppressive splat after the other, I felt surprisingly powerful and free. One especially big blotch landed at the bottom of the canvas. I could almost make out a being down there. It seemed to crouch on the ground in an effort to hide.

I felt called back to the first image, intuitively determined to envelop the archetypal child in every color of the rainbow. With a careful brush, I transformed her outstretched arms and hands into fireworks. Each arm blasted music and light out into the universe. I painted onto the earth (that held up the child's body) two big eyes and a mouth. The earth, now wearing a huge grin, looked up at the radiant child. The whole world rejoiced in the child's existence.

Gradually, I turned the sky around the earth and child from powder blue, to cobalt, to the deepest night navy. As the image unfolded, it became increasingly obvious to me that this archetypal child wanted to be the major source of light, not the sun. She needed to be the focal point, the very center of the universe. She stood there, lighting up the cosmos, unabashedly loving, connected and beaming.

I could only take so much of this 'hallelujah child' before the emotional nausea kicked in. This was definitely not the child I remembered or experienced growing up. I couldn't have imagined anything more forbidden, actually. I even found myself looking over my shoulder, hoping no one would notice her. She embarrassed me.

Back to the other painting I went, this time with a combination of gusto, and relief. Flinging thick rain-like sheets of black, purple and blue onto the canvas, I made a mess. Trusting my animal instincts, I felt free and unfettered.

I also heard that old familiar voice, pouring through the rain. "Down, down with you, little girl! Who do you think you are?! You're nothing special. How dare you shine like that! How selfish you are! Think of how your light is going to make the others feel. You're hurting people. Hide, Rosy, hide!"

Another voice joined the choir, "Don't be a threat, Rosy. Remember, your safety lies in your invisibility. Stay small and quiet if you want to survive…if you want our approval. Remember, you can't live without our approval."

I continued to paint to the sound of internalized voices from the past. A figure fully emerged out of the blotch at the bottom of the canvas. It was definitely a human being, huddled in a ball, protecting itself from the violent rain. The rain, now splattered with yellow blotches, gushed down mercilessly upon the figure. Inspired by the imagery, I gave the completed painting a title: *The Shower of Approval.*

I returned to complete the image of the archetypal child, adding a big green heart on the little girl's chest. And then, in big letters, across the smiling globe, I painted the title: *Welcome, Me!*

During the entire process, bits and pieces from my childhood story surfaced.

My coming to this world was (understandably) not the best news my sister had received in her very young life. Though she is my best friend today, when we were little, she regularly demonstrated her disappointment and ambivalence about my existence. I, a typical younger sibling, worshipped her. For much of my early childhood, I did not understand why 'Goddess' seemed to dislike me so much, concluding at a very early age, "I must have done something wrong, or there must be something very wrong with me, to deserve this treatment."

My insightful, sensitive mother did her best to appeal to our understanding. She told my sister, "You're hurting Rosy. Can't you see she loves you? Be nice. Don't be so mad all of the time." My sister heard, "How can you be so mean and feel so angry at someone who loves you so much!? There is something wrong with you. You are bad and guilty." To me, she said, "Your sister feels guilty every time she is hard on you. She doesn't mean to hurt you; she just feels insecure and envious. Try to understand her. Don't outshine her. Let her have the attention." I heard, "Rosy, your existence, needs and natural abilities are hurtful and a threat to the people you love. People who are not nice to you feel bad about themselves. Instead of standing up for yourself, understand them, and know that their guilt is sufficient punishment. The best way to love people is by hiding your light."

These basic beliefs (the CliffsNotes version!) made up the backbone of my conscious and unconscious self-image and worldview for years. They still do on occasion. My poor mother's only mistake was overestimating the psychological sophistication of a four and five-year-old! Needless to say, she wound up with quite a handful, two terribly guilt-ridden daughters, equally determined to prove their self-critical thoughts about themselves right.

Revisiting these messages, I could better understand why I actually felt more free, powerful and comfortable when painting *The Shower of Approval* than I did *Welcome, Me!*

Painting the archetypal child—the little girl who was happy, who could shine, and to whom everything came easy—was fun, but my energy did not flow as freely as it did while painting *The Shower of Approval*. I felt self-conscious around her. Painting myself as a grandiose radiant success, in public, felt about as scary and awkward as *being* a success in life did.

Putting myself down in public, however, was much more familiar territory for me. No wonder painting of *The Shower of Approval* felt so natural. As long as I was representing myself as undesirable, weak and oppressed, I was (ironically) free to be visible, take space, and be powerful.

Once the process was complete, I sat for a while and looked at the two contrasting paintings. Though they were opposite in many ways, they shared one quality. They were both extreme. One shouted, "I am the very center of the Universe!" The other exclaimed, "I am nothing. I don't even exist." One expressed, "I am the cause of everything. I am doing it to the world!" The other confessed, "I am the victim of everything. The world is doing it to me."

These paintings reflected the two extreme survival options available to me when growing up: I could be absolutely perfect (winning the love of my father by 'doing well'), or an invisible failure (avoiding the wrath of my sister and earning the attention and approval of my mother, by being a combination of sick, invisible, insecure, humble, self-loathing and self-sacrificing).

Of course, neither of these *idealistic* options—neither painting—provided me with much room for being human. Neither model for the inner child made intimacy easy. It can be just as difficult to intimately connect with an exploding bomb of love and light, as it can be with a turtle retreated into its shell. While these two extreme aspects and strategies of my inner child were worthy of recognition and compassion, I knew that a more balanced, middle-of-the-road version also existed. I longed to get to know her.

The Bridge

Using the completed paintings as inspiration for a movement exercise, we were instructed to find two body positions—one to reflect the essence of the archetypal child, the other to reflect the essence of the emotional response to that child. Once the body positions were found, we were asked to slowly move back and forth between the two.

As I physically explored my two positions, vacillating between them, I became increasingly aware of their extreme natures. Neither position allowed for much flexibility. When we were asked to move around the room and experience what it felt like to move back and forth between the two positions in the presence of others, the rigidity of my positions became even more clear. I found it very difficult to come into contact with people when my body was 'filling up the room' with my grandiose *me, me, me* child. I found it equally impossible to connect with those around me when huddled in a self-effacing, groveling crawl. Either way, I felt alone and separate.

Eventually, we were instructed to find an embodied middle position, one that combined the two extremes equally. Strangely enough, my middle position turned out to be an absolutely normal standing position. My head was up; my arms were relaxed at my sides; and my back was straight. The first message I heard when I assumed this middle stance was, "I have the right to be here."

What a feeling that was! I had a right to be here, as a human being—with good days and bad days, happy feelings and unhappy feelings. I also discovered that when I moved around the room, in this relaxed and upright state, relating to others came much more easily to me. I felt so much more physically comfortable. Accepting and feeling into the positions of the other participants felt equally effortless and non-threatening.

We were then asked to use this middle position as a springboard for a new painting. This painting would be of our true inner child, a more balanced picture combining archetypal strengths with our deeply human qualities.

As I faced the new white sheet of paper, I imagined how I wanted this child to look, feel and think. I wanted her to embody the thought, "I have the right to be here, and so does everybody else."

I painted a little girl, standing up straight, yet relaxed. I placed her on green nurturing grass and gave her a soft, relaxed smile. When the girl was complete, I looked at her and felt peaceful inside. She was who she was. Nothing more and nothing less. She had nothing to flaunt and nothing to hide. I could instantly feel her connectedness—to her parents, to her family, to her friends, to nature, to the universe. I painted two symbols beside her to represent friendship, connection and support. A little girl stood to her left, and a little boy stood to her right. I saw them as both her inner girl and inner boy, as well as her outer playmates.

I then painted a rainbow above the three beings to symbolize all of the colors of life, the vast range of feelings, thoughts and experiences which make all of us uniquely human. Painting this little girl, together with others, provided pleasure as well as relief. It filled me with a wonderful physical sensation. There was space for all of me. I felt safe and supported.

The Projection Which Hit Home

We had a guest teacher during this particular week. She was a music therapist who guided us through a process which turned out to be very illuminating for me. Each group member was asked to find a partner, preferably someone in the group with whom we had felt some sort of uneasiness. This request alone was quite provoking. I ended up with the perfect partner for me. After we found each other, we were each given a task. One was to play the role of the child throughout the exercise. The child's job was to play, have fun, and reach out for the attention and encouragement needed. The other partner was to parent.

This exercise was divided into three phases. During the first phase, the course participants playing the parents were instructed to be rejecting parents. During the second phase, the parents were to compete with their children for attention. They were to embody the thought, "Look at me!" During the third phase, the parents were to be supportive, loving and encouraging of their children.

My partner and I picked straws to decide who should play what role. She was to be the child first, and I was to be the parent. "Oh, no!" I remember thinking to myself. I was intimidated enough by this process as it was. Now I had to be intimidating?! Despite my fear of being a 'bad parent,' I decided to go for it. It was difficult, but I knew my willingness to dutifully play my roles would eventually benefit both of us. As I acted out the rejecting parent and the 'see me' parent, I witnessed how painful it was for my partner, the child. I remember how determined she was to win my love and attention, and how long it actually took for her to give up.

I also remember the awkward transition between the second and third phases of the exercise. Suddenly, I was supposed to be a sweet and supportive parent, despite the fact that I had just betrayed my partner's every last bit of trust! As most children do, she gave me another chance, returning to the same optimistic and innocent state from which she'd started. Quickly getting over my initial guilt, I entered the supportive role and enjoyed it. It felt like home.

Later, when the group talked about the experience, my partner shared that the most difficult section for her to deal with emotionally was the last one. Being rejected and competed with was uncomfortable for her, yet, familiar. Being seen, listened to, reflected, and given space to explore, on the other hand, were totally new and strange occurrences. Hearing this made a very strong impact on me. The guest teacher said we would continue the process the following day, reversing roles. My partner had to leave the next day for personal reasons. I see this as no coincidence. This left me without a 'parent.'

The next day, when the teacher found out about my parentless position, she gave me a choice. Either I could be in a group as a twin, or I could observe the whole thing from the outside. I decided to observe from the outside. Part of me wondered if I was copping out. Was I afraid to involve myself, afraid to feel? Was I reliving my old pattern of avoiding sibling competition for a parent's attention? Or, was it really my intuition speaking to me? Most likely, my decision had mixed motives. Instead of getting stuck in over-analysis, I put my faith in the fact that every experience brings its own gift. I surrendered to the choice I made, trusting I would not be deprived of a lesson.

My choice to observe turned out to be just what I needed. Between my acting as a parent the previous day, and observing this day, I realized something. I had not experienced blatant rejection or competition from or with my parents. Relatively speaking, my parents had been encouraging, supportive, and had given me lots of space to be creative. I could see that for me to get in touch with my inner child's feelings of rejection, it needed to happen in a less direct way. Luckily, it did.

While I observed the group, I sat in a chair to the left of the video camera documenting the process. The teacher sat in a chair to the right of the camera. I remember witnessing all of the little innocent playful 'children' in the room, being ignored, scolded and rejected by their 'parents.' I saw how differently each child reacted to the same parental attitude. Some gave up immediately. Some kept on trying. Some rejected their parents even more strongly than their parents rejected them. Some managed to manipulate their parents into giving them what they wanted anyway. It was fascinating.

Amazing as it was, most of the children were able to return to their original enthusiasm at the beginning of each phase. A few, however, could not make that shift. The experience of having been rejected, or competed with, had gone too deep. They had become so completely identified with their given roles that they simply couldn't distance themselves from the exercise enough to move on to the next phase. The painful dynamics hit too close to home.

What also struck me, as an outside observer of the entire process, was how the rejecting, oppressive 'parents' looked like little children themselves. I have intellectually grasped many parents' childish helplessness, but watching the events of such a blatant process imprinted a very clear picture of how parent/child relationships are created, evolved and repeated from generation to generation.

Although I had a great deal of compassion and empathy for the 'children,' as well as for the 'parents,' it was not until the process was over and the partners went off to exchange experiences that something really hit home for me.

While the partners shared with each other, I sat and watched them. So did the teacher. Slowly, I found my attention shifting over towards my teacher, who was still sitting a couple of meters away from me. I looked carefully at her face, studying her expressions. I sensed she was feeling sad and alone.

All I could think about was, who would support and encourage the teacher? With whom was she to share *her* experiences? It took all of the restraint I had not to go over to her and offer her a massage! Instead of rushing over to take care of her, I explored what could be lying behind my strong impulse. I was clearly projecting something onto her. In that moment, I realized that I had created the perfect parent and partner for myself—the teacher and the entire group!

A Bit More Background

My Jewish mother was, in fact, a teacher. In her large circle of friends and family, she was literally (and ironically!) known as 'the Saint.' My mother dedicated much of her life to caretaking those who could not take care of themselves. She met her own needs primarily through meeting the needs of others.

Due to a complicated family background, she never had the opportunity or the conscious desire to 'individuate' from her parents. During most of her adult life, she took care of her parents. Never rebelling, she worked hard to remain a 'good girl' in their eyes.

Needless to say, the woman I am describing is the woman through whose body I was born, the woman I love very deeply, and whose thoughts and feelings I once thought were my own. I have spent the larger part of my relatively conscious adult life attempting to honor the loving and generous aspects of my maternal inheritance, while freeing myself from the oppressive reigns of an internalized (and exaggerated) 'Saint' and 'good girl' living within me. Much of my personal development has been spent discovering that I actually have a self.

My father, on the other hand, is a highly creative man, who as a child, did not receive the kind of attention and understanding he needed from his parents, two practical people understandably focused on making ends meet. Their competitive tendencies and inability to fully appreciate and nurture his sensitive and artistic nature left him with a deep need to be seen and acknowledged. Since my mother's job of taking care of everyone was time-consuming, she often relied on her daughters to provide their father with the attention she couldn't. The more my sister and I admired him and the more we achieved in ways that made him proud, the less guilt my mother felt for prioritizing others over him, and the less my father felt the painful feelings which lay beneath his strong need for external validation.

Born with a nature and temperament similar to my father's, I have also needed to discern between the inherited traits which were healthy for me—the creative and sensitive—and those less healthy. I've spent years learning to free myself from my own deep need to be affirmed by others, to receive positive attention without becoming a slave to it, and to let go of the tendency to equate my self-worth with how I performed, looked or was measured by the mainstream culture. In my intimate relationships, I have needed to learn and trust that the men I partnered with were strong enough to survive without my stroking their egos, downplaying my power or sacrificing myself.

Successfully practicing self-restraint, I refused to go over and give the teacher a massage. It was time for me to look the projection square in the face. I asked myself, "How are *you* feeling, Rosy?" In that moment, I realized that I felt alone, abandoned, and rejected! Ah-ha!

"And how did you learn as a child, Rosy, to get your needs met?" I got my needs met by meeting the needs of others, my father included. By becoming my mother's little support elf, by giving my full attention to whomever was deemed 'neediest' in the moment, I was sure to not only win her approval, but also lessen her load. If her job of saving the world was minimized just a little, perhaps she would have a bit of energy left over for me. If I saw, acknowledged and approved of my father enough, if I did everything in my power to make him proud, maybe one day he would turn around and notice me as a real person, not just an extension or reflection of him.

Suddenly, I felt a very old pang in my heart. The pain and hurt of my own inner child and my parents' inner children were visible in my teacher's face, in the vision of the group. I recalled the countless times in a group situation when I had felt responsible for rescuing the teacher, for making sure the teacher's needs were being met—just as I remembered all the times when I had disappeared into the role of witness, listener, encourager. It all fell into place.

The Gift of Expressive Arts Therapy

After this process, I felt vulnerable and alone, consciously longing for positive parents, and finally understanding why. Part of me expected someone out there to play that role for me. But there were no lovey-dovey Rebirthers around to give me lots of hugs, or to reassure me. I was on my own, and it felt ice cold. I asked myself, "What is the purpose of all of this art-therapy-mental-bologna? Where is the heart in this work?"

Something then happened. Our group had reassembled together with Vibeke Skov, our Institute director, to talk about the different processes which had taken place during the past few days. As the group shared, it became obvious that many people in the group felt as I did, hopelessly lacking and longing for a positive parent. Instead of trying to be that parent for us, Vibeke calmly said, "Well, why don't we all go up to the studio and paint our positive parents."

In that moment, I understood. *There* was the heart. *There* was the power. Where we felt lack, we ourselves were called upon to fill the space. We were reminded of our true power, the power to literally and physically create what we wanted, what we thought we did not have. Just the thought of being able to paint my positive inner parents gave me a sense of empowerment and hope. Since then, I have appreciated this knowledge and used it in my work with others.

APPENDIX II

Jung's Model of the Psyche in Practice

At another week course at the Institute for Art Therapy in Denmark, I had the honor of meeting and exploring more of my own beloved—and not so beloved—inner counterparts. In this specific course, the Jungian model of the psyche was introduced to me by two guest teachers, Bente Ploug and Ulrikke Strandbygaard. I'd like to share about four paintings I created during this course—the Persona, the Body, the Shadow, and finally, one which neared the Self, or at least the inner woman who might take me there. My emphasis will also be on the face. As you will learn, the faces I painted during this week changed dramatically from picture to picture, from process to process. Having been able to witness the transformation of my own changing face through the creative process, I was able to witness false layers of myself being peeled off.

The Persona (mask)

Sitting quietly in a circle with eyes closed, course participants were asked to think about the masks we wear in our everyday lives. What part of ourselves did we allow others to see? With what face did we meet the world around us? When we received a clear enough inner picture of our mask, we were asked to create it in physical form, with whatever materials and methods we saw fit. The only requirement was that our mask be created so it could be worn physically.

I allowed the picture of my outer mask to appear before me. Determined to receive as honest and revealing an image as possible, I let the mask emerge in its exaggerated form until it clarified. Dutifully, I opened my eyes and manifested this inner image on a piece of paper with meticulous accuracy. While I painted, I was not thinking. I was too busy trying to be true to what I saw just moments before. Only when the painting was complete did I stand back and take a look.

When I saw my creation, I felt queasy. It was not that the face I saw was not nice to look at. It was too nice. It was sweet, smiling, warm, understanding, loving and happy. It was also uncomfortably pleasing, panic-stricken, and practically painful to look at. I quickly became aware that while my mask had served me well for a long time, it had its limitations.

The process continued. Instructed to put on the masks we had just made, we interacted with each other—and each other's masks—through a dance. As I danced and existed behind my mask, I found myself wanting to melt into the wall or crawl under the carpet. Everyone else's masks seemed so real, honest, lively, abstract and freeing. Mine was one big white-toothed grin, as real and relatable as a toothpaste commercial. Yet, it was my mask, the mask which had protected me for so many years, helped me win the love and approval of my parents, friends, even strangers. Why was I not feeling thankful? On the contrary, I was devastated and ashamed. I felt trapped, misunderstood and strangely guilty. I was sure others would just write me off as some depthless plastic dummy, or be intimidated by me, which would be even worse.

Old experiences surfaced—my need for approval, my fear of rejection, my tendency to withdraw before anyone had a chance to reject me. I had seen and lived it all before. In that moment, even though I did not understand this at the time, the experience of wearing my mask led me directly to my shadow. I could not help but hear another part of me just screaming to get out.

"Hey! What about me!" she screamed. "What about me who gets pissed off, who cries, who doesn't give a shit about anyone or anything!? I'm here too! And I CAN'T BREATHE IN HERE! Let me out!" The more I danced, the more I withdrew, and the more acutely aware I became of the painful imprisonment my shadow had been experiencing most of my life—consciously and unconsciously. While the curious part of me could observe this revealing process with growing fascination, another part of me just couldn't wait to take that stupid mask off.

The next part of the mask-exploring exercise involved the use of interviews. Each group participant had a chance to be interviewed by the group while wearing their masks. The questions asked by the group were to be directed to the mask, not the person wearing the mask. Similarly, the people wearing their masks were to answer as their masks, not as themselves. We were encouraged to think of our masks as separate beings, as story book figures possessing their own names, backgrounds, and narratives. This helped us distance from our masks.

I volunteered to sit in the hot seat as quickly as possible, feeling anxious and vulnerable. As I sat on the chair, wearing my mask, the group asked the mask many profound, appropriate questions. Like the good girl which my mask was, I followed the rules of the game, responding as the mask would answer. "Yes," I said in answer to one of the questions, "everything is under control." "Me? Needs? No." I continued, "My only need is that all of you wonderful people have your needs met."

The revealing responses went on. "What might happen if I made space for myself and stopped trying to save you all? Well, you would all leave me, of course!" "Does my jaw ever get strained from all this smiling? Well, sometimes, but it's worth it." Finally, "Me? Angry? Never!" The mask could have gone on with her self-denial all evening.

Luckily, she did not. The teacher asked me if I was willing to take a risk. "Yes, I guess so," I responded with a trembling voice. The teacher then asked me if I was willing to take my mask off, turn it inside out, and put it back on. I was. She then asked me to express something which I did not normally allow myself to express. It was up to me to choose the expression, as long as it felt honest. Before I tell you what I ended up expressing, I want to share how the simple act of turning the mask inside out made me feel. I felt surprisingly freer than I had felt in a long *long* time—in my real life, not just during the course. Suddenly there was space for me, for all of me.

My first thought regarding the expression I was asked to share was that it should be something really forbidden, like anger. The only problem was that when the mask was finally turned around, anger was the last thing I felt. What I felt was space, and the space I felt made me feel sad. I had spent most of my life longing for space to be me and space to feel however I felt, but I had so rarely given myself permission to claim that space. The most honest expression I could share was my sadness. So I did. I began to cry, and what a relief it was! In this particular process, space was created for me and my sorrow, and I experienced that the group did not leave the room. They stayed and were very supportive. During this poignant moment, I could feel a deep healing taking place. I was filled with gratitude and felt ready to face the next day, and peel off the next layer.

The Body

The next day we were all given two hours to paint a body. The painted body was to be inspired by outlines of our own bodies which were traced onto large sheets of paper. Instead of forming a specific picture in my mind, I decided to see what would happen if I just let go. I painted and painted, surrendering to the process, not thinking much about anything other than what color called out to me and what strokes felt right.

As I painted, I felt happy—happy to have such a big sheet of paper on which I could express myself, and happy to feel the freedom of being able to do what I wanted without the burden of introspection. I used my usual bright colors and big strokes, and built a body, layer upon layer. The next thing I knew, our time was up. For the first time, I stood back and took a look at what I had created. There in front of me stood an absolutely wild and overpowering Amazon woman. Her arms were outstretched; her black hair was writhing like snakes around her blatantly sexual body; and she was glaring back at me with wide green eyes.

Well, this was certainly not the little Goody Two Shoes from the day before! In fact, my mask would have blushed like a tomato at the sight of this sensual powerhouse. As I studied the being before me in surprise, I began to register fear in my own body. While she was beautiful in a way, she scared me. As the minutes passed, I looked more closely at her face and more deeply into her green, glaring eyes. I examined her expression and realized something.

This Amazon goddess was even more terrified of herself than I was of her! She had so much power, and no idea what to do with it. Her thick strong hair, enveloping her neck and torso, was nearly strangling her. It was as though she was trapped in her own body, and by her beauty. Although she seemed confident, in that she had no trouble making eye contact, at second glance, it became clear that her intense stare was a protective one. It felt as if she was trying to scare people away with her intensity.

The group helped me look deeply into her fear, into my own fear of the power hiding within me. How did I plan to use all of my power? Was my power safe? Could I trust myself to use it? Were others safe with me when I expressed it? What was I so afraid of? The exploration continued…

The Shadow

The next day, our teachers guided us through a meditation. With eyes closed, we were asked to think of a person. This person was to be someone we found fascinating, or someone we found repelling. I figured with the rate I was going that week, I might as well take option number two. I picked a woman I had been working with in a hospital setting. While we had grown close to each other and I cared about her, she possessed a unique ability to get under my skin. Samantha was like most people are deep down, a basically good person who longed to love and to be loved. Also, like most people, she had some insecurities stemming from a complicated past I won't detail.

What made Samantha special to me was the particular way she dealt with her insecurities. When she felt afraid or threatened in any way, she turned ice cold. Her ears, her eyes and her heart would pull down their shutters in the flash of an instant. Whenever she perceived even the slightest hint of danger, her normally nuanced worldview instantly coagulated into two distinct clumps—a glob of guilt and bowl of blame. Figuring that someone had to be wrong in any given conflict, and knowing from experience that her survival depended on her *not* being that someone, Samantha blamed someone *else*. On occasion, to my dismay, that someone else was me.

To the warm, understanding and enlightened diplomat that I liked to think I was back then, the ice-cold rejection and blatant judgment Samantha dished out in my direction brought up my greatest fears and most uncomfortable feelings. Being shut out made me feel insecure and forced bad memories to surface from my childhood. Even though I did not like to admit it to myself, it brought out the judgmental and critical part of me too.

Now, back to the expressive arts therapy process. Once we had chosen a person that we wanted to explore further, we were asked to paint the person's qualities, colors and rhythms, as well as all the feelings we associated with the person in an abstract picture. Totally opposite to the pretty and smiling mask, I painted a face which was grotesque and warped. An angry ice blue, crying eye stared out from the face's upper left hand corner; a grimacing mouth dripped blood from its fangs; a heart remained trapped in a cage; and two hands stuck out like stop signs at the bottom of the painting, as if they were screaming, "Stay out!"

I also painted a woman in the front of the picture. She stood with her arms folded in front of her chest. Her eyes were closed, and her nose was turned up to the side. Icicles formed on her nose and body, hanging down like sharp daggers. I painted two small children. They were trapped in the prison of the big grimacing mouth. One stared with wide-eyed desperation out from her jail. Her mouth was gagged. The other crouched in the corner, hiding. Finally, I painted a key to the cage where the heart was trapped, yet the key was far away from the cage itself.

In an exercise designed to help us bring our shadows home, we were all asked to hang our paintings on the walls in front of us. One at a time, we were encouraged to own the qualities we had projected onto the people we had painted by describing ourselves out loud *as if we were* the very objects of our envy or irritation. One at a time, each individual was instructed to confirm our self-descriptions. When it was my turn to give Samantha a voice, I exclaimed "I am enraged!"

"Yes, you are enraged," answered the group.

"I am cold."

"Yes, you are cold," the group replied.

I continued the process, "I am alone. No one loves me. I have been abandoned. I am terrified. I am guilty. I cannot receive anything from anyone. I am rejecting. I am rejected. I have given up all hope."

The group responded with an echoing yes. "Yes. Yes. Yes. Yes," they said.

This particular process was especially provoking for me at the time. I had spent so many years perfecting my positive thinking skills that declaring such blatantly negative thoughts out loud, and having twenty people repeat them back to me simultaneously, felt blasphemous. Still, I instinctively knew this process was good for me. At some deep level, I must have understood that allowing myself to own the projections I had given to Samantha would somehow free me to become the whole person I knew I was.

I went along with the exercise. I described myself as Samantha, and when the group began to ask me/Samantha questions, I answered them to my best ability.

Over time, an atmosphere of frustration developed in the group— as well as in me. It was as if I could not be reached. Though going through all of the right motions, I just could not identify with this picture. I could not see that Samantha was a part of me. I talked as if she were me, but it still felt like I was describing Samantha, the woman I worked with. I, Rosy, was not *that* angry. I had not suffered *that* much.

I had not felt *that* abandoned. The list of "had not's" went on, until an insight fell on our heads like a giant clump of hail.

I was indeed *just as* cold, just as shut down, and just as rejecting of my own painting as Samantha had ever been of me, or of anyone else. By totally disassociating myself from my painting (my shadow), I exposed just how real, present and active the shadow was in my life. Only then could I take the picture into my heart. I could see the two children imprisoned in the woman's mouth, and I could see and feel that they were parts of me. I could see the cold, rejecting, negative mother and see that she was a part of me, too.

So often the children within me cried out for my attention and love. And just as many times, I shut myself down to them. I did not have time for them. They were too difficult, too needy. A part of me understandably feared that if I took them seriously, I would have no choice but to meet their needs. Accepting the responsibility of taking care of these children would complicate my life. It would require saying no to others who needed or wanted my attention, and part of me could not bear the potential consequences of being experienced as rejecting and cold as Samantha. For so many years, my survival was guaranteed by my warmth and helpfulness.

With aid from the group and the teacher, I began to realize how my shadow manifested itself in my everyday life. By refusing to own the rejecting part of myself, by doing anything and everything possible to avoid being cold and withholding, I became a slave to my need to be seen and experienced as warm and giving. Any time anyone needed me or my attention, I said yes—regardless of my needs. If someone served me food I did not like, I ate it anyway. If someone wanted me to be their friend, I would be their friend. If the phone rang, I would answer it. And I did it all with a smile.

The smile was only half-real. I had not known it at the time, but the smile shut people out. It said, "Everything is fine in here. Just leave me alone, and let me take care of you." In that way, I was cold or at least distant. My one-sided caring meant I could only be the 'giver.'

Beneath the smile was fear, sadness and anger. Behind the smile sat two children starving for my love and attention, powerless to break free from their imprisonment. Under the smile was Samantha, the overwhelmed, underpaid mother in me, desperately trying to protect herself and her hungry inner children from a demanding, insatiable world.

With time, I could see the genuine love and the desire to protect lying behind my shadow's coldness. Her ability to deny her anguish and to push people out had spared me from a great deal of pain in my life. She helped me to survive in the winter, when I was surrounded by snow and ice. She taught me how to be self-sufficient, stay safe, and avoid the pain of reaching out and being rejected. She saved me from experiencing the disappointment which would have come from facing the truth that some of the people I loved the most were not capable of giving me the support or love I needed.

Although my shadow helped me survive in the past, she was now preventing me from creating and experiencing the true intimacy I longed for in the present. If I wanted to experience the give and take of real friendship, I would have to embrace her. I would have to learn how to say no, so I could feed my hungry inner children. I would need to reject, so that when I said 'yes,' I would know that the 'yes' was genuine, that it was coming from a space of surplus, self-love and a willingness to receive—not desperation, self-hate and a fear of abandonment.

With these discoveries, I began to feel again. Tears flowed, and my heart opened to myself and those around me. Later that evening, my group gave me a gift. They sculpted a key out of clay for me, a symbolic key to my heart. Practicing my new skills, I received their gift as fully as I could. Holding it in my hand, I walked upstairs with the deep desire to paint a painting—just for me.

That Which Nears the Self

I approached the studio determined to paint a woman who felt safe and at peace being who she was. I chose every color I could find, black included, and pasted two huge sheets of paper together for a spacious canvas. I played some music, surrendering to the process. After several hours, I had painted a big dark woman sitting under a tree. She was definitely not smiling. She looked a bit sad, pensive, yet peaceful. Her naked body was powerful and sensual. The tree beside her was full of life and colors, and she was sheltered by it, although she looked away from the abundance. I looked at the painting and felt happy. Compared to my original mask, she felt much more honest to me.

Just when I felt satisfied with the level of personal growth I had reached during the week, a male member of the group sauntered into the room, and his own shadow followed him! He took one look at my painting and exclaimed, "She's too perfect." He didn't stop there. "And by the way, you should know that when I first saw you, I thought you were superficial and not very intelligent because of the way you look. If you want people to think you have a brain, do something about your appearance."

While a part of me realized more than a few of his statements carried some hefty projections, another part felt a sting of truth in his words, a truth that existed long before this man entered the room.

At a very early age, I'd learned two lessons for survival. One was that if I wanted love and approval from those around me, I needed to look a certain way. Like so many women living in our appearance-obsessed culture, I learned to think that I *was* my body. Especially during my pubescent and early teen years, I measured much of my self-worth in terms of how I looked.

The other lesson I learned was that although I wanted and needed attention and approval from others, the kind of attention I received from 'looking good' was not the kind I wanted or felt comfortable with. I learned, in fact, that being in a woman's body, being in a beautiful woman's body, was dangerous. It almost always resulted in my being objectified, and my inner self being ignored.

For many years, I rebelled against my own inner as well as concrete outer 'objectifiers.' I did so by hiding, rejecting, even disrespecting my body. In this way, I made sure that when people looked at me, it was *me* they were seeing, not the shell.

Of course, my self-destructive methods revealed whose oppressive thoughts I was truly rebelling against. My own. Several years actively involved in the women's movement helped me recover a sense of worth, pride in being a woman, and an ability to value myself as a person with power and substance.

The human potential movement took that process one step further, helping me love and care for myself, and seeing my body as a divine temple, an instrument through which all of my creativity and sexuality was meant to flow. I learned that the way I treated my body did not have to be about pleasing men (or anyone else) and living up to contorted cultural standards imposed on me, nor did it have to be about refusing to please men (or anyone else) and using the rest of my life rebelling against an oppressive sexist system. I needed to learn how to choose to dress in a way which made me feel good, which made me feel taken care of.

When this man shared his personal opinion about my appearance and picture, I had not yet reached a state of total self- and body-love. (I still have not reached this state, but I'm much closer today!) Hearing someone tell me that I was dressing for men, or that I appeared superficial ignited a spark of horror in me. It did so, because somewhere deep down, a little voice inside me still believed the same thing about myself.

With the support of another group member, I was able to regather the pieces of my broken self-esteem. I was reminded of the truth: I was not shallow, and I certainly didn't walk around begging people to slobber over me. In fact, objectively speaking, my appearance was very low key. The group member helped me to see that no one else perceived me in the same way that the man did, and that what he said revealed more about him than it did about me.

Feeling better, I sat and looked at my painting for a while. Two other course participants entered the room to see what I was doing. One of the two women quite innocently said, "Her face is so smooth, and the rest of the painting quite rough." That was feedback I could use. As I contemplated why this was the case, the valuable essence of the man's critical feedback was brought into the light.

Although the woman in this new painting wore an expression which was much more honest than the one possessed by my original mask, the method through which the face was painted was reminiscent of the original perfectionism. I reflected and realized that I had spent much more time and energy working on her face than I had on any other part of her body, and I had done so meticulously. It was time to rid myself of the last remnants of the flawless face.

I got up and bravely applied rough, blotchy strokes onto the woman's face. I made her hair wild, and I risked destroying the whole painting to which I had grown so attached. Afterwards, I could see that this roughening was essential. I could feel the relief. She was still beautiful, yet she was honest, raw, and definitely not 'just a pretty face!'

Shadow Integration

In the beginning of any conscious integration process, it is important to remember that most people feel awkward and uncomfortable, like they're too much or too little. This only makes sense, for they are trying on old and forbidden qualities for size. They are doing exactly what they learned not to do. It can take time to find the desired balance, but things eventually ease. The freedom people feel in the end is well worth the temporary discomfort.

Take Samantha and I, for instance. The shadow she mirrored for me was coldness. She set harsh limits, said no, blamed others, and withheld her love. The fact that her coldness bothered me as much as it did reflected the fact that these behaviors had all been forbidden to me as a child. To survive, I learned to do the opposite as well as to identify with the opposite.

To become whole and make space for greater intimacy and honesty in my life, I needed to be more like Samantha: to practice saying no; to set healthy limits and be more honest and selective in relation to others, including Samantha. I did *not* need, however, to become rejecting and icy. That would be unhelpful and inappropriate, replacing one form of the same shadow with another, for Samantha's coldness was a shadow expression itself.

Like my unconsciously stiff smile, her cold persona was just an unconscious expression of her own shadow. The truth is that Samantha and I had a lot in common. We were both caretakers. We both perceived ourselves as giving, vulnerable and unprotected in relation to others. We were both guilt-ridden, and doing what we thought we must to survive. While Samantha was convinced she could not survive if she revealed her vulnerability to others, I was convinced I could not survive if I revealed the strong and discerning part of me.

APPENDIX III

A Guideline for Parenting Professionals

Many people today are turning to alternative paths instead of to organized religions to meet their spiritual, ideological and psychological needs. Instead of using community elders, biological parents or early caregivers as role models, they are relying on alternative leaders and teachers.

The alternative professional's job has become an all-encompassing one, no longer confined to the traditional psychological goals of changing people's behavior or controlling their primitive destructive drives. It has taken on the profound—even sacred—purpose of helping people connect with their spiritual and psychological potential. The professional Wisdom Keeper has become spiritual advisor, mentor, role model, counselor, helper, listener, container, challenger, teacher and parent all in one.

In this final Appendix, I'd like to look at the parenting role in therapy, or any healing relationship. As I reformulate Vibeke Skov's five-phased theory in the context of the parent/child relationship during the child development process, feel free to use the model to look at your own parenting history. This chapter is especially meant to help professional Wisdom Keepers find out what their strengths and weaknesses are as 'professional parents.'

If you are a Wisdom Keeping professional, you may find that your own areas of strength and weakness reflect compensations you have made for the strengths and limitations of your own parents. When you know where your ability to parent tends to crack, you can more easily recognize when it is cracking, and ultimately, take charge of transforming the pattern, as opposed to letting the pattern take charge of you.

Whether your inner family structure directly reflects the actual family in which you grew up, or the distorted picture of that family which evolved within your psyche over time, it is important to acknowledge the impact this structure can have (and probably has had) on your ability to parent and support others.

Just as it requires courage, commitment and consciousness to develop and grow as an individual, it also takes courage, commitment and consciousness to assist another through a similar growing process.

I invite you to look at the following family model symbolically, as opposed to literally. When I speak of *Mother* and *Father*, I am speaking of archetypes, not actual people. Just as there is a *masculine* and a *feminine* aspect of every person regardless of gender, I see a *fathering* and *mothering* aspect in each of us.

All parents, caregivers, therapists and professional Wisdom Keepers—whether LGBTQIA, straight, gender-fluid, single, polyamorous or married—can benefit greatly by cultivating their ability to *mother* as well as to *father*, to nurture and support. Keep in mind that too much of a 'good' thing can be bad, and just enough of a 'bad' thing—if handled with sensitivity and good timing—can be good. Also, while ideas like *feminine* and *masculine* can be very useful, they are also culturally relative and often used in association with an increasingly outdated dualistic model of gender, and are thus worthy of being held lightly.

Parenting the *Empty Phase* Baby

The first experience on the hero's journey is birth itself. When it comes to the parent/child relationship, birth opens the door to 'emptiness.' The baby, once merged with *Mother*, once one with the body and mind of its carrier, is now on its own: open, unformed, a separate entity.

After birth, all is chaos for the infant, in the sense that the conscious and the unconscious are fused together. Without an ego identity to separate self from other, waking life from dream life, or individual consciousness from the collective unconscious, the baby senses and experiences intensely, yet still lacks the psychological sophistication necessary to understand, interpret or express its self in a comprehensive way. The baby certainly feels, learns, and contains a unique spiritual core and genetic signature, yet its inner psychic, emotional and spiritual life remains unassimilated.

In this 'empty' state, what babies need most is safety experienced through physical and emotional closeness. Infants need parents who can provide a loving environment for them. Infants need to be held, nurtured and cared for, just as they need to experience devotion and support.

Regardless of the specific family constellation, or how a particular parent or significant caregiver embodies these archetypes, the *Father's* task is to hold the space, provide the faith, and create the safe and balanced surroundings needed by the archetypal *Mother* and child to surrender into an intimate space together.

If babies experience sufficient amounts of positive parenting at this stage, they can move to the next stage of development with the inner core of safety that they need. If the *Maternal* energy they experience is cold and distant, and/or the *Paternal* energy rejects the *Maternal* or feels jealous of the child for winning the *Mother's* attention, the passage that babies make through the empty or chaotic stage of development will be hindered.

Babies neglected or mistreated in this way can later in life turn into people who have difficulty containing chaos, who have trouble nurturing and caring for themselves and others, or who seem helpless in some way. They can be clingy or appear desperate when dealing with caregivers or when in the process of caregiving. They can experience anxiety or psychosomatic illnesses whenever they move through a change, ending a cycle and beginning another, or whenever they are called to surrender to the unconscious. A fear of the creative process, their sexuality, and spontaneity, can easily develop in such people if sufficient damage has been done during this first developmental phase.

Parenting the *Idealistic Phase* Toddler

The next stage of a child's development opens the door to idealism. This is the second experience young heroes experience on their journey. During this phase, positive archetypal parents are activated. Something comes into the empty void, and a magical world is created.

As babies continue to grow, they begin to need something more from their parents than basic safety and support, although safety and support are always needed. What becomes essential for young toddlers is that they are given ample opportunity to explore their own bodies, rhythms and senses. During this stage of development, they begin to repeat movements and sounds. They are learning how to control the miraculous instrument known as their bodies.

The job of positive parents here is to provide safe physical conditions and to encourage their toddlers to explore their own bodies and develop 'body awareness.' The positive archetypal *Mother* in parents mirror their children's own rhythms, allowing toddlers to experience their physical selves through the mirroring process. If a child laughs, the positive *Mother* laughs. If a child seems sad, the positive *Mother* reflects back a sad face.

By mirroring in such a way, positive *Mothers* help their children believe in themselves. They help their children gain the self-confidence which comes from having their own physical impulses affirmed.

The positive *Father* in parents has a different job. Theirs is to physically play with their children, helping them to feel, experience and test their own limits. By helping children experience their bodies as different from the bodies of others, as autonomous, positive *Fathers* enable their toddlers to experience their own physical boundaries.

During this time in a child's development, being seen through the eyes of others is exceptionally important. A certain amount of what can be called 'shame' is necessary here. Think of a toddler who suddenly realizes that they are being watched when they pee. They become *self*-conscious, and perhaps for the first time in their life, they blush or cry from a primitive form of embarrassment. All young children need to experience this kind of self-consciousness to be able to move to the next stage of development where they develop a psychological consciousness, an 'ego' identity.

Depending on how these kinds of shame experiences are handled in this idealistic stage, children can either develop healthy relationships to their bodies or shameful ones. If the parents are positive enough, children are free to fall in love with their bodies, take up space, and unfold as physical beings. They learn to trust their own senses, and to enjoy their sensuality as well as their sexuality later on in life. If parents are unable to properly mirror or support their children during this phase of development, children may end up associating rejection and un-lovability with their bodies and sexuality.

Many parents have difficulty sharing in their children's 'irrational' infatuation with their sensual experiences. Without realizing that this is what they are doing, parents can teach their children that there is something wrong, dirty or 'insensible' about being so sensual. At this stage, negative *Mothers* in parents either mirror the opposite of what their children experience back to the children, or they mirror something different, or nothing at all. This kind of confusing mirroring (or non-mirroring) lessens the degree of self-confidence children feel in relation to their own physical impulses.

Negative *Fathers* in parents, on the other hand, do not respect their children's physical boundaries. Such archetypal *Fathers* (regardless of gender) can be physically violent or sexually abusive. This can cause children to have difficulties in setting physical boundaries in relation to others as independent and autonomous beings.

Toddlers who receive such negative messages from their parents can end up attracting further physical rejection or abuse later on in life whether from someone else or from themselves. Many adults who never learned that it was OK to trust their bodies, for example, learn to overcompensate for this lack by becoming overly intellectual, or by developing self- and body-destructive tendencies.

Parenting the *Confrontation Phase* Child

After children have had ample opportunity to explore their physical selves, their psychological selves come knocking at the developmental door. A concrete concept of *I*, of self, begins to form. With this self comes a personality and a will. The minds of young children begin to engage in independent and organized thought. As their mental and verbal skills develop, they give voice to an increasingly conscious inner world.

For these young children, a chance to explore, use and move their bodies on the physical plane is no longer enough. They now want to enter another plane, a magical one. They want to imagine, to role play and to tell stories. Using their newfound power to create and impact reality as psychologically autonomous beings, they rejoice in a world of symbols.

During this time in a child's life, the best thing positive *Mothers* can do is communicate with their children on a symbolic, not logical plane. They can do this by asking imaginary questions which honor the reality of their children's psychic experiences. By doing so, the positive *Mothers* in parents demonstrate trust in their children and the validity of their children's inner lives. They allow their children to explore and experiment in the infinitely wondrous imaginary world.

During this phase of their children's development, positive *Mothers* are also willing to let go of their children. They happily set them free so that their children can spend more time on their own, basking in their inner worlds, or with their *Fathers* (or whomever holds this role in their life).

The positive *Fathers* in parents play an important role during this particular phase. Their job is to play with their children and join the imaginary world in which their children are living. Positive *Fathers* also teach their children how to set limits through the act of play. Not taking themselves too seriously, such ideal *Fathers* enjoy being able to help their children to live out their imaginary life actively.

In this symbolic stage, both positive *Mothers* and *Fathers* have something in common: the ability to appreciate and understand the realness of the symbolic world in which their children find themselves. These parents take this imaginary world seriously, somehow understanding that as far as the human psyche is concerned, imagination has just as much power and value as that which is physically experienced.

When children are fully supported in this particular phase, they learn to believe in themselves and to trust their own feelings. Even if other people experience the same situation or object differently than they do, they can still trust in their own inner experiences. This eventually leads such children to find an individual form of expression later on in life, as well as develop the ability to resist external pressures to conform.

The worst thing negative *Mothers* in parents can do during this stage is to cling to their children, or to disregard the importance of the magical world. Negative *Mothers* can use their children to give their own lives meaning. They can demand their children's constant attention as opposed to letting their children go off and explore on their own.

Negative *Mothers* in parents can try to make their children think rationally and logically about what is magical by nature. They can teach their children to be afraid of the unconscious, to feel guilty about being different, and to mistrust their own feelings. Negative *Fathers* in this case can misuse their power and authority in relation to their children by turning what was supposed to be play into performance and judging the results.

Parents unable to see or value the magical reality contained by symbolic explorations can end up blocking their children's development. Just as their parents probably did with them when they were little, these parents pass on discouraging and condescending messages to their own children, saying, "The monster living under your bed does not exist," or "that doesn't look like an elephant at all!" or "stop all of this nonsense!"

By communicating to their children that their inner lives are unworthy of being taken seriously, or by judging the primitive state of their newly discovered expressions, negative parents manage to stunt their children's creative growth, helping their children to internalize unhealthy thoughts and judgments.

Since most negative parents are children of negative parents themselves, they often fear their own inner symbolic worlds, since those worlds most likely brought them rejection, condescension and criticism from their parents when they were little. Because of this, making the decision to reenter a magical space—even if it is with their own children—can feel threatening, even though they've grown up.

Some parents intellectually understand the importance of imagination and play, but their unconscious fear of engaging in unpredictable play is greater than their conscious desire to support and join their kids. Such parents can fall into the trap of over-praising or analyzing their children's expressions, or of dealing with the expressions from a moral or theoretical perspective. When they do this, they unintentionally reduce or trivialize the true meaning of their children's inner worlds. Such parents can also risk sabotaging play time by prioritizing other more 'important' tasks in life, like washing the dishes and making phone calls.

This sad phenomenon is exacerbated by the fact that many of us live in a world which prioritizes logic, rationality and productivity over the intuition, imagination and play. Parents with the best of intentions can feel guilty about 'wasting time.' Modern life gives them countless reasons to avoid reuniting with the magical worlds that they left behind years ago—the worlds still waiting to be rediscovered from their own childhoods.

Parenting the *Forgiveness Phase* Child

During the next stage of development, children begin to form a social consciousness, a sense of living in the world together with others. A collective reality comes into play here, a reality shared with other people who possess their own unique needs, thoughts and feelings.

Positive *Mothers* for children in this phase of development know how to support their children's own ability to create happiness for themselves and to get the loving care needed. Embracing their children's individuality, the positive *Mothers* in parents encourage their children to honor their own feelings. They teach their children to take care of their own physical and psychological needs while simultaneously respecting the needs of others. Their children learn to connect with others without losing themselves.

Positive *Fathers*, on the other hand, allow their children to be their own authority, and they give their children sound advice regarding the setting of practical goals, education and social consciousness. Their advice is more responsive than intrusive, grounded in their children's individual interests and talents.

Negative *Mothers* during this phase reject their children's needs by prioritizing the needs of others over the needs of their own children. In this way, the negative *Mothers* in parents teach their children to reject their own needs in order to make room for the needs of others, the parents' included. Negative *Mothers* can misuse their children's emotional dependencies on them, and they can be emotionally distant.

Negative *Fathers* during this stage judge their children's social interests and ways of expressing themselves. The judging paternal voices provided by such *Fathers* are ultimately internalized by the children. They take on a life of their own as the children grow older. This kind of constant internal criticism, if powerful enough, can prevent children from even trying to express themselves in an individualistic way later on in life. It is in this way that the negative *Fathers* in parents support conformist and conservative behavior in children, and society as a whole.

The *Free* Child

When parents or caregivers have thoroughly supported their child through all phases of development, the child ends up experiencing a great deal of personal freedom. They have a deep trust in their instinctive and intimate consciousness, in their bodily sensuality, in their psychological realities, as well as trust in themselves as unique human beings, equally worthy yet different from all other human beings.

On the other hand, if children have received more negative parenting than positive during childhood, chances are that their ability to trust themselves and healthfully connect with others will be damaged in whatever areas lacked parental support.

Being a Professional Parent

Whether consciously or not, the moment we assume the role of parent to someone else, our own experiences from childhood and adolescence are inevitably and automatically triggered. Some of the triggered experiences will be positive; others will not.

Most of us, including professional Wisdom Keepers, had parents or caregivers who were well-equipped to support us through certain aspects of our growing up process, and less equipped to support us through others. There is no need for blame or judgment here, just a willingness to see things as they were, and a desire to find out how and if these learned ways of parenting could be affecting our life and work today.

Keep in mind that parenting does not mean better-knowingness or a lack of respect for our clients' own wisdom. It means an ability to nurture and support them appropriately, in a way that allows them to heal unfinished business from their past and embrace their sovereignty.

For a creative and synchronistic approach to *Shadow* work and
for support in liberating your inner *Wisdom Keeper*,
please check out:

The *Wisdom Keepers* Oracle Deck & Inner Guidebook
&
The Designed to Blossom Foundational Course
& Creative Workbook in Human Design

www.WisdomKeepers.net

ABOUT THE AUTHOR

Rosy Aronson, PhD, is an Artist, Blossoming Guide and ordained Spiritual Counselor with a Masters in Expressive Arts Therapy and a Doctorate in Intuitive Listening and the Creative Arts. In addition to *Walking a Fine Line*, Rosy has created the *Designed to Blossom* Course/Workbook and Resource Book, the *64 Faces of Awakening, The Wisdom Keepers Oracle Deck* and *Inner Guidebook, The 64 Faces of Awakening Coloring Book* and *A Tale of Serendipity, Part One* of *The Wisdom Keepers Adventure Tales Series*, to reflect essential healing archetypes that lie at the foundation of our universe. Her deepest intention is to provide empowering tools for people to awaken their inner *Wisdom Keeper* and bloom into their authentic selves.

An avid permission-giver, pressure-dissolver and embracer of the unknown, Rosy believes we are literally designed to blossom, and the more each of us radically trusts, honors and expresses our True Nature, the more magic we can create together.

To learn more about Rosy and her work:
Wisdomkeepers.net

Made in the USA
Lexington, KY
10 April 2019